The Tao of Star Trek

Finding Your Inner Self Through Outer Space

What Sun Tzu and Lao Tzu Teaches us About the Dueling Philosophies

Of War and Peace

In the Very Best Star Trek Stories

Star Trek: The Original Series,

Star Trek: The Animated Series and Star Trek: The Next Generation

(Volume One)

Written By

Dr. Joseph Daniel Di Lella

The Tao of Star Trek:

Finding Your Inner Self Through Outer Space

What Sun Tzu and Lao Tzu Teaches us About the Dueling Philosophies

Of War and Peace

In the Very Best Star Trek Stories

(Star Trek: The Original Series, Star Trek: The Animated Series and Star Trek: The Next Generation)

Volume 1

By Dr. Joseph Daniel Di Lella

Copyright © July 21, 2021

For permissions contact: jdilella79@gmail.com

Cover by Canva.

E-book ISBN number: 9798527361339

Dedication

This book is dedicated to my father, Paul, who inspired the love of reading and the creation of fantastic tales – written and in oral storytelling. Exciting stories of frightening monsters and heroic men and women fighting and defeating the ugly and powerful beast were a nightly bedtime reward. I never fully understood the importance of this nightly ritual nor how it would shape my curiosity of creating my own fantastic tales later as an adult.

I truly hope that my current twelve year old, Daniella Paulina Di Lella, will one day repeat this nightly ritual with her children, if decides to start a family, and instill creativity in the minds of her young ones, too.

Acknowledgements

First and foremost. I would like to give special thanks and acknowledgements to the creator of the *Star Trek* franchise, Gene Roddenberry. It was a great honor to be a freelance pitch artist with Jack Trevino (*Star Trek: Deep Space Nine* story writer for the two episodes, *Little Green Men* and *Indiscretion*) and submit stories to staff writers for *Star Trek: Enterprise* from 2000-01.

I would also like to give special recognition to all of the staff writers for each one of the series over the years, starting with founding television show, *Star Trek: The Original Series* to the most recent ones of *Star Trek: Discovery* and *Star Trek: Picard.*

Lastly, a very loving acknowledgement to Lucile Ball, who strongly backed the original series with Paramount executives, convincing them that Roddenberry's vision for the future deserved their strong promotion for a slot on the weekly NBC schedule in 1965.

Table of Contents

The Tao of Star Trek:

Finding Your Inner Self through Outer Space

What Sun Tzu and Lao Tzu Teach us About the Dueling Philosophies

Of War and Peace

In the Very Best Star Trek Stories

(Star Trek: The Original Series, Star Trek: Animated Series

Star Trek: The Next Generation)

Lessons 1-34 & Episode Titles: 1. Where No Man has Gone Before, 2. The Enemy Within, 3. The Corbomite Maneuver, 4 The Cage, 5. The Menagerie, 6. The Conscience of the King, 7. Balance of Terror, 8. The Squire of Gothos, 9. Arena, 10. The Return of the Archons, 11. Space Seed, 12. A Taste of Armageddon, 13. The Devil in the Dark, 14. Errand of Mercy, 15. The City on the Edge of Forever 16. Amok Time, 17. The Changeling, 18. Mirror, Mirror, 19. The Doomsday Machine, 20. Day of the Dove, 21. Journey to Babel, 22. The Trouble with Tribbles, 23. A Piece of the Action, 24. The Immunity Syndrome, 25. The Enterprise Incident, 26. The Tholian Web, 27. The Empath, 28. Let this be your Final Battleground, 29. The Cloudminders, 30. All Our Yesterdays, 31. Star Trek II: Wrath of Khan, 32. Star Trek III: The Search for Spock, 33. Star Trek IV: The Voyage Home and 34. Star Trek (2009).

Preface

During the 2020-21 pandemic year, everyone in the world needs heroes in their lives. Role models represent a way to stand tall in our struggles against a deadly illness that plagues all of humanity. *Star Trek*, viewed through the lens of Sun Tzu and Lau Tzu's philosophical takes on war and peace, can show us the best way to battle inner demons and problems seemingly beyond our control – ones that demands we act thoughtfully, quickly, and efficiently when confrontations with nearly unstoppable forces push us to our limits.

The Tao of Star Trek: Discovering Our Inner Selves Through Outer Space – What Sun Tzu and Lao Tzu Teach us about the Dueling Philosophies of War and Peace Illustrated in the Very Best Star Trek Stories provides parameters for each of us as we go about our daily lives in 2021 and beyond through a critical literacy approach to ninety of the best *Star Trek* stories in franchise history, covering the first three television series in *Star Trek: The Original Series*, *Star Trek: The Animated Series* and *Star Trek: The Next Generation*. If one understands the essence of *Tao Te Ching* and *The Art of War* as guideposts, any individual can see the wisdom of the ideas of both Lao Tzu and Sun Tzu when applied to Trek character behavior in compelling storylines that are a metaphor for daily lives in 2020 – nearly 45 years after the first Roddenberry episode broadcast on NBC in October of 1965.

The late Gene Roddenberry, after writing for a television detective series (*Police Story*) in the early 1960's, wanted to move beyond the standard cops and robbers genre and into a more meaningful, episodic series that promoted the development of humanity rather than merely the good vs. bad wrapped up in a tidy 60 minute network show. "*Wagon Train* to the stars" is what Gene termed the original *Star Trek*, and from it, it spawned nine more syndicated series after the initial one's limited run of 3 years.

Yet, what it gave its viewers, and science fiction and fantasy fans in America and other countries throughout the world, were more than weekly sessions of 'Must See TV' – it brought about a template for how to live their lives on a daily basis. From the *Star Trek: The Original Series* to *Star Trek: Next Generation*, to Deep Space Nine, Voyager, Enterprise, the movies and animated series, and currently, *Star Trek: Discovery* and *Star Trek: Picard*, people from all corners of our planet easily relate to the five courageous captains – James T. Kirk, Jean-Luc Picard, Benjamin Sisko, Kathryn Janeway, and Johnathan Archer, and their fearless crews successes from peaceful first encounters to fierce military battles encounters with dangerous alien civilizations. Not all of the stories end-up as best they can for either humans or those they make contact with, but the heart of the adventures rest in the best of their intentions, without cruelty or hatred for others, who represent a different, more tolerant culture and way of life that embraces diversity throughout the galaxy.

As a fan, I started to watch the original series as a teenager, and even bought a model of the starship, *Enterprise*. Yet, today, the profound messages of Gene Roddenberry's vision resonate with me, and I use my interpretation of single story problems and solutions through character actions that can be translated from war – Sun Tzu, and peace – Lao Tzu, landmark collection of sayings for all of us to better understand in today's dangerous world.

As a professional, with experience as a freelance pitch person to *Star Trek: Enterprise*, short story writer, screenplay author, consultant and convention spokesman, I make my case to not only all fans of Gene's franchise, but those of us who still need heroes in our lives in 2021 and beyond. Lao Tzu and Sun Tzu may not have been as dynamic or dramatic as the fictional world of Star Trek characters, but application of their critical ideas on life, nature, the Way, and how to fight battles when pushed to the brink, extend beyond the pages of their most famous works.

As a 21st century human being forced to fight almost unbeatable odds, you need the best possible role models to base your everyday life on in 2021 – and how better than to use *Star Trek* to change your inner self through the adventures of outer space?

Chapter One

Why the Exploration of Space to Find Oneself?

A Personal Story

When I was a teenager, I was a bit lost, searching for my purpose in life. Was I any different than any other teenage boy? No. But was I aware that life needed a direction, a positive one that could benefit others and put me on a path of self-realization? Yes.

Have you ever felt directionless in personal, life choices or career decisions? Each us of face obstacles many times in our lives, but who helped you find clarity of purpose? Was it a parent, a poet, a particular author who sparked an idea, a concept of what it meant to be the very best human in this world?

My father, Paul, immigrated to American from a small village just north of Naples in southern Italy, and needed to find his own identity in a land that still does not embrace language nor ethic differences. My Pop always reminded me, as I was growing up, that a person's main reason for living was to contribute to society. His mantra and his direction was an ethical, moral and decent direction to go down the path of life.

Besides loving and principled parents, television, too, can act as a moral compass.

In the mid-6o's, when I was a child in love with science fiction and fantastic stories, a new television series hit the airwaves. I loved following Kirk, Spock and McCoy over three seasons. Captain James T. Kirk would typically fall in love and fight the bad guys with guile or his fists. Mr. Spock used logic to determine the best solutions for his friends, *Enterprise* or himself. Dr. Leonard McCoy, the ship's physician, used his medical expertise to save lives. To a pre-teen, all of this action was entertaining and a bit thought provoking – at least for the better stories told in the series, like *City on the Edge of Forever*, *Arena*, and *Enemy Within*, to name a few of the more allegorical tales of the series.

At the time, I realized the stories were more than whimsical fables and more like 'life lessons' for me on character building. Was I going to be as daring and resourceful as Kirk? Would I be as logical as Spock when a puzzling dilemma arose? Could I apply an empathetic ear to my friends like McCoy who were having trouble with parents, girlfriends, and in school? For me, these three Starfleet officers represented a type of archetype human being I aspired to in my daily life.

Star Trek: The Original Series – pushing aside several of the unspeakably poor ones like, *Spock's Brain*, but more like, *Taste of Armageddon*, spoke to the idea of the ease politicians and over-zealous military leaders could embrace the notion of human suffering and death in war. *Let this be Your Final Battleground* empathetically not only reminded the audience of the absurdity of racism but also taught as that this ridiculous notion was both ultimate danger for humans and aliens and their civilizations alike. In the popular episode, *The Return of the Archons*, the theme of state control and how autocratic leadership destroys individual freedom speaks to Americans during the rise of the Vietnam War. Overall, Gene Roddenberry, creator of the science fiction series, used allegory to represent the best and worst of poor government, wars, and racism overrunning the United States during the years the show ran from 1965-68.

In 1968*, Star Trek's* adventures were cancelled after only three years I, like so many fans rejoiced when the series reappeared in syndication shortly afterwards late at night and in the afternoons. University freshmen could skip their classes and sneak back to the dormitory and re-watch Kirk match maneuvers with a Romulan commander, see Spock's blood boil while fighting his captain to the death for the love of a Vulcan woman or, laugh at Bones try to patch-up his pointy-eared friend's brain synapses. All was right with the world again – at least for young adults still trying to find his place in an equally strange new world on a college campus.

The Tao of Pooh, Star Trek and Me

As Trek re-entered our lives with movies a decade later, *Tao of Pooh* also captured our minds and hearts. In 1982, A.A. Milne's sweet Winnie-the Pooh was reunited with his equally cute friends in the forest, but not for a typical children's stories, but one promoting the heart-warming children's character to a Taoist master. He, Piglet, Rabbit, Owl and Eeyore and others showed us the importance of Chinese philosophy of Taoism and the basic tenets to our everyday life. Remaining opened minded, and the ease of doing nothing, which Pooh seemed to do so very well, made us laugh, but also taught us the value of his instinctive problem solving nature methods employed by Taoist masters. Benjamin Hoff's take on the metaphorical significant of Winnie's life and adventures reminded me of a not so distant space opera allegory where humans fought their worst instincts to make important, ethical decisions with strangers in very strange lands and worlds.

An epiphany hit me – Kirk and company's adventures were just as allegorical as Winnie and friends misadventures deep in the woods. Somehow the intimate connection of Trek and Taoism blossomed as beautifully in me as a primrose after sunset.

Clearly, Taoist ethics that concerned itself with performing good acts and living in harmony with others was exactly what Roddenberry's television show promoted for all of us. Trek stories also illustrated the worst of humanity's behaviors through alien civilization, or mankind itself – such as in the Seven Deadly Sins of greed, lust, gluttony, sloth pride, envy and wrath.

Tao Te Ching, Star Trek and the Search for Peaceful Coexistence with Nature, Humanity and the Universe

Today, as I look closer at the stories in the many incarnations after the original such as *Star Trek: The Next Generation*, *Star Trek: Deep Space Nine*, and *Star Trek: Voyager*, to name only three, I also see that they undoubtedly expressed military strategies that Sun Tzu promoted in his work, *The Art of War*, too. There are ethical standards and way to conduct military battles to minimize bloodshed and suppress the enemy without needless slaughter. Did Captain Kirk need to kill the Gorn when he easily could? No – and the Metrons were impressed with the human race because of the compassion the human showed to the opponent.

In 2021, there are now nearly 800 original episodes (including *Star Trek: Discovery* and *Star Trek: Picard*) in the 11 television/streaming series, plus twelve movies. Of these I have selected over 250 TV adventures, movies and cartoons that are considered cannon of the Roddenberry dream that best represent both Lao Tzu's and Sun Tzu's strategies on how to live a more thoughtful, more connected one to nature, society and yourself, but also how to defend oneself in the midst of battles one must fight to save one's community and way of life.

Let's first look at a brief overview of Lao Tzu's philosophical stances before examining what Sun Tzu taught us the importance of strategies on saving ourselves in the midst of life threatening circumstances.

Tao's origins

Although Lao Tzu is credited with the writing of the *Tao Te Ching*, the basic philosophical beliefs of Taoism started with shamanism. Taoism started in 142 C.E. credited Tao to Zhang Daoling as a god. Zhang Daoling was credited with becoming the Celestial Master and founder Taoism (Livia Kohn, 2020). Tao Te Ching was published between the 3rd and 4th centuries, and the religion of Taoism was adopted by the Chinese during the Tang Dynasty. When Confucianism became more popular, Taoism was relegate to a less popular religion among the Chinese.

Due to Communist Party's takeover in 1945, Taoism practice fell to nearly nothing, but was adopted in Taiwan as their people had greater religious freedom. After the end of the Cultural Revolution in the mid-1960s, Taoism was revived in China; and today, temples dedicated to Lao Tzu and his teachings flourish throughout the country.

The Moral Philosophy of Tao

Those who believe in Taoism must change themselves, and not others, and live as an example on how to be in complete harmony with society and the universe. Each person has an obligation to each other, and should be more attuned to nature and their place in the world. If one is in *wu wei*, free from desires, a person can remain calm. In today's world, technology may act as a way to make us anxious, like any job, and force us to obey the dictates of others. This creates an unnatural way for human beings to behave, and must be remedied by accepting a harmony and simplicity as stated in the Taoism. Within the eighty-once chapters of the *Tao Te Ching*, Lao Tzu gives us a way to act more simplistic and natural in the hurried everyday world of the 21st century.

Important Values of Taoism

There are five critical areas of Taoism that must be addressed for humans to attain a high level of inner peace and harmony with others **(Translation Compiled by Shih-ming Hwang (Tsan Huah Temple):**

> *The Five Bonds of Human Relationships* – between sovereign and minister; parent and child, husband and wife, brother and sister, and friend and neighbor.
>
> *The Eight Cardinal Virtues* – filial piety, brotherly love, loyalty/honesty, truthfulness/trustfulness, propriety, righteousness, integrity/purity, and shamefulness.
>
> *The Four Ethical Principles* – propriety, righteousness, integrity/purity, and shamefulness.
>
> *The Three mainstays of Social Order* – between sovereign and minister, parent and child, husband and wife.
>
> *The Five Constant Virtues* – benevolence, righteousness, propriety, wisdom, and truthfulness or trustfulness.

If the majority of people throughout the world follow these principles, the world should be a safer place to live. For every man, woman and child who practice as many of these virtues as possible are easily on a path to follow the Way that Lao Tzu believed each one needed to make their lives the best as humanly possible.

Taoism: Discovering Oneself and The Way

In Lao Tzu's book, readers are encouraged to start a journey within themselves to understand their path in life and discover their Way in the Taoist tradition. If one truly accepts one's nature and does not go against it that is the beginning of knowledge.

If we look at all of the *Star Trek* series (nine and counting), multiple characters explore their identity – a more humane one, throughout the stories. In Taoism, that is the constant in the philosophy: looking to improve one's life through simplicity, patience and compromise. Although one can never truly complete one's journey to ultimate tranquility – even Taoist masters – it never stopped the brave souls in the *Star Trek* sagas.

TOS: Mr. Spock's Battle Balancing Logic and Emotions

After their split with their cousins, the Romulans, centuries ago, the Vulcans regard logic as the most important tenant to living a balanced life. Yet, for Mr. Spock, who is the child of a Human and a Vulcan, his life has always been complicated. His desire to maintain an emotionless life has always haunted him because emotions cannot be so easily repressed, even for a full-blooded Vulcan. Once in Starfleet, Mr. Spock was always challenged to make hard decisions, ones that were supposedly made on pure logic, but this imperative was not always followed. In fact, when Spock sacrificed his life for his crewmates in the movie, *Star Trek II: The Wrath of Khan*, it is done for everyone in the most logical manner. Regardless, James Kirk and Leonard McCoy know that he did it to save his friends – a love for them that he never admitted, but made obvious in his final act to save *Enterprise*. Even though he was resurrected in the next movie, In Search for Spock, he never admitted this act was one of love and devotion – something that goes Vulcan philosophy.

TNG: Data's Attempt to Understand Humanity

Commander Data's positronic net was capable performing of amazing calculations and intellectual deductions. His physical strength was double than of humans. Still, he was always searching to better understand the behavior of his crewmates and alien species. Emotion was something Data could not process because he had none. Ironically, when Q could have made him fully human in the story, Q Who, Data quickly warned him not to do so. The Federation officer was always quizzical and curious about motivations on love, hate, anger and rage, to name a few of them, but never wanted to fully embrace a biological state of being to sustain such complex understanding of emotions. Instead, his discussions with Captain Picard, Chief Engineer Gordi La Forge, Counselor Troi, and others, elevated his understanding of what it was to embrace the best of humanity.

DS9: Odo's Origin Search

In Deep Space Nine, Odo – the Constable of DS9 – is unlike the Founders, though he was once a part of the Great Link. His journey to self-awareness is the essence of any Taoist in the true tradition. He knows not where he comes from, but he is aware that when he finally meets the female shape shifter that the path before him is one of choice: to retain solid form and take the side of humanoids or return to the home world?

For the Constable of DS9, his internal journey of learning what he is, is linked to where he came from after being found by a Bajoran scientist. His sense of self becomes manifested through a greater need to keep order and laws for a space station next to the Wormhole. But is his need for strict compliance of first Cardassian law, then transformed to Bajoran and Federation rules and regulations truly any better?

Odo's path best exemplifies the path of anyone trying to overcome self-doubt, emotional pain and misery. Even after finding the road home, the shape shifter does not know if it is any better than the path he is one with the true love of his life, Kira Nerys, a solid. Although he eventually decides to leave the Federation-Bajoran space station to live with his people, it is not an easy choice, but one he does to keep the peace with his people and the rest of the galaxy. Still, he gives up the one person who brings him joy, happiness and purpose. A reasonable choice? Perhaps not, but one Odo does for the greater good of everyone, solids and Changelings alike.

Voyager: Seven of Nine's Quest for Individualism and Selfhood

After assimilation, Annika Hansen became a mere number – Seven of Nine – in Tertiary Adjunct of Unimatrix 01, serving the Borg Queen's most vile of intentions towards other beings and civilizations. Though she still had memories of Magnus and Erin, her human parents who explored space as scientists, she was forced to suppress them. When Seven disconnected from the Borg Collective, a necessity for her survival after a Borg and Voyager alliance deal fell apart, she gradually reclaimed her humanity through interactions with the Voyager crew. Though she never reclaimed her human name, Seven learned lessons in humanity mostly through life teachings of The Doctor and Captain Janeway.

Enterprise: T'Pol's Trepidation with her Human Crewmates

Like her counterpart, Mr. Spock from the USS *Enterprise* NX 1701-A, Sub-Commander T'Pol also struggled to maintain her truest Vulcan perspective on life aboard her new ship. With Captain Archer, Trip Tucker, and others, she is constantly challenged to be more 'human' and emotional, to express her strongest of feelings and even to share her fears while exploring the galaxy.   T'Pol refuses to be one of her newest companions, but gradually bonds with them and supports her friends even more than her Vulcan superiors.

Discovery: Burnham's Reconciliation of Human and Vulcan Culture

In *Star Trek: Discovery*, Michael Burnham had a rough beginning, and as an adopted child of Vulcan Sarek and Human Amanda, the young girl learned how to balance emotion and logic – or did she? Once serving the USS *Discovery*, Michael finds her Vulcan upbringing helps her in the routine nature of serving her commander and exploring the known galaxy. Once challenged by a mythical race, the Klingons, Burnham has to make a choice of following her Vulcan's father's advice or adhering to Starfleet protocol – and she chooses the former, causing her to mutiny against her captain. After attacking the enemy first, provoking a war, and leading her captain into a dangerous situation that sees her friend and mentor killed, Michael faces charges of mutiny, and serves six months of a life sentence until Captain Lorca rescues her and gives her the option of serving aboard the USS *Discovery* or return to prison. Burnham choose to remain relevant on the starship as her path towards redemption begins.

Star Trek's Other Side: Sun Tzu's Tactical Strategies

As mentioned earlier, *Star Trek* may represent a peaceful path to live our lives, but it is in the real sense also a war drama. The best of Trek shows the balance of light and darkness, the individual growth of characters, across the Federation as well, but also shows in the later incarnations of the series such as Next Generation, Deep Space Nine, Voyager, Enterprise and Discovery the horrors of war and those who perform the duties (Section 31, Obsidian Order, Romulan Tal Shiar are examples of undercover operations).

The Art of War: Sun Tzu's models

In the *Art of War*, Sun Tzu presents the best methods and strategies to military victories, not necessarily how to start battles, but how to contend with them if necessary. The thirteen chapters are: 1. Detail Assessment and Planning, 2. Waging War, 3 Strategic Attack, 4. Disposition of the Army, 5. Forces, 6. Weaknesses and Strengths, 7. Military Maneuvers, 8. Variations and Adaptability, 9. Movement and Development of Troops, 10. Terrain, 11. The Nine Battlegrounds, 12. Attacking with Fire and 13. Intelligence and Espionage. For Sun Tzu, all warfare is divided into three distinct ways – strategic, operational and tactical. Those who follow the very basic, but successful approach can minimize death and destruction to one's troops. Perhaps the most important elements of the book is the approach towards deception and maneuvers in battles.

What is most interesting, in relationship to Lao Tzu, is that Sun Tzu believes that all wars are presided by five factors: Moral law, Heaven, Earth, Commander and Method and Discipline. Lao and Sun agree about a moral approach to conduct war. Lao believed that those who used weapons of violence, and grew to enjoy bloodshed, fame and glory of battles lost sight of the hideous nature of the formal action. Sun, too, agreed that to linger and make war last long would savage a nation and its people. Essentially, the morally of war is determined as one of the most important codes to use in any large-scale conflict.

The Art of War, Sun Tzu's most important manuscript, was used by the Japanese, the French – especially Napoleon Bonaparte, and the Chinese in the 1959 civil war. The book has also been used by Russian, Vietnamese and American military schools to instruct their young leaders on the proper use of strategies in any conflict. In dealing with philosophy and psychology, the Art of War, teaching about morale building and how to build confidence.

Star Trek Conflicts: How to Avoid War *if* Possible

Most importantly, *The Art of War* teaches us that a military leader can win with ever fighting – the ability to avoid conflict is critical in any potential battle. How many times did we see Captain Kirk talk their way out of a possible deadly battle – *The Corbomite Maneuver* is just one such example. Captain Jean-Luc Picard often found a way to confront Romulans, but avoid costly battles and an ultimate war with the aggressive species.

Any conflict is expensive, and keeping costs down is critical to any organization. Look at the battle of Worf 359 with the Borg in the TNG episode, *The Best of Both Worlds*. The Federation lost thousands of lives and over thirty starships. No one can measure the loss of any person in battle, and certainly their lives were not in vain because Commander Riker and crew finally found a way to disable the Borg Cube, with Picard's help, and save Earth. Still, the destruction of any military or scientific vessel in the *Star Trek* universe shows the cost of any war.

In *Star Trek*, as in life, the most important weapon we can use is our mind. Strategies that limit conflict saves lives, resources, and prevents prolonged wars that can destroy civilizations or federations. In *Yesterday's Enterprise*, we saw what would have happened to the Federation if the Klingons and Romulans joined forces. If not for Guinan's intuition, and convincing Jean Luc that their timeline had been changed, millions of lives were saved. Using one's mind and even gut instincts, can shape the beginnings or ends of conflicts anywhere in the universe.

The Art of War in *Star Trek*: Leadership in the Galaxy

TOS: Captain Kirk's Balancing Act in the Unknown

Although James T. Kirk is prone to use non-violence as a Starfleet officer, he defends his starship, his crew and innocent alien civilizations with well-calculated maneuvers and strategies becoming a Sun Tzu follower while maintaining a Lao Tzu, peaceful approach to first contact encounters through the galaxy. Still, when pressed to save his crew and ship, Kirk will do whatever it takes to defeat the enemy – as seen in the story, *Balance of Power.* Although he nearly loses the battle, he cripples a Romulan warbird. Afterwards, he offers to take the survivors aboard, showing compassion and diplomacy, though the enemy captain self-destructs his ship rather than be captured.

TNG: Captain Jean-Luc Picard is the Voice of Reason

Through his alert and brilliant move to save the USS *Stargazer*, a very young Jean-Luc Picard earned his captaincy through his ingenuity and battle performance against the Ferengi. Much later, Captain Picard combating foes with ease, through strength of character and a show of force – but only when necessary. Once on the USS *Enterprise* NX 1701-D, Jean-Luc Picard uses the voices around him before making command decisions unilaterally. Rallying the troops provides a democratic platform before any major decisions are made that could prove unwise against potential enemies.

DS9: Captain Benjamin Sisko's Dual Role as Emissary and Commander

As Emissary to the Prophets/wormhole aliens and Starfleet commander of Deep Space Nine, Benjamin Sisko must use unorthodox methods to protect the people of Bajor and from Klingons, Cardassians, and not to forget the fiercest opponent, The Founders and their Dominion forces intent on conquering the Alpha Quadrant. Sisko, like Picard, listens to his fellow officers before making big decisions. Still, when the time comes when a show of strength is needed against the enemy as seen in the story, *Sacrifice of the Angels*, Captain Sisko makes the tough choice and attacks the opponent as Sun Tzu recommends in his teachings.

Voyager: Captain Kathryn Janeway's Sacrifice

Choosing to save the Ocampian civilization, and thus committing her starship to a 75 year journey home, Captain Janeway faces early battles with the Kazons, time altering and deadly struggles with the Krenim Imperium and the always menacing Borg Collective. Captain Janeway always uses wits along with technological innovations and keen strategies to save her ship and crew dozens of time in her flight home to the Alpha Quadrant. Seven years into their return to the Alpha Quadrant, Admiral Kathryn Janeway returns to the past to help Captain Janeway to destroy a Borg transwarp conduit system connecting multiple quadrant of the galaxy, eliminate the Queen, and help *Voyager* return to Earth to a regatta of starships escorting her to port. Future Janeway makes the ultimate sacrifice, but one that is well worth it for a family she made in the Delta Quadrant.

Enterprise: Captain Johnathan Archer's Life and Death Decisions

Although Captain Archer sought peace in his early missions, Temporal Agents forced Johnathan's hand in fighting with force and cunning. When the Xindi murdered tens of thousands on Earth, and with total annihilation in mind, Captain Archer may have sacrificed principles at times, but steadily fought the enemy with guile and did his best to convince The Counsel to reconsider implementing the Superweapon. Eventually, Archer and crew prevented the destruction of their home world, but pushed themselves to finally win a battle they had to win.

Discovery: Captain Lorca and Captain Philippa Georgiou of the Mirror Universe

Both Lorca and Georgiou are the most militaristic of the *Star Trek* leaders because both originate from an alternative universe, where fighting for power and status is most important goal. Their strategies are to attack first and never question their decisions – or allow anyone to do so either. Lorca is murdered by Georgiou when he returns to his universe in his quest to overthrow his enemy. When Michael saves Georgiou, the mirror universe leader is forced back to a reality inhabited by normal, peaceful human beings. Although she hates her life in a gentler universe, comes to accept it and work towards the better good for the Federation, Starfleet and her mentee, Michael Burnham.

Critical Literacy: A View on *Star Trek* Characters

This book takes a critical television and film literacy approach on character development and story themes as how both relate to society and Lao Tzu and Sun Tzu works on nine series that also includes original and reboot movies, animated cartoons plus the newest in the franchise – *Star Trek: Discovery* and *Star Trek: Picard*.

In film and television criticism, most academic critiques discuss how stories work either on an aesthetic, political or societal level. Such critiques typically include a summary of the story, and character development by placing both in the cultural context of the times. Major themes of the stories are examined for their intelligent takes on real-life problems for individuals and nations who confront historically troublesome legacies.

Thus, as we read the stories of each Trek series, there is an obvious connection of the stories and Taoist beliefs as told by Lao Tzu as well as military strategies exposed by Sun Tzu. In his book of *Tao Te Ching*, a likely composite of sayings, expressions and beliefs for the average person to abide to for a better physical, spiritual and emotional life. In the *Art of War*, the strategies of how to defeat an enemy without violence, but if necessary, use whatever it takes to defend oneself and a nation, is also illustrated by Trek characters confronting imperiled situations.

We shall focus on major characters of each series and tell of their adventures, but not one of physical confrontations but their emotional growth through Taoist belief system brought about in the eighty-one chapters of *Tao Te Ching* and the thirteen chapters of, *The Art of War*.

Star Trek and Taoism: Stories and Character Growth

This depends on the type of person you are today and what you aspire to be tomorrow.

It is hoped that you, as a fan of *Star Trek*, can more easily see what you have learned subconsciously through tales of bravery and emotional and spiritual growth, per se, of Gene Roddenberry Federation characters like Benjamin Sisko. Ben was not a man who believed God or a higher power could intervene into his life in a powerful way – certainly not after he lost his ship, most of his crew, and especially his wife, to the Borg in the attack of Wolf 351. Regardless, he was reassigned to Deep Space Nine and was taken in by the Wormhole Aliens (or better known by the Bajorians as the Prophets) who used him as their emissary to the people who created a religion based on them. Sisko's life changed for the better and (MAJOR spoiler alert!) eventually joined the Prophets after he lost his life taking down his arch enemy Gul Dukat in the Fire Caves of Bajor in the final episode of DS9, "*What you Leave Behind*."

Star Trek Episodes: Which ones illustrate the most important ideas on peace and war?

As famous fantasy and science fiction story teller, Rod Serling, said over 50 years ago, only one-third of any television episodes are worthy of re-watching. In the eight *Star Trek* series and over 726 episodes shown, about a third of them resonates today for this writer today.

In our case, nearly 30% of all Gene Roddenberry-inspired tales are discussed in this book. After watching and re-watching each episode from all of the series multiple times, I have drawn from 250+ of the most fascinating and still noteworthy stories. Of these Trek adventures, I have written a brief summary to reacquaint you with the key elements to refresh your minds with the initial conflict, which character was featured prominently, and how the dilemma was solved.

Personal Growth of the Reader: Can you become more of a Taoist?

As you read over the ninety episodes of three *Star Trek* series (plus movies and animated cartoons) in this first volume of three, you will learn about character arcs of Taoist behavior displayed in intense interactions with alien species and among themselves. I ask you to reflect on the main social, personal, political, and other issues of each episode. Lastly, you will be urged to consider taking action on the Taoist tenets presented in the 'lesson' and in your life.

Chapter Two

Star Trek: The Original Series

Exploring Humanity through the Exploration of Space

Lesson 1

The giant pine tree grows from a tiny sprout.

The journey of a thousand miles starts from beneath your feet.

Lao Tzu Chapter 64

Season 1 Episode 3: Where No Man Has Gone Before

Story Summary

While exploring the outer edge of the galaxy, the USS *Enterprise*, captained by James T. Kirk, locates the last known message of the USS *Valiant*, a starship that had vanished over 200 years earlier. In the message, the ship's captain tells of his ship swept away by a highly charged ion storm as his crew was desperately looking for information on extra sensory perception (ESP). The message ends with the captain ordering a self-destruct of his ship.

Breaking the 'great barrier' at the rim of the galaxy may be a dangerous move for Captain James T. Kirk. All that he knows about the potential crossing is that it may have caused space madness – as seems evidenced by the *Valiant's* captain calling for the self-destruct of his ship and the death of the entire crew.

Although in theory, it is possible for the starship to break through the energy barrier circling the known galaxy, it may severely damage *Enterprise*. Regardless of the risk, Starfleet orders Kirk and his crew to test the waters, to examine the rim, and decide if the gamble is doable for the sturdy *Enterprise*. Science Officer Spock provides advice to Captain Kirk, and after a serious discussion with other bridge members, including Dr. Dehner, the decision is made to pass through the rim.

As *Enterprise* proceeds across the barrier, powerful energy waves hit the hull, but also move through the ship and randomly strike members of the crew – with Dr. Dehner and helmsman Mitchell the hardest hit. Somehow, both Mitchell and Dehner survive.

Soon, Mitchell starts to exhibit incredible telepathic and telekinetic power likely caused from the energy field. Seeing the rate of Mitchell's power increase exponentially, The Vulcan science officer, Mr. Spock, recommends that the crew member be marooned on a nearby world to save the crew. Kirk agrees and steers the *Enterprise* towards a lithium mining facility in Delta Vega. Once there, the Kirk and Spock try to confine Mitchell, who has been under sedation, to a holding cell on the planet but he awakens. After he kills Navigator Kelso, he knocks out Kirk and Spock and escapes. He brings along Dr. Dehner who now exhibits the same powers. The captain follows him onto the planet's surface.

> **Dehner**: Before long we'll be where it would have taken mankind millions of years of learning to reach.
> **Kirk**: And what will Mitchell learn in getting there? Will he know what to do with his power? Will he acquire the wisdom?
> **Dehner**: Please go back while you still can.
> **Kirk**: Did you hear him joke about compassion? Above all else a "god" needs compassion! Mitchell.

Dehner distracts Mitchell him before he can murder Kirk. Dehner, instead, is killed by Mitchell, and in that moment, Kirk grabs his phaser rifle, fires a shot at a nearby mountain, and starts a minor tremor. A huge boulder falls on Mitchell, killing him instantly.

Onboard *Enterprise*, the captain puts in his log that both Dehner and Mitchell gave their lives in the performance of their duty, explaining to his science officer that the two did not deserve what happened to them.

Notable Dialogue:

> **Mitchell**: Time to pray, Captain. Pray to me.
> **Kirk**: To you? Not to both of you?
> **Mitchell**: Pray that you die easily.
> **Kirk**: There'll only be one of you in the end. One jealous god... if all this makes a god. Or is it making you something else?
> **Mitchell**: Your last chance, Kirk.
> **Kirk**: Do you like what you see? Absolute power corrupting absolutely.

Character Arcs: Dr. Dehner and Gary Mitchell

In this story, the two antagonists represent a real threat to the safety of the crew due to their increased telepathic and telekinetic skills. In a sense, the Federation crew soon become childlike and limited intellectually to both Helmsman Mitchell and Dr. Dehner – whose arrogance and sense of superiority forced Captain Kirk to abandon them both on a desolate planet.

In the Taoist tradition, a human being should look at personal growth as the most important aspect of his/her life. Certainly, Helmsman Mitchell lost any sense of this once he realized that his new-found abilities transformed him into an all-powerful, God-like human. Dr. Dehner, quickly grew to understand she also possessed these dangerous powers, but also realized, just in time, that her humanity rested in compassion, as Captain Kirk called on Mitchell to remember.

Everyday Reflections

As Lao Tzu reminds us, the greatest journey starts with the smallest of steps. In *Star Trek*, although the adventures takes humanity to exotic, but dangerous locations throughout the known galaxy, each story is truly about the personal growth each character takes and learns from in lands far from home.

Up to this point in your life, what type of chances do you typically take in your personal relationships or career challenges? What type of personal growth can you say you made last year? Professional Accomplishments? Your baby steps away from your comfort zone may not take you to other worlds, but each move may bring you greater joy and satisfaction as you live a life that Lao Tzu would have been keen to see in himself.

Everyday Actions

In your journal, please take a few moments to write the answers to these few questions:

What can you do to change your approach to life, at a basic level, to begin a new adventure, a new direction in life, one worthy of your heart and soul and mind?

Lesson 2

What is and what is not create each other

Lao Tzu Chapter 2

Season 1 Episode 5: Enemy Within

Story Summary

After a seemingly normal transport from Alpha 177, a geological team member, Technician Fisher, returns to *Enterprise*, but brings back with him an unusual ore dust on his uniform. Mr. Scott notices that this material may have interfered with the transporter's lock on Fisher, but cannot find anything wrong with the unit.

Captain Kirk beams up next, but he re-materializes disoriented, and Scotty helps him to sickbay. A few moments later, another Captain Kirk materializes on the transporter pad with an evil look in his eyes. Evil Kirk walks the ship, and at one point, harasses Yeoman Janice Rand.

Mr. Scott, unaware of the duplicate Kirk, tries an experiment with the transporter by beaming a native canine from the planet. Scotty finds that two pups beam up, one after the other, with different personalities. The transporter chief alerts Mr. Spock of this problem, and shuts down the machine, stranding the rest of the away team on the cold, desolate planet as night approaches.

The evil Kirk, now drunk, goes to Yeoman's Rand's quarters. This James T. Kirk pushes the subordinate into a corner and tries to force himself on her. Janice screams, slaps him and scratches his face. Ensign Rees rushes to her quarters and tries to defend her. Kirk fights with him, but leaves, angrily.

Rand reports this incident to Mr. Spock. Spock deduces that Kirk must also have been divided into two halves, like the canine of the past experiment, and alerts the crew of this over the ship loud speakers.

> **Spock**: We have here an unusual opportunity to appraise the human mind, or to examine, in Earth terms, the roles of good and evil in a man-- his negative side, which you call hostility, lust, violence, and his positive side, which Earth people express as compassion, love, tenderness.
>
> **McCoy**: Are you aware it's the captain's guts you're analyzing?
>
> **Spock**: Yes, and what makes one man an exceptional leader? We see indications that it's his negative side which makes him strong, that his evil side, controlled and disciplined, is vital to his strength. Your negative side removed from you, the power of command begins to elude you.

Although Evil Kirk is now running around the ship with a severely scratched face, the evil one puts make-up on his cheek so no one can identify him. After he grabs a hand phaser, he hides in Engineering. Good Kirk anticipates the move and confronts him. Both scuffle, and the Evil Kirk scratches the good Kirk to confuse Spock who meets the two. The Vulcan gives Evil Kirk a nerve pinch, knocking him out, and escorts them both to Sickbay.

Dr. McCoy believes that if the two Kirks are reunited, like the dog was earlier by Mr. Scott, they too will die like the canine. Spock disagrees, saying that the dog did not have the emotional intelligence to withstand the reintegration.

> **McCoy**: Jim, you can't risk your life on a theory!
>
> **Spock**: Being split in two halves is no theory with me, Doctor. I have a human half, you see, as well as an alien half, submerged, constantly at war with each other. Personal experience, Doctor. I survive it because my intelligence wins out over both, makes them live together. Your intelligence would enable you to survive as well.

With the away crew near death on the freezing planet, Scotty must try to rescue them, but not risking the worst outcome, he dare not. The good Kirk has to convince his double to join him in transport, stating that they need each other to survive. He reluctantly agrees, and both stand on the transporter pad. Scotty energizes and reenergizes. Only one Captain Kirk reappears, seemingly like his real self. Scott immediately beams up Sulu and his away team - saving the *Enterprise's* crewmen.

Notable Dialogue:

> **Kirk**: *[about Evil Kirk]* I have to take him back inside myself. I can't survive without him. I don't want to take him back. He's like an animal. A thoughtless, brutal animal. And yet it's me. Me!

> **Spock**: What makes one man an exceptional leader? We see indications that it's his negative side which makes him strong, that his evil side, controlled and disciplines. It is vital to his strength. You negative side removed from you, the power of command begins to elude you.

Character Arcs: Good vs. Evil James T. Kirk

James T. Kirk, like all humans, has both an evil and decent side to him. According to Mr. Spock the negative side makes Kirk strong, and as a controlled side of his personality, makes him a strong leader.

Lao Tzu would disagree with Spock, saying that the evil that rests inside us is a part of us that is not on the Taoist path to the Way. The Way, in this regards, does not seek self-satisfaction at the expense of others (like Kirk's attempt to force himself on Janice Reed). Rulers in China at Lao's time might also be seen as giving into the base instincts by taking control of their people in a selfish, hateful manner as well.

The good part of Kirk, Lao might say, is the person who knows that there must be a better way to interact with those around him. Strength comes from compassion, patience and simplicity of life. Seeking power over others, like rulers do, is not in line with a Taoist existence.

Everyday Reflections

We have both good and evil parts to our core being, one being controlled over the other in times of necessity action with others. For Kirk, like others, the embrace of both sides, make him what he is as a leader.

What are your dominate personality traits? Are you an introvert or an extrovert? Are you a leader like Captain Kirk, or would you rather be a bridge officer or an engineer?

What type of actions have you taken recently (in your school, your job, your family, etc.) to change your behavior so that you can either control the roughness inside you or become more outspoken?

What type of leaders do you believe would make great leaders in your society today? What type of issues would they need to tackle?

Everyday Action

Do something extraordinary in your daily routine. In a few encounters with a stranger, do a kind, compassionate act you normally would not on any day. With a teacher or a supervisor, take a strong stand on an issue affecting you and others. In both instances, see what comes of your uncommon acts.

Lesson 3

The good fighter is able to secure himself against defeat,

but cannot make certain of defeating the enemy

Sun Tzu Chapter 2

Season 1 Episode 10: The Corbomite Maneuver

Story Summary

On a mapping expedition, *Enterprise* destroys a marking buoy of the First Federation that had appeared dangerously close to the ship. Minutes later, a ship of enormous size saddles alongside the much smaller Federation starship. Commander Balok of the *Fesarius* alerts Kirk that their move to cross into their space is an act of war, and the consequences, their immediate death. Balok gives Kirk and crew ten minutes to make peace with their god before meeting a very uncomfortable end to their lives.

Spock fixes on a visual of Commander Balok, a creepy, haunting image of a bald, bulbous, blue head with large eyes and mouth. His appearance is more than terrifying and causes one crewmen, Bailey's hysterical reaction and impending doom. Ushered off the bridge by Dr. McCoy, the physician blames the captain for putting Bailey and the others in this dire predicament.

Knowing the *Enterprise* cannot match the firepower of the *Fesarius*, Captain James T. Kirk bluffs Commander Balok.

> **Kirk**: This is the Captain of the *Enterprise*. Our respect for other life forms requires that we give you this... warning. There is one critical item of information that has never been incorporated into the memory banks of any Earth ship. Since the early years of space exploration, Earth vessels have had incorporated into them a substance known as... *corbomite*. It is a material and a device which prevents attack on us. If any destructive energy touches our vessel, a reverse reaction of equal strength is created, destroying --
> **Balok**: You now have two minutes.
> **Kirk**: -- destroying the attacker. It may interest you to know that since the initial use of corbomite more than two of our centuries ago, no attacking vessel has survived the attempt. Death has... little meaning to us. If it has none to you -- then attack us now. We grow annoyed at your foolishness.

At the end of two minutes, Balok does not fire on *Enterprise*, but instead tells them that he will tow out of Federation space, imprison the crew and then destroy their starship. A small scout vessel sets a tractor beam on *Enterprise* and begins its tow towards enemy territory.

Spock devises a plan to serve the ship at sharp angles to break the enemy vessel's hold – which works well, crippling the smaller ship. A distress call to the mother ship is not answered, so Kirk, Bailey, Spock and McCoy board the alien vessel to render aid.

There, they are greeted by a small humanoid child, who appears no more than six years old. The boy is the real captain of the *Fesarius*, the boy tells Kirk that Balok is his alter ego, and admits he was only testing *Enterprise* for its true intentions. The child welcomes the small contingent to stay, perhaps even send a crewman to teach him about humanity on Earth. Bailey volunteers for the away mission.

Notable Dialogue:

> **Kirk**: Captain to crew. Those of you who have served for long on this vessel have encountered alien life-forms. You know the greatest danger facing us is ourselves, an irrational fear of the unknown. But there's no such thing as the unknown-- only things temporarily hidden, temporarily not understood. In most cases we have found that intelligence capable of a civilization is capable of understanding peaceful gestures. Surely a life-form advanced enough for space travel is advanced enough to eventually understand our motives. All decks stand by. Captain out.

> _____

> **Spock**: I regret not having learned more about this Balok. He was reminiscent of my father.
> **Scotty**: Then may heaven have helped your mother.
> **Spock**: Quite the contrary. She considered herself a very fortunate Earth woman.

Character Arcs: Balok and Captain Kirk

Although James T. Kirk is always a strategist of skill and cunning, with Balok's superior ship and weaponry, the enterprising captain uses more guile than muscle or bluster. Although it is later revealed that both ship captains were bluffing, neither are sure of the other's intention or words. Balok and Kirk draw a stalemate, and surprisingly, both accept it. Neither wish to use force, so instead use diplomacy and patience with the other when all other options fail. A good move by both in this first contact scenario.

Everyday Reflections

Sun Tzu would applaud the way Kirk prevented the situation from escalating, and instead, used his mind to out think his opponent. The *Enterprise* captain used guile, and due to his strategy, prevented his ship from possible destruction, saved his crew, and also brought about a truce between both the enemy and himself.

In your life, when have you acted like Captain Kirk and you bluffed your way out of trouble? Did you eventually reconcile the problem with your opponent, boss or co-worker?

Everyday Actions

The next time you watch a detective, crime or mystery on Netflix or on television, take notice where the bluff occurs between the characters. Any *Columbo* (1968-78) episode, staring the inscrutable actor Peter Falk playing the supposed dim-witted police investigator, would be perfect for this assignment.

Lesson 4

The skillful fighter puts himself into a position which makes defeat impossible, and does not miss the moment for defeating the enemy

Sun Tzu Chapter 2

Season One: The Cage (Original Pilot Episode of the Series)

Story Summary

With the USS *Enterprise* 1701-A captained by Christopher Pike, the starship answers a distress call from Talos IV. Sending a landing party to the surface, Captain Pike immediately becomes entranced with a beautiful young woman named Vina, who has survived a crash landing along with other members of a science team thought lost eighteen years ago. Christopher and Vina take a short walk to a nearby mountain to talk, but suddenly, the Talosians knockout Pike, and take him to their underground home.

Just as quickly, the science team and their camp vanishes. Number One, 2nd in charge of *Enterprise*, Mr. Spock, the Doctor and the rest of the away team realize that they have been fooled to believe in the Talosian illusion. Spock rushes to the last known spot of his captain, but his hand phaser cannot cut through the sheer rock blocking the entrance to the underground cavern. Spock asks for a much larger phaser from *Enterprise*. After it is beamed down, Spock focuses the energy on the mountain, but not even at the highest setting does the weapon affect the rock face.

Inside the cavern, Christopher Pike awakens, with Vina by his side. She tells him of the Talosian's plan to repopulate the planet with humans, starting with them. Pike, angered by the kidnapping, is more interested in escaping back to the surface, barely listening to his cell mate.

To excite Pike's interest in the human female, the Talosians present Vina in different seductive forms for the starship captain. First, they create a pastoral area, a horse, and a country girl persona to Vina. When this scenario does not work long, Vina's image is transformed, making her next a high princess. Finally Vina appears as a green skinned, seductive Orion slave girl. Pike calls out the Talosians to stop the game and demands his release.

Back in his prison cell, Number One and an attractive crew member from the ship appear next to Pike. A Talosian tells the captain that if Vina does not interest him, perhaps he will better enjoy the pleasures of one or both of these earth women. Neither crew members are thrilled with the thought of confinement either. Pike goes into a rage and lunges at the see through force field, frightening the Talosian. Christopher guesses correctly that reading his primitive emotions are the way the Talosians can be defeated. The captain fires his hand phaser at the cell's force field – seemingly without effect.

Later that evening, a Talosian returns to feed the humans, slips the tray through the door, and Pike grabs him and pulls him into the cell. The captain pushes the phaser to the Talosian's head.

"I bet this phaser has ripped a hole in this cell – and I also believe that if I pull this trigger again, I can put a hole in your head as well," Pike tells the Talosian. The keeper stops the illusion and Pike and the other women see reality – a hole in the cell large enough for them to escape to the surface. The Talosian stops the illusion and proves Pike's suspicion valid. The captain goes to the surface with his Number One and the yeoman along with Vina.

After Pike calls his ship, Vina walks away, telling him that she cannot go because her life is tied to the planet. Realizing that Vina's illusion of health and beauty is important to her, he asks the Talosians to give that image back to her. They oblige. Captain Pike, Number One and the yeoman beam, back up to the ship as Vina watches from the planet.

Notable Dialogue:

> Talosian: "She has an illusion and you have reality. May you find your way be as pleasant."

Character Arcs: Captain Christopher Pike

Sun Tzu would be proud of Captain Christopher Pike who used his mind against a superior force to free himself, his ship, and squash the Talosians plans to repopulate their planet with his crew. In this military scenario, weapons could not win, only mental acuity. Fighting an enemy with one's mind is the key to any battle, but in this instance, it was the only one to secure Pike's release.

Everyday Reflections

What is illusion and what is real? That is the question of our existence, but one that is hardly answered with certainty. For example, in the case of the Talos IV incident years earlier during Captain Pike's first venture onto the planet, Christopher experienced the pain and the agony of illusion during his captivity on the world by the Talosians. When Pike realized Talosian mind control kept him from achieving his goals, he knew that it was he who had imprisoned himself. Not think about your existence in the world today. What is it that truly keeps you from achieving your most precious life goals? There are no Talosians on Earth, but are there people in your work or personal life that imprison you by their words? As metaphysical as a discussion like this could become, reflect on how you allow others to control you by intimidation, mental or physical. How can you ever break that imprisonment if you never challenge that person/people who try to bind you to slavery or to bend you to their wills?

Everyday Actions

How do you encourage others to be all they can be in school, work, family challenges? Try to find a road to help someone close to you dream bigger, try harder and be bolder in their everyday lives. As you know, even the smallest of actions will cause a cascade of confidence in others. Write the action down in a journal and collect the stories.

Keep track of your good deeds. During the next month, write down the number of times you have performed such acts of kindness. How many human beings you have directly assisted in a way that should put them on a path to personal and professional success?

Lesson 5

The value comes from what is there, but the use comes from what is not there

Lao Tzu Chapter 11

Season 1 Episodes 11 & 12: The Menagerie

Story Summary

The USS *Enterprise* goes to Station 11 to answer a distress call made by Captain Christopher Pike, the first leader of starship. When the ship enters orbit, Captain Kirk and Mr. Spock beam down to the Starfleet base to answer the hail by Pike. Commodore Mendez tell both officers that the former captain could not have possibly made a call due to a severe radiation accident Pike was in years ago that has rendered him relatively helpless and with no ability to communicate with anyone except in yes and no answers. Christopher Pike wheels into the room, scared and unable to speak. Kirk goes outside the room to talk more about this with Mendez, whereas Spock speaks to his close friend and former captain, telling him about his plan. Repeatedly, Pike signals a *no* answer with his chair buzzer.

Ushered into another briefing room, Commodore Mendez confirms that Pike did not send a message to *Enterprise*. Mendez also discusses Pike's visit to Talos IV years earlier, which is now classified information, and how the planet is off limits to all Starfleet personnel.

During this meeting, Spock has beamed up to *Enterprise* with Pike and has placed him in Dr. McCoy's care in sickbay. Additionally, Mr. Spock has given false information to the crew, telling them that Captain Kirk has been delayed on Station 11, but that the ship is to immediately travel to Talos IV on a secret, emergency mission.

Soon afterwards, Captain Kirk is informed by Mendez that *Enterprise* has left orbit. Kirk and Mendez speed towards the starship in a shuttle, but cannot maintain the speed to catch *Enterprise*. Out of fuel, and nearly out of life support, Spock turns the ship around and picks up the shuttle. Immediately, the Vulcan admits his behavior is mutinous and demands a court trial. Although Mendez is furious with Spock, and Kirk confounded, the commodore tells the first officer that they cannot hold a court martial on *Enterprise* without three ranking officers. Spock disagrees, and asks for Pike to join the proceedings.

The court martial begins, and as evidence, Mr. Spock displays a video transmission from Captain Pike's mission to Talos IV. Although Mendez cites the evidence inadmissible, both Kirk and Pike overrule the commodore. The trial goes on as Pike's entire adventure on Talos IV starts to play for the four Starfleet officers.

By the end of Pike's story on Talos IV, *Enterprise* has reached the forbidden planet. Mendez mysteriously disappears from the courtroom. Spock admits that it was the Talosians who created the image of the Starfleet leader and the courtroom drama was merely a distraction to keep Kirk from preventing the starship from reaching Talos IV.

Captain Kirk, more understanding of Pike's situation, asks his friend if he would like to go to the planet and live out his final days there with Vina. Pike buzzes yes. Spock wheels the former captain out of the room. Kirk smiles as he watches the viewscreen and sees Christopher on the planet, hand in hand with Vina.

Notable Dialogue:

> **Kirk**: Mr. Spock, when you're finished, I want to talk to you. This regrettable tendency you've been showing lately towards flagrant emotionalism --
> **Spock**: I see no reason to insult me, sir.

Character Arcs: Spock

In a very unusual occurrence, Mr. Spock succumbs to his human side, and tricks his current commanding officer, James T. Kirk, to help his former captain, Christopher Pike, so the wheelchair-bound man can return to Talos IV and live out his days in the illusion of vitality. As Lao Tzu said elegantly, the use of something comes from what is *not* there – and in this case, what is unavailable to Pike is use of his body. The illusion of health and youth is something many of us yearn for as old age ravages our physique. With the help of the Talosians, Mr. Spock gives his first captain the illusion of youth, and with Vina by his side, yet another human who suffered from physical limitations, both were able to live out their lives in a joyful manner.

Everyday Reflections

Was Spock's actions truly against the best interests of his crew, starship, Kirk and Federation laws? What were his true motives? Do you find it odd that a person who professes not to be an emotional being would do such an emotional act to help his former captain attain a better life in another world? Would you have endangered your career like this to help a close friend, one you respected and believed deserved to live out his/her life in peace and joy? Can you think of any actions by your friends or family members who have done something unusual or heroic for another person?

Everyday Actions

Take a risk and stand up for a fellow co-worker, family member, perhaps even a stranger, and do what is necessary to make their life better for at least one moment, one day, in an important way. Can you channel your inner-Spock, and do what it takes to be a hero to someone who needs a helping hand like his former ship's captain.

Life is not about playing it safe, but by contributing to the betterment of others, even in the smallest of ways.

Lesson 6

Good leaders reach solutions, and then stop. They do not dare to rely on force.
Lao Tzu Chapter 30

Season 1 Episode 13: Conscience of the King

Story Summary

Based an accusation by a friend, Dr. Thomas Leighton, Captain Kirk investigates an actor named Karidan, who is thought to be *Kodos the Executioner* – a former governor of Tarsus IV, who had half the Earth colonists put to death to avoid chaos and confusion over a food shortage. Leighton and Kirk were both eye witnesses to the executions – unnecessary murders especially in light that a supply ship reached the planet shortly afterwards. The body of Kodos was allegedly found, but burned beyond recognition. Unsure, but curious, Kirk assures his close friend that he will do whatever it takes to bring the man to justice if he is indeed the despot.

Back on board *Enterprise*, the captain investigates the acting troupe. The photo of the actor and the governor seem to match, but without more evidence, Kirk cannot bring charges against Karidan.

To prove Leighton's claim, the captain invites the troupe to the ship to have them perform a Shakespeare play to further observe the man. The crew enjoys the performance, but the actor covers his face on stage and refuses to attend the after party. Kirk does meet the daughter, the beautiful Lenore, who flirts with James in the botanical garden.

Spock also does his own investigation and tells the captain that nine more eye witnesses to the crime have been murdered – all of them with the Karidan acting troupe has performed in the immediate vicinity. When Kirk finds out that Lieutenant Riley, too, was also a witness to the massacre, he is reassigned to Engineering, to keep him out of harm's way in case he is recognized by the possibly villainous Kodos. Regardless, Riley is poisoned, but survives. Once he learns of Karidian possibly be Kodos, he sneaks backstage to have his revenge on the man who murdered his family.

Captain Kirk learns of the sneak attack and grabs Riley backstage at the performance. The crewman surrenders his weapon. Karidian hears the conversation onstage while performing Hamlet. He stops the performance to confront his daughter. Lenore admits that she has murdered nearly all of the witnesses to protect her father and she will complete the task by killing Kirk. Kodos steps in front of the captain, and takes the phaser shot meant for Kirk. As the actor dies in his daughter's arms, Lenore breaks down completely.

Later on the bridge, McCoy assures Kirk that Lenore is under the best care, though now believes that her father is still performing to sellout crowds across the galaxy.

Notable Dialogue:

> **McCoy**: What if you decide he is Kodos? What then? Do you play God, carry his head through the corridors in triumph? That won't bring back the dead, Jim.
> **Kirk**: No. But they may rest easier.

> **Lenore**: There is no mercy in you.
> **Kirk**: If he is Kodos, then I've shown him more mercy than he deserves. And if he isn't... then we'll let you off at Benecia, and no harm done.
> **Lenore**: Captain Kirk. Who are you to say what harm was done?
> **Kirk**: Who do I have to be?

> **Kodos**: I am tired! ... The past ... is a blank.
> **Kirk**: Those beautiful words, well-acted, change nothing.

Character Arcs: Kirk, Riley, Spock, McCoy, Kodos/Karidian and Lenore

Lao Tzu knows that the perception of any ruler rests in the eyes of the people.

Rulers of lands in the past and the present day kill people in war, justifying the deaths to protect the land of his/her people. Is that type of rhetoric fair and just or simply a way to prevent the possible takeover of nations by foreign powers?

As a ruler, was Kodos a monster? Did the governor of Tarsus IV save the entire population from riots over food shortages?

Were his actions similar to Hitler's, condemning people to death who else need not have died?

Both Kirk and Riley see Kodos as the 'wicked leader' who condemned millions to death in response to an impending food shortage. Are they quick to judge and condemn an innocent man before seeing evidence?

Was Kodos also responsible for his daughter's murders? Lenore killed nearly a dozen eye witnesses to her father's crime. If she were judged mentally fit to go to trial, should she have also been as harshly judged as Kodos?

Everyday Reflections

Was Kodos's action on his home world heroic or murderous? If he had to do it again, do you think he would have done things differently and not execute half of the world's population before the late expected food shipment to his world? Was he a coward to run away and live another life with his daughter? Was he a hero when he stepped in front of his daughter's phaser blast to save Captain Kirk? Do you believe that his daughter acted to protect her father or that her act was that of treachery? Did Lenore, in essence, become the murderer like her father?

Everyday Actions

Take a moment and read a chapter of a book, an article, or an essay on any military leader or a small group of soldiers who was accused of a massacre. Read multiple sources to confirm this opinion. Are they correct in their assessment of the scenario that transpired in a war or conflict?

Or, you can watch, *Casualties of War*, a 1989 movie starring Michael J. Fox and Sean Penn. The true story about a US troop in Vietnam, on Hill 192, who repeatedly raped a Vietnamese hostage then murdered her. The real life cover up and consequences this action is chilling.

Lesson 7

If you know your enemies and know yourself, you will not be imperiled in a hundred battles

Sun Tzu Chapter 3

Season 1 Episode 14: Balance of Terror

Story Summary

While officiating a wedding about *Enterprise*, Captain Kirk is stopped in mid-ceremony, when the ship receives a distress call from Outpost 4, a science station near the Romulan Neutral Zone. Although James wishes to continue to ceremony, he dismisses himself and calls all crew to battle stations.

Spock briefs Kirk about the Neutral Zone – a symbolic but real area of space that has kept both Federation and Romulans at peace for over 100 years, with neither crossing the border nor inflicting harm to the other side – except today. It has been so long in place that neither side has seen each other in that time period.

In a live communication, a single survivor aboard the outpost reports to Kirk and Spock an unseen enemy wrecked devastation on the station, and destroying the phaser team, with a weapon of immense power. As Kirk speaks to the officer, he sees the ship reappear on the Outpost 4 viewscreen and fire one final volley that obliterates the station.

Captain Kirk goes to Red Alert and *Enterprise* chases after the unseen enemy by tracing their warp signature. Kirk assumes that the enemy, as Spock suggests, is likely a Romulan battleship, using a cloaking device. Ensign Stiles finds a coded message and shows it to the bridge crew. The visual is of a humanoid with pointy ears – not unlike Spock's appearance. Lieutenant Stiles looks to Spock and overtly questions his loyalty, at which time Kirk chastises the crewmen for his callous statement.

Stiles apologizes for his remark, but suggests that *Enterprise* pursue and destroy the Romulan ship before it reaches the Neutral Zone. Spock agrees, stating that his distant cousins, the Romulans, will likely perceive any weakness by Starfleet as a just call for war. Unlike the Vulcans who have a peaceful philosophical side, the Romulans have given into a warlike posture for generations. Both groups split up centuries ago to pursue their own cultural and military agendas, according to the Vulcan.

> **Spock**: If Romulans are an offshoot of my Vulcan blood, then attack becomes even more imperative.
>
> **McCoy**: War is never imperative.
>
> **Spock**: It is for them, Doctor. Vulcan, like Earth, had its aggressive colonizing period, savage even by Earth standards. If Romulans retain this martial philosophy, then weakness is something we dare not show.

Over the course of several battles, and although *Enterprise* is faster and easy to maneuver, the Romulan's ship has cloaking and more deadly weapons. Both captains use their most brilliant tactics against the other, and several times, both nearly defeat the other. Eventually, when the *Enterprise* appears severely damaged and is left adrift in space intentionally by Kirk to lure in the enemy, the Romulan commander is pressured to destroy their opponent.

Against his better judgement, the Romulan orders his ship to decloak, moves closer to the starship and prepares to fire. Unable to execute Kirk's command to fire the kill shot, Mr. Spock rushes to the phaser control room, saves his crewmembers who were overcome with gas, and shots, disabling the enemy's vessel.

> **Kirk**: Captain. Standing by to beam your survivors aboard our ship. Prepare to abandon your vessel.
>
> **Romulan Commander**: No. No, that is not our way. I regret that we meet in this way. You and I are of a kind. In a different reality, I could have called you "friend".
>
> **Kirk**: What purpose will it serve to die?
>
> **Romulan Commander**: We are creatures of duty, Captain. I have lived my life by it. Just one more duty to perform.

Although Kirk offers to take survivors aboard, the Romulan refuses, and self-destructs his own ship.

Notable Dialogue:

> **Romulan Commander**: Danger and I are old companions.
>
> **Centurion**: We've seen a hundred campaigns together, and still I do not understand you!
>
> **Romulan Commander**: *I* think you do. No need to tell you what will happen the moment we reach home with proof of the Earthmen's weakness. And we will *have* proof. The Earth commander will follow, he must. And when he attacks, we will destroy him. Our gift to the homeland: another war.

> _____

> **Romulan Commander**: *[referring to Kirk]* He's a sorcerer, that one. He reads the thoughts in my mind.

Character Arcs: James T. Kirk, Spock and the Romulan Commander

In the short battle between Kirk and the Romulan commander, both men use their wits to out run and out fight the other. Both military leaders know that weapons alone cannot save their ships. Kirk carefully scans for the strength of the enemy vessel, but nonetheless nearly loses the first skirmish.

The Romulan commander uses guile before nearly destroying the *Enterprise* several times, but loses nonetheless. In the end of the encounter, the Romulan like a samurai warrior, accepts death rather than surrender.

Everyday Reflections

What made James T. Kirk a wise tactician in the battle with the Romulan commander? Did either military leader over-extend themselves in the battle? Did the Romulan commander act out of instinct, military training, or strict adherence to his culture by destroying his ship and crew when defeated by Captain Kirk? Why was surrendering not an option here?

Everyday Actions

Are you competitive to a fault? Is winning above all costs a lesson you live by today?

In you journal, write down at least three different times when you fought to win in sports or work-related activities.

For example, did you train well beyond your normal schedule to win a city track meet for your high school? Did you practice your hitting in the cages for a league championship for a community softball league? Or did you put in overtime to impress your supervisor to earn a promotion over a fellow worker for your company?

Lesson 8

Ancient masters of excellence had a subtle essence,

a depth too profound to comprehend

Lao Tzu Chapter 15

Season 1 Episode 17: The Squire of Gothos

Story Summary

The *Enterprise* speeds through a star dessert on an eight day supply run to Colony Beta VI. Spock spots a rogue planet directly ahead of them. As Lt. Sulu attempts to put *Enterprise* in orbit, which prevents it from crashing into the planet. Moments later, he and Captain Kirk are beamed off the ship, shocking the bridge officers.

More surprisingly, a message, in old English comes on a small viewscreen: "Greeting and Felicitations!" Spock orders McCoy and LaSalle, a geologist, to beam to the surface with to search for their captain and navigational officer.

Once on the surface, Spock and company find a medieval castle. They are ushered inside and find Kirk and Sulu – frozen in mid-motion. Nearby is a strange being dressed in gothic military garb who calls himself, General Trelane, Retired. Trelane welcomes the crew compliment to his planet, Gothos. With Trelane's permission, McCoy examines the alien but finds no life as he knows it.

After reviving the landing party that had been paralyzed by General Trelane, Kirk beings to lose patience with the being who is more of a braggart than anything else. As Trelane plays a piano, Spock guesses that the instrument holds his power. Kirk shots the musical instrument, upsetting Trelane, and beams his party back to Enterprise. As the starship takes off at a high warp speed, Trelane moves his planet and catches up with Kirk. Knowing that they cannot escape, Kirk transports down to the world once again to confront his nemesis. Immediately, the captain is put on trial in a English courtroom of long ago.

Dressed in a white wig and black robe, Trelane accuses Kirk of treason, conspiracy and insurrection. He condemns the captain to hanging – and produces a noose. Kirk proposes a hunt, with himself as prey, a more challenging proposal to Trelane, for the freedom of his ship and crew. Trelene agrees.

Cornered in front of the castle shortly in the hunt, Kirk slaps Trelane in the face, bringing the alien to tears, Just then, two energy being appear and order their son to come along home. The two parents apologize for their son's misbehavior. Kirk accepts their apology and returns to his ship.

Notable Dialogue:

> **Trelane**: You do realize that it's in deference to the Captain that I brought you here.
> **Spock**: Affirmative.
> **Trelane**: Well, I don't know if I like your tone. It's most challenging. That's what you're doing, challenging me?
> **Spock**: I object to you. I object to intellect without discipline. I object to power without constructive purpose.
> **Trelane**: Oh, Mr. Spock, you do have one saving grace after all - you're ill mannered. The human half of you, no doubt.

Character Arcs: Trelane, Spock and Kirk

When confronted with illogical actions by the emotionally delicate Trelane, neither Kirk nor Spock know how to deal with him. Is he a man-child or a cruel alien who is judgmental, arrogant and spiteful to a fault? How does anyone play with such a being with powers of life and death?

The seemingly all-powerful Trelane, (who we later find out is a member of the Q Continuum and godfather to Q seen on TNG) endangers the *Enterprise* crew repeatedly like a petulant child – which we find out at the end, is just that, a boy playing with what he thinks are his new found toys. The Q, Trelane, tries to replicate the history of old Earth form over 900 years ago, due to the Continuum's beings living in three separate timeline simultaneously (according to author Peter Gerald in his 1994 novel, *Q-Squared*), but neither master's the ancient ones wisdom nor their patience.

Both Captain Kirk and Spock do their best to show patience with the alien being at first, but eventually the *Enterprise* commander realizes that he must treat the strange being as a child –

and just say no to anything he demands of them. Spock tries to reason with Trelane, but children cannot use rational thought over their emotions.

Everyday Reflections

Are you as viscously playful with fellow human beings as Trelane? Do you view others as puppets to manipulate and dance to your songs like children do with their toys? If not, then you are more like the Ancients, as Lao Tzu said, who show wisdom and compassion?

Everyday Actions

As mentioned earlier, I suggest you pick up a copy of the book, *Q-Squared*, by Peter Gerald, published by Pocket Books. This *Star Trek* big book novel spent three weeks on the New York Times Best Seller List back in 1994.

Lesson 9

Those who relish manslaughter cannot reach their goals in the world

Lao Tzu Chapter 31

Season 1 Episode 18: Arena

Story Summary

As Captain Kirk responds to a distress call of a Federation science outpost, he, Spock and Dr. McCoy and a security force team beam to the surface to defend the scientists. One man survives, telling Kirk before he dies that an unknown enemy fired upon them without reason. Once again, the enemy attacks Kirk's men, killing several of them as they also fire at the *Enterprise*. Kirk and Spock use a cannon to scatter the enemy, and *Enterprise* defends itself. Soon, the unknown attacker leaves with Captain Kirk and crew in high warp pursuit to seek revenge if not an answer for the unprovoked attack on innocent Federation citizens.

As the two ships race towards an unexplored area of space, both lose power. Neither ship can move nor fire weapons at the others. The Metrons, an isolationist alien race, condemn the intrusion on their space. Since the two warring factions show little regard for life, the Metrons announce they the two representative from both ships will fight to the death in hand to hand combat on a nearby planet. Neither ship's crew nor any of its weapons may be use in battle. The winner will be allowed to go on their journey, but the loser will be condemned to death.

Both crews are allowed to view the one-on-one fight on their respective ship's viewscreen, but neither can offer advice or interfere in any way.

Soon, James T. Kirk and the Gorn captain appear on the planet. Kirk attacks the Gorn, but finds himself overmatched. He escapes, and figures out how to create gun powder from the planet's natural minerals. Eventually, he shoots a cannon off into the Gorn, stuns it, and as Kirk is about to kill the opponent, he stops, showing mercy towards the enemy. The Metrons are impressed. Kirk recommends that the Metrons spare the life of the Gorn, which they do, and send his ship and the *Enterprise* on their respective journeys home.

Notable Dialogue:

> **Kirk**: *[to the helpless Gorn]* No, I won't kill you. Maybe you thought you were...protecting yourself...when you attacked the outpost. *[louder, to the Metrons]* No, I won't kill him! Do you hear? You'll have to get your entertainment someplace else! *[helpless Gorn disappears, and a Metron appears]* You're a Metron?
>
> **Metron**: Does my appearance surprise you, Captain?
>
> **Kirk**: You seem more like a boy.
>
> **Metron**: I am approximately 1,500 of your Earth years old. You surprise me, Captain.
>
> **Kirk**: How?
>
> **Metron**: By sparing your helpless enemy who surely would've destroyed you, you demonstrated the advanced trait of mercy, something we hardly expected. We feel that there may be hope for your kind. Therefore, you will not be destroyed. It would not be...civilized.
>
> **Kirk**: What happened to the Gorn?
>
> **Metron**: I sent him back to his ship. If you like, I shall destroy him for you.
>
> **Kirk**: *[calmly]* No. That won't be necessary. We can talk. Maybe...reach an agreement.
>
> **Metron**: Very good, Captain. There *is* hope for you. Perhaps, in several thousand years, your people and mine shall meet to reach an agreement. You're still half-savage, but there *is* hope. We will contact you when we are ready.

> Kirk: We're a most promising species, Mr. Spock, as predators go. Did you know that? I frequently have my doubts, but not anymore. And maybe in a thousand years or so, we'll be able to prove it.

Character Arcs: Kirk, Spock, the Metrons and the Gorn

After centuries of spiritual and emotional growth, the Metrons know that aggressive behavior is the worst quality of any intelligent species. Like ancient Taoists from a far-off galaxy, the Metrons hope to learn which species, human or Gorn, show the most promise.

No Taoist would have both battle to the death, but in this contest, they do give both captains a chance to show mercy – which Kirk does. Both human and Gorn are allowed to continue their journeys with the blessing of the Metrons.

Everyday Reflections

What did James T. Kirk learn from his fight with the Gorn? Do you believe that the lesson learned from by *Enterprise* captain will be taken this into his next battle?

In general, why do human beings often prejudge people based on actions that seem insensitive or just plain wrong by social norms of our society? Are our judgements based on what our perceptions of what we should do in certain situations rather than accepting a less than perfect reaction from others from a culturally different way of life?

What type of fights have you had in your life? Physically? Psychologically? Why did they occur? On reflection, should you have turned the other way when challenged?

Everyday Actions

In your journal for the upcoming week, keep track of your interactions with others on the street, at work, in school, wherever you spend time in a public setting. How often did you feel challenged by others in an unfair way? What was your reaction to a stranger, co-worker, fellow student, friend or family member who you believed treated you badly?

Lesson 10

In ancient times, those who followed the Way

did not try to give people knowledge,

but kept them ignorant

Lao Tzu Chapter 65

Season 1 Episode 21: Return of the Archons

Story Summary

The *Enterprise* travels to Beta III to search for the USS *Archon*, a Starfleet vessel lost over 100 years earlier near the planet. Lieutenant Sulu beams down to covertly investigate, but when he returns, he appears under a spell that renders him hopelessly peaceful and without direction. Due to his inability to convey any useful intelligence on the planet, Kirk, Spock and McCoy beam down to Beta III to better understand what or who transformed their navigations officer into a mindless drone.

Once on the planet, Kirk and the others find a 19th century community with Lawgivers and an all-powerful leader known as Landru. As night approaches, the citizens begin to riot in the street, attack each other violently and men sexually assault women. Kirk discovers that he evening of Festival is a frequent event on Beta III.

To avoid conflict and injuries, Kirk, Spock and McCoy hide in a boarding home of a local named Regar. The local tells them of a legend that a starship was pulled from the sky by Landru many years earlier. Thanking the man for the information, Kirk contacts *Enterprise*. Mr. Scott tells his captain that a heat ray from the planet is draining the ship's shielding, and at this rate, *Enterprise* will fall into the atmosphere in less than twelve hours unless the beams are turned off.

Landru's projection appears to the landing party. An ultrasonic high pitched sound renders Kirk, Spock and McCoy unconscious. After the trio are imprisoned, McCoy is 'absorbed into the body', and put under Landru's control. Surprisingly, Marpion, a member of the underground resistance rescues a subdued McCoy, Kirk and Spock. Reger, too, is a resistance member, and both he and Marpion tell the two Starfleet officers that Landru saved their society 6,000 years ago and created a simple society, but now, it was corrupted, without any personal freedom allowed apart from the leaders' commands.

Kirk and Spock overwhelm two guards and use their robes to disguise themselves so as to commune with Landru. Once inside, the leader threatens Kirk and Spock, but after the captain blast through the wall with a hand phaser, Landru is revealed to be a supercomputer. Using logic inside the hidden fortress, Kirk convinces Landru that the people must be governed by free will. Landru agrees and self-destructs, saving *Enterprise* and allowing the Beta III people to run their own society.

Kirk, Spock and McCoy leave the planet but the people agree to accept Federation advisors to help create a better society.

Notable Dialogue:

> **Landru Computer**: I am Landru. I am he. All that he was I am, his experience, his knowledge.
> **Kirk**: But not his wisdom. He may have programmed you, but he could not have given you a soul. You are a machine.
> **Landru Computer**: Your statement is irrelevant.

> _____

> **Kirk**: Without freedom of choice there is no creativity.

> _____

> **Kirk**: It's time you learned that freedom is never a gift. It has to be earned.

> _____

> **Spock**: How often mankind has wished for a world as peaceful and secure as the one Landru provided.
> **Kirk**: Yes. And we never got it. Just lucky, I guess.

> _____

> **Spock**: I prefer the concrete, the graspable, and the provable.
> **Kirk**: You'd make a splendid computer, Mr. Spock.
> **Spock**: That is very kind of you, Captain!

Character Arcs: Mr. Spock, Captain Kirk and Landru

Is Landru an enlightened leader, an ancient that Lao Tzu would recommend to run a planet? Unlikely. This form of government is a dictatorship, a religious cult-like organization that would offend any Taoist follower.

In this story, Landru, keeps the people in the dark about who or what 'it' is – something that also promotes stagnation and state control, even outward expressions of aggression by its people.

Landru rule represents Stalinism or totalitarian rule found in Russia under Putin today. This government leader is more like the Borg we find in TNG.

Captain Kirk and Mr. Spock are Taoist in nature, and promote individualism, social progress and self-expression. They are Starfleet, but also represent an American model of political freedom and equality.

Everyday Reflections

Even though both Kirk and Spock interfere with the culture of the planet by exposing Landru to the people, the captain claims they are not going against Federation's Prime Directive on Beta III. The culture on the planet is stagnant, and thus the directive does not apply here.

Still, what allows Captain James T. Kirk to interfere with a civilization if it chooses to worship a god-like leader? Is this the right call?

In 2020, would a Prime Directive, like Starfleet's, be appropriate for all governments today so as to prevent any strong-armed leader to take over other countries for mineral resources or strategic military bases?

Everyday Actions

Perform a literary search on the topics of Stalinism, totalitarianism, socialism and communism. Compare historical definitions of all countries that used these in the past, and ones that do it today (Russia, Cuba, and others). Do these countries provide well for the people or do they manipulate the nation for political power, wealth and personal glory

Lesson 11

I have three treasures that I cherish.

The first is compassion.

The second is moderation.

The third is not claiming to be first in the world

Lao Tzu Chapter 67

Season 1 Episode 22: Space Seed

Story Summary

The *Enterprise* finds the USS *Botany Bay* adrift, a derelict, but still with precious cargo aboard: genetically altered humans from the Eugenics War of the early 21st century. As Kirk and company board the *Botany Bay*, they find 84 stasis pods; 72 of which are still contain living Augments. Historical expert, Marla McGivers, recognizes the leader, but does not tell her captain his name. As he is revived, and has difficulty breathing, Kirk has him beamed to sickbay.

In the medical bay, Khan Noonien Singh awakens, and grabs a scalpel from a tray. As McCoy goes to examine the Augment, Khan slips the scalpel under the physician's throat. Leonard makes a joke on how to bring quick death to him, Khan smiles slightly, and lets McCoy his hostage go.

Kirk comes to sickbay and questions his quest, but does not receive much detail in the answers. The captain welcomes him aboard and tells him he has freedom of the ship when he is strong enough to move about.

Soon afterwards, Khan is cleared by McCoy. Khan visits McGivers in her quarters and recognizes a painting she is working on: himself. The Starfleet officer knows his background as the power-hungry, madman who started the Eugenics War on Earth, then escaped capture when he lost. Khan gives her an option: join him or die. McGivers, charmed by the dangerous, handsome man, or death.

Within the hour, Khan attacks the main transporter chief, beams aboard the Botany Bay, and works with McGivers to revive the other seventy two augments.

Shortly after this, Khan's group boards *Enterprise* and take over the ship – placing all the senior officers in the Ready Room, except for Kirk – who Khan places in a decompression chamber. The terrorist threatens to kill Captain Kirk if Spock does not give him Enterprise's commands codes. Spock refuses to hand over the ship to the lunatic.

As the entire crew watches Kirk gasping for air, the transmission ends, and Khan hails his death as a new beginning for his people. Little does he know that McGivers has betrayed him by overpowering the guard with a hypospray, disabling the security camera and sets her captain free from impending death in the decompression chamber.

Kirk works to free his other crewmates before he meets Khan in Engineering. The Augment sets the ship on a self-destruct mode by overloading the warp core, challenging Kirk to hand to hand combat to save *Enterprise*. Khans' overwhelming strength nearly defeats he captain, but Kirk finds a way to defeat him and return the engines to normal working order.

Now in custody, Captain Kirk, Spock and McCoy oversee a brief hearing on Khan's actions. Instead of bringing him to Starfleet Headquarters for imprisonment, he sentences him and his group to Ceti Alpha V, a desolate world. Khan accepts this challenge, citing Milton from *Paradise Lost*. Kirk also grants his officer, McGivers freedom with Khan, who accepts the strong woman to be his companion on the new world

McCoy asks Kirk what Khan was referring to in Milton's book, and the captain paraphrases the idea saying that Eugenics War criminal he would rather rule in hell than peaceably live in heaven.

As they leave the makeshift courtroom, Spock speculates what life would be like on Ceti Alpha V in 100 years under Khan and his band of super humans.

Little does the Vulcan know that merely 15 years later, Khan will have his revenge on Captain Kirk and his friends, killing Kirk's only son and being responsible for the death of his best friend, Mr. Spock.

Notable Dialogue:

> **Khan**: Where am I?
> **McCoy**: You're in bed, holding a knife at your doctor's throat.
> **Khan**: Answer my question!
> **McCoy**: It would be most effective if you would cut the carotid artery, just under the left ear.
> **Khan**: *[releasing McCoy]* I like a brave man.
>
> **Khan**: Improve a mechanical device and you may double productivity, but improve Man, and you gain a thousand fold

Character Arcs: Khan Noonien Singh and Captain James T. Kirk

Lao Tzu understood that compassion and moderation were two important values humans need to possess. Also, Lao knew that those who sought power would never lead for long in any society.

Is it the seed of engineering or the advancement of greed and lust for power that goes along with it that makes genetic enhancement so dangerous?

In this story, Khan represents what is terribly wrong with genetic engineering. Does the lust for power prove dangerous because humans with enhanced abilities think of themselves as gods? From the earlier Trek story, *Where No Man has Gone Before*, Gary turns into a god-like being, and others around him, are like ants, according to Mr. Spock. Is it the same here with Khan, or is there rush to take over the galaxy proof alone of this question?

Everyday Reflections

What is so dangerous about genetic engineering? Why is this banned in the medical community across the world? Are we afraid enough about this type of behavior happening like it did in this *Star Trek* adventure?

Everyday Actions

If you have not seen the movie, *Star Trek II: The Wrath of Khan*, please take a few hours to watch it today. The story continues the tale of *Space Seed* and is widely regarded as the best *Star Trek* feature length movie.

Lesson 12

The fish cannot leave the deep waters. The state's weaponry should not be displayed.

Lao Tzu Chapter 36

Season 1 Episode 23: The Taste of Armageddon

Story Summary

The *Enterprise* ferries Ambassador Fox to negotiate diplomatic relations between the Federation and Eminian VII. Little is known about the political dynamics of the government but that they have been at war with a neighboring planet, Vendikar, for many years.

When about to take orbit around Eminian VII, Captain Kirk is warned not to approach. The captain ignores the request, and continues the diplomatic venture. Spock, Fox and Kirk beam to the planet and are escorted to the war room where they meet Anan 7 and walls of supercomputers conducting wargames.

The Starfleet officers and diplomat are told that the Vendikar and Eminian use computer simulations to wage war. Minutes earlier, *Enterprise* was hit and destroyed in the attack. Kirk shrugs to the news, but Anan 7 is deadly serious. He tells them *Enterprise* has less than an hour to surrender and order its entire crew compliment to the disintegration chambers. The captain refuses to honor that or any other request from Anan 7. Spock, Kirk and Fox are lead to a holding cell.

Anan 7, using a voice modulator, pretends to be Captain Kirk as he speaks to Mr. Scott. Suspicious that his commander would ask for all *Enterprise* personnel to beam to the planet, Scotty analyzes the voice and finds it to be a fake recording. Scott puts up shields before Anan orders an unprovoked attack on Enterprise.

Apologizing for the skirmish, Anan 7 says that is was a mistake, and that Kirk, Spock and Fox were accidently killed in a fight on his home world. Unknown to him, Spock tricks the security guard to release the landing party. Spock, Kirk and Fox escape and beam back to *Enterprise*. The real war begins.

Soon, Kirk convinces Anan 7 that both worlds, now involved in true to life war, must confront the horrors of death and destruction before either one commits to a peace treaty. A ceasefire is called and Ambassador Fox soon acts as mediator between the two worlds.

Notable Dialogue:

> **Kirk**: Death. Destruction. Disease. Horror. That's what war is all about. That's what makes it a thing to be avoided.

> _____

> **Kirk**: [War] is instinctive. But the instinct can be fought. We're human beings with the blood of a million savage years on our hands! But we can stop it. We can admit that we're killers... but we're not going to kill today. That's all it takes! Knowing that we're not going to kill - today!

Character Arcs: Captain Kirk, Mr. Spock, Ambassador Fox and Anan 7

In this story, Anan 7 is nothing more than a dangerous bureaucrat attempting to perform a job without considering the impact of his insidious task. The basis of such character to a Nazi soldier showing his Jewish prisoners into a gas chamber is obvious. Anan 7 may say that his is doing his job, but at what costs to millions of others in his planet? The humanoid alien may believe he has no blood on his hands, but he does.

Ambassador Fox, in the end of the story, may indeed have value to the mission. His future work on the planet may save countless lives if he can negotiate a treat with the waring planets.

Captain Kirk and Mr. Spock save the day once again by forcing the two planets to take real action in their wars.

Everyday Reflections

Could war to end all wars truly occur in the 21st century? How do you feel about people in power in various nations with the capability to wage Armageddon and ultimately destroy the world? What safeguards are or should be in place to prevent leaders from waging destruction like we see in this story – or worst?

Everyday Actions

In your journal, keep track of the readings you cover on the issue of nuclear weapons in the 21st century. Where are they kept – and which countries are the most prolific in building up such massive stockpiles? Is the U.S. the only country to do this in 2021?

In terms of actions, what can you do, as a private citizen, to raise awareness of nuclear weapon stockpiles in your community? Is there anything an individual or civic group can do to prevent wartime polices in America or abroad? You may wish to contact such organizations locally to see what role you could take to bring everyone's attention to such dangerous weapons that could easily destroy the world.

Lesson 13

To fight and conquer in all your battles is not supreme excellence;

Supreme excellence consists in breaking the enemy's resistance without fighting

Sun Tzu Chapter 3

Season 1 Episode 25: Errand of Mercy

Story Summary

As peace negotiations between the Klingons and the Federation have hit a roadblock, Captain Kirk is sent to Organia, a planet near the borderland, in hopes of forming an alliance of the strategically important post in the galaxy. Once near Organia, *Enterprise* is intercepted by a Bird of Prey, but it survives the sneak attack and destroys the Klingon ship.

Kirk and Spock beam down to Organia to start a peaceful negotiation for a Federation alliance. Avelborne, the Council spokesperson for his civilization, tells the captain that they do not wish to take a side in the battle between the two warring groups. Even using the threat of war against their people by the Klingons as a negotiating point, Kirk cannot seem to get through to the peaceful and confident Avelborne.

Soon, three Klingon ships head towards Organia. Kirk orders the *Enterprise* to leave orbit. To save the two Starfleet officers from capture, the Organian advises Kirk and Spock disguise themselves as citizens.

Immediately, Commander Kor arrives on Organia, and without any resistance, appoints himself as the governor of the planet. Suspicious of Spock as a Federation spy, Kor uses a mind sifter device on the Vulcan. Of course, Spock passes the test due to his superior mental strength. Kirk is appointed as a liaison between the Organians and the Klingon occupation force.

Taking action, Kirk and Spock blow-up an ammunitions dump later that night, hoping to incite resistance of the Organians against the Klingons. Kor is outraged and demands to know which one of his people destroyed his weapons of mass destruction. Ovelborne tells Kor the truth, and expose the two Starfleet officers.

Before the two can be tortured, Avelborne frees Kirk and Spock as both hide from their enemy. For this act of betrayal, Kor promises that he will kill 200 Organians if the two Starfleet officers do not turn themselves into him immediately. Avelborne and the Council seem unworried and do not respond with any animosity towards Kor.

To save the citizens from death, Spock and Kirk raid the Klingon headquarters and capture Kor, but before a final showdown occurs, the Organians reveal their true selves: non-corporeal beings with advanced philosophy and technology.

Rendered powerless, both sides are politely reprimanded for their violent tendencies. Before leaving the Council Room as beings of pure energy, Avelborne predicts Kor and Kirk will one day work together.

After the Organians leave the room, Kor brazenly scoffs at the notion that both Klingons and Humans will one day form a military and political. Doubtful but hopeful, Spock and Kirk act more amendable to the Organian's suggestion. The three military men leave not as friends, but as opponents who may see truth to the Organian's way of logic, and perhaps, on their way to a peace accord one day in the future.

Notable Dialogue:

> **Kirk**: I'm embarrassed. I was furious with the Organians for stopping a war I didn't want. We think of ourselves as the most powerful beings in the universe. It's unsettling to discover that we're wrong.
> **Spock**: Captain. It took millions of years for the Organians to evolve into what they are. Even the gods did not spring into being overnight. You and I have no reason to be embarrassed. We did, after all, beat the odds.
> **Kirk**: Oh, no, no, no, Mr. Spock, we didn't beat the odds; we didn't have a chance. The Organians rigged the game.

Character Arcs: The Organians, Captain James T. Kirk and Klingon Commander Kor

Like Sun Tzu would agree, obtaining territory is one of the most important aspects of any war. Kor, certainly believes in this proposition; and Kirk does as well.

Negotiations between nations is always a tricky business. The Klingons, as a warrior race culture, cannot simply stand by and allow others to take a strategic position in the known galaxy.

Even though Captain Kirk had no intention of striking the Klingons vessel first, he was forced to defend his ship and crew. The Federation and the *Enterprise* captain see that Organia could be the pivotal post that the Klingons could launch a pre-emptive strike against Federation allies.

The Organians have no need for war, and for that matter, peace is a state of being, not a pretense to hold material possessions or territories. As mediators between the Federation and Klingons, they do their best to maintain neutrality. Lao Tzu would very much like this alien race because they take the path of a Taoist and hold true to the ideals of non-interference and peaceful relations with everyone they meet in the galaxy. As Mr. Spock tells Captain Kirk, the Organians have taken thousands of years or longer to master this approach. Humanity, he guesses, is far behind this learning curve.

Everyday Reflections

For the Organians, neither the Klingons Brid of Prey nor the Federation's *Enterprise* posed any military threat to their home world. Neither Kirk nor Kor are true threats to the planet or the non-corporeal beings, and as such, there is no need for violence of any kind. The Organians are truly an enlightened species who could have undoubtedly simply negotiated a settlement between the Klingons and the Federation, but they knew that both sides needed to learn from each other rather than be given something that did not earn through a true dedication to the peace process.

Everyday Actions

When in world history has peaceful protests brought about an important change in government policies? Spend some time researching at a local library, or on the internet, on the effectiveness of protest movements.

For example, look into the India's 1930 Salt March, led by Gandi, against the British rulers. The 1913 Suffrage Parade in America brought attention to the lack of women's equal rights. The 1960's Delano Grape Protest – with a 25 day hungry strike by Caesar Chavez, brought attention to the poverty wage of Mexican workers in the California fields. The Montgomery Bus Boycott of 1955 and Rosa Park's refusal to sit in the back of the bus gave rise to an historic Supreme Court decision on Civil Rights in the South that had profound affects and gave rise to the Civil Rights Movement of the 1960's in America.

Once again, *Star Trek* illustrates humanity's social problems can easily be translated into science fiction stories for viewers.

Lesson 14

What's the difference between beautiful and ugly?

Must one dread what others dread?

Oh barbarity! Will it never end?

Lao Tzu Chapter 20

Season 1 Episode 26: Devil in the Dark

Story Summary

Captain Kirk, Mr. Spock and Dr. McCoy beam down to Janus VI to help colonists put an end to the murders of innocent, perigum miners. With fifty miners already dead and buried, the trio must come up with a way to find a mysterious creature responsible for the deaths.

Examining everything available to him, Spock notices a silicon nodule on the desk of Chief Engineer Vanderberg. The engineer discounts it as a natural oddity of the planet.

Soon, the Chief is alerted to the trouble at the colony's nuclear reactor. Yet another miner is murdered, and a critical part of the reactor stolen. Mr. Scott tries to solve the problem, but his solution will only hold for ten hours – and afterwards, the reactor will blow, destroying the mines and endangering everyone on Janus VI.

While investigating the mine tunnels, Spock tells Kirk that he suspects the creature is a silicon base life form, and to adjust their weapons to injure it. When they find the creature, they fire on it, but it escapes by creating a tunnel with a corrosive it produces, the same substance it likely used on the unsuspecting miners.

A search of the creature bring Kirk and Spock to a chamber filled of the same silicon nodules that Vanderberg had on his desk. By using his proximity detector on his tricorder, Spock determines that the creature is the only one of its kind for 50 miles around, perhaps the entire planet.

Suddenly, the creature appears, and causes a cave-in, trapping Kirk and separating him from Spock.

In the chamber alone, the captain raises his phaser at the creature, but decides not to fire as it back away from him.

Soon, Spock finds a way to reach Kirk, and he too agrees that the native creature is not a threat to them for the moment.

In the ultimate effort to make peace with the life form, Spock offers to mind meld with it. Kirk agrees to the dangerous plan. The Vulcan gently places his hands on the being and relates the message to Kirk: No kill!

Spock finds out that the creature is a Horta, and that every 50,000 years its kind dies off except for one mother who guards the next generation – the silicon eggs found by the minders, and broken apart, murdering her children. The Horta agrees to return the missing nuclear reactor part if Spock promises to protect her babies before she dies from her wounds.

Just then, the miners, led by an angry Vanderberg locates Spock and Kirk, tell them to stand back so they can exact retribution on the murderer. Kirk stands between them and the injured Horta. Spock tells them that they, in fact, had murdered hundreds if not thousands of her babies. The Horta was simply trying to protect itself and her people.

Dr. McCoy is called to help save the life of the Horta, and somehow, with his keen medical expertise and a load of silicon cement beamed from *Enterprise*, the physician repairs the damage from a phaser blast.

Although the miners are still fearful of the Horta, Spock and Kirk reassure them that the creature will not pose any danger to them as long as they leave her children alone.

Notable Dialogue:

> **Spock**: The Horta is badly wounded. It may die.
> **McCoy**: It won't die. By golly, Jim, I'm beginning to think I can cure a rainy day.
> **Kirk**: Can you help it?
> **McCoy**: Helped it? I cured it.
> **Kirk**: How?
> **McCoy**: Well, I had the ship beam down 100 pounds of that thermal concrete. You know, the kind we use to build emergency shelters out of 'em. It's mostly silicone. So I just troweled it into the wound, and it'll act like a bandage until it heals. Take a look. It's as good as new.
> **Kirk**: Well, Mr. Spock, I'm gonna have to ask you to get in touch with the Horta again. Tell her our proposition: She and her children can do all the tunneling they want, our people will remove the minerals, and each side will leave the other alone. You think she'll go for it?
> **Spock**: It seems logical, Captain. The Horta has a very logical mind - and after close association with humans, I find that curiously refreshing.

Character Arcs: Kirk, Spock, McCoy, the Horta and Chief Engineer Vanderberg

With a dead miner and a stolen circulation pump, Vanderberg fears the Horta are dangerous to his people and the mining camp. Yet, can he reason why such creatures could so different than himself and do such an act against a human? Labeling the oddly different life forms as murderers limits the possibility of their sentience or communication with the Horta.

Mr. Spock, a sensitive Vulcan ruled by logic instead of fear and anger, soon realizes that the creature who attacked the miner was merely protecting the thousands of young, living in egg-shaped shells, ones that the minders had destroyed by the hundreds through the caverns. Once Spock shares this knowledge with Captain Kirk, and Dr. McCoy finds a way to repair, and thus save the mother Horta, a peace between the miners is established to the mutual benefit of both humans and Hortas alike.

Everyday Reflections

Why do so many humans consider themselves the ultimate creation? Why do they dismiss the value of other life forms – such as horses, animals of burden, bovines, or canines or felines? Do we fear them because some possess the power to kill us? Why do we subjugate many of them for food? What gives us the supreme ruler of their fates so we may eat beef, chicken, or fish?

Everyday Actions

The next time you come across an injured creature, whether it be a baby bird, a lost kitten or puppy, take it home or bring it to an animal shelter. Your kindness may not be immediately rewarded, but the act itself will bring peace to and comfort to the lost and distressed life.

Lesson 15

Solve it before it happens.

Order it before chaos emerges

Lao Tzu Chapter 64

Season 1 Episode 25: City on the Edge of Forever

Story Summary

After McCoy inadvertently injects himself with a powerful drug during a turbulent orbit around a strange planet putting off huge waves of temporal energy, Leonard becomes manic and paranoid. Although security tries to bring him to the infirmary for treatment, Bones eludes them and transports himself to the planet.

With a small security team, Captain Kirk, Mr. Spock, Scotty and Uhura search for their friend among the ruins. They fail to find him at first, but do stumble upon the Guardian of Forever, a being with the powers to present history to whomever requests it. The Guardian, a mechanical-looking, donut-shaped device speaks to the group. As Spock begins to record earth history his tricorder, McCoy is chased by security – and through the open center of the Guardian.

After his disappearance, Uhura tries to contact *Enterprise*, but cannot reach the starship. There is no USS *Enterprise*, no Starfleet Command or Federation of Planets – thanks to McCoy.

The Guardian tells the Kirk that all they knew is forever changed due to McCoy's actions in earth's history. Captain Kirk asks if history can be reverted back to what it was. The Guardian promises Kirk that if the goes back in time and prevent their friend from making a critical error of judgement, Earth history will go back to the way it was.

By entering the Guardian of Forever, a portal into the past, James T. Kirk and Mr. Spock must find Dr. Leonard McCoy who somehow dramatically changed the history of humanity. If Kirk and Spock fail to stop McCoy from making a dangerous mistake, their timeline, and that of millions of others will be forever be changed for the worse, causing suffering and death to those who did not die before.

When they step through the portal, Kirk and Spock immediately find themselves in an old Chicago neighborhood of the 1930's. Both men steal clothes, run from the police for their misdeed, and hide away in the basement of a men's shelter. Hidden downstairs, they meet Edith Keeler, a beautiful and headstrong woman who rules the center for the homeless. Keeler keenly knows the two need work, so hires them to clean and work at the 21st Street Mission.

Working with primitive but effective vacuum tubes and copper wiring, Spock finds a way to create an advanced mnemonic memory circuit board. Connecting his tricorder into the board, Spock uses old video footage and newspapers to go back in history. Unsurprisingly, he finds that Edith Keeler and their lives are intimately connected. The Vulcan science officer discovers that Edith must die before she can lead a pacifist movement that delays the entrance of the USA into World War II and allows the Germans to develop nuclear weapons first. Carrying the A-Bomb on their V-2 rockets, the Nazis will then bomb all allied target cities and conquer the world.

If Ms. Keeler does not die in a street accident, Mr. Spock tells his friend, their timeline will not exist; and instead billions of people on Earth will die who did not before, and the start of the Federation let alone Starfleet, will never happen. Jim sees this as what must occur, but admits that he has fallen in love with Edith. Spock reminds him that if he leads with his heart and not his mind, humanity will suffer like it never has before or ever will.

Soon after the conversation, a disoriented McCoy stumbles into the mission. Edith sees his plight and offers him a cot in the back storage area, as they both just avoid running into Spock serving coffee in the kitchen area. McCoy thanks her a few days later as he comes out of his drug-induced fog and asks if he can help around the mission. Edith thanks him and tells the doctor that her gentleman caller are going to a Clark Gamble movie in the evening – but Leonard seems bewildered at the actor's name, making Keeler laugh.

As Kirk picks up his date for the evening she mentioned McCoy's lack of pop culture awareness. James grabs her and asks where McCoy is – and the physician shows up on the street. Kirk tells his date to wait as he runs across the busy street to hug his friend. Spock comes out as well, and a confused Edith walks across to meet the three – but is hit by a speeding truck and dies. McCoy condemns Jim for holding him back from saving the woman, but Spock tells him Kirk knows.

Time is restored. The Guardian of Forever asks the crew, once Kirk, Spock and McCoy return through the portal, if they wish to take more adventures.

Notable Dialogue:

> **Edith Keeler**: One day soon, man is going to be able to harness incredible energies, maybe even the atom... energies that could ultimately hurl us to other worlds in... in some sort of spaceship. And the men that reach out into space will be able to find ways to feed the hungry millions of the world and to cure their diseases. They will be able to find a way to give each man hope and a common future. And those are the days that are worth living for.

> _____

> **Edith Keeler**: I think that one day they're going to take all the money that they spend now on war and death...
> **Kirk**: And make them spend it on life.

> _____

> **Edith Keeler**: You know as well as I do how out of place you two are around here.
> **Spock**: Interesting. Where would you estimate we belong, Miss Keeler?
> **Edith Keeler**: *[to Spock]* You? At his side. As if you've always been there and always will. *[to Kirk]* And you... you belong... in another place. I don't know where or how... I'll figure it out eventually.
> **Spock**: I'll finish with the furnace.

Edith Keeler: '..., Captain.' Even when he doesn't say it, he does.

Scott: What happened, sir? You only left a moment ago.
Spock: We were successful.
Guardian: Time has resumed its shape. All is as it was before. Many such journeys are possible. Let me be your gateway.
Uhura: Captain, the *Enterprise* is up there. They're asking if we want to beam up.
Kirk: Let's get the hell out of here.

Character Arcs: Edith Keeler, McCoy, Spock and Kirk

Although Edith Keeler speaks a 'truth', one that needs to be heard by the U.S. President, it is too early, and allows the Germans to conduct heavy water experiments that leaders to world domination. Her death in a street accident seems destined, and saves millions around the world. Though a sage in the truest Taoism sense, her philosophy was years before time.

Mr. Spock, unmoved by the physical beauty or charm of Ms. Keeler goes about his work with 'buck knives' to ascertain the truth – no matter the ugliness it may reveal. He is surprised to find that Edith must die to allow Earth history to continue on a path of democracy and freedom.

James T. Kirk falls in love with the lovely Edith Keeler, and will not accept that she must die to save the world and their prime timeline. Spock's research shows that he must accept the fact and not interfere with Edith's death – or thus condemn the Earth to Nazi rule for generations.

Although McCoy was the one who originally saves Edith from a street car death and alters the timeline, once told the truth by Spock, accepts James T. Kirk's actions to let her die. The truth for Bones is painful, but not as much as it is for his friend.

Everyday Reflections

In the last few years, what type of self-sacrifices have you made for the benefit of strangers, friends, co-workers, family? Would you say that these sacrifices truly made a difference in the lives of these people? Was your sacrifice a monetary one, or one of a spiritual, emotional, or intellectual contribution to these people (for example, did you volunteer to tutor a child after school, or read to the blind?). Is there anything in the future you could change in your behavior to be more civic minded?

Everyday Actions

Let's consider doing two activities for this everyday action, shall we?

First, perform research on how pacifist movements in the United States have brought attention to the potential of nuclear war between the Superpowers of the world. Look into the Committee for Non-Violent Action, formed in 1957, and how their demonstrations worldwide have brought all of us awareness of atomic weapons and the dangers of wars throughout the globe.

Secondly, take at least one afternoon or evening of your busy schedule to volunteer at a church, a crisis center, or at a school to help those less fortunate. If you find yourself enjoying this volunteer job, perhaps make a habit of it once a month or more. Edith Keeler made a difference in the lives of many down-and-out people in her neighborhood. You can do the same, perhaps on a more modest level, in your life, too.

Lesson 16

Free from desire you see the mystery. Full of desire you see the manifestations.

These two have the same origin but differ in name.

That is the secret, The secret of secrets,

The gate to all mysteries.

Lao Chapter 1

Season 2 Episode 1: Amok Time

Story Summary

Mr. Spock asks his captain if he can take leave and go to his home world to tend to personal matters. Kirk questions his motives, but the Vulcan is tight lipped and only says it is important for him to be home at this time. Regardless of the lack of a specific lack of reason, the captain agrees to his friend's request.

At the same time, Starfleet Command order the *Enterprise* to a diplomatic ceremony. Kirk acknowledges the request and changes course. Shockingly, Mr. Spock changes course back to Vulcan. When asked why he did this, he claims to have no memory of his action.

With Spock's behavior under scrutiny, Dr. McCoy determines that the emotional and physical changes to the Vulcan is attributed to *pon farr*, a normal malady that affects the males of his species. Unfortunately for Spock, if he does not mate in the next eight days, he will die from the condition.

Captain Kirk decides that the health and life of his first officer is more important than a direct Starfleet order.

Upon arriving at Vulcan, Kirk and McCoy join Spock to his wedding ceremony to T'Pring. She arrives with Stonn, a pure Vulcan, who she prefers to Spock. T'Pau, a respected matriarch, who calls for a *kal-if-fee* – a match of physical prowess to win the hand of T'Pring. The bride to be picks Kirk over Stonn. Kirk accepts the challenge, and soon learns it is to the death.

Kirk battles his friend with traditional Vulcan weapons, and is soon winded by the ordeal. McCoy is allowed to inject James with a tri-ox compound to offset the atmospheric effects. No matter, Spock strangles his captain, and Kirk collapses to the ground dead. McCoy requests that he take his captain with his to the ship.

Back to his senses, Spock no longer wants T'Pring. When he asks why she chose Kirk over Stonn she explains that if the captain had won, he would not have taken her, and if Spock won, he would also renounce her. The Vulcan compliments her logical approach, and leaves for *Enterprise* and his punishment.

Upon returning to the ship, Spock resigns his commission and asks for his murder trial to commence – but discovers a much alive Kirk, who had been knocked out with a neuro-paralyzer drug that made it appear he was dead. Spock is overjoyed and nearly hugs his friend, but stops short.

Notable Dialogue:

> **T'Pau**: Live long and prosper, Spock.
> **Spock**: I shall do neither. I have killed my captain... and my friend.
>
> ———————————————
>
> **Spock**: *[After realizing that Kirk is not, in fact, dead.]* Jim! *[Catching himself before he displays further emotion]* I am...pleased to see you, Captain; you seem...uninjured.
>
> ———————————————
>
> **McCoy**: There's just one thing, Mr. Spock. You can't tell me that when you first saw Jim alive that you weren't on the verge of giving us an emotional scene that would have brought the house down.
> **Spock**: Merely my quite logical relief that Starfleet had not lost a highly proficient captain.
> **Kirk**: Yes, Mr. Spock, I understand.
> **Spock**: Thank you, Captain.
> **McCoy**: Of course, Mr. Spock. Your reaction was quite logical...
> **Spock**: Thank *you,* Doctor.
> **McCoy**: ...in a pig's eye!

Character Arc: Spock

To see beyond the surface, to see the world for what it is beyond the most frightening or hopeful of events to come means we are on our path to understand the Way. The surface of it is just as important as the depth. Both, opposites, need the other to survive. It is the Way.

As a Vulcan, Spock is ruled, most of the time, by logic. He sees beyond the emotional, and looks to the depth of others, their motives and their innate needs. Spock detaches himself from the trappings of the world, which frees him to see its beauty. When he does this, Spock is not tempted by people or the distractions of the world.

As perhaps the most Taoist-centered character of the *Star Trek* series, Spock should not be moved by emotions of love. Yet, for Vulcans, a hormonal build-up to mate is beyond even the strongest of logical beings. When he believes he has killed his best friend and captain, his *pon farr* is gone. He now sees clearly what he did as a result of the emotions, and the blood lust he had for T'Pring is gone completely.

Everyday Reflections

What is it about the passion of love that makes people do the most dangerous of things and the deadliest of acts to each other? Is love a choice, or is it a hormonal or emotional attraction beyond our control? What have you done over the years for a taste of it from intimate partners? Have the actions justified the means – and have the brought you greater pain or sorrow?

Everyday Actions

There are many wonderful books on love and relationships – some old, some new. Pick up one and start your adventure. *Pride and Prejudice* (1813) by Jane Austen, *The Thorn Birds* (1977) by Colleen McCullough, *Love Story* (1970) by Eric Segal or *The Fault in Our Stars* (2012) by John Green are just a few of the most popular.

One of the most treasured books of all time as is *Romeo and Juliet* (1597) by Shakespeare. *Ana Karenina* (1877) by Leo Tolstoy is also a beloved and respected novel that should be read by those who yearn for a romance tale of grand proportions.

For a more modern take on relationships, the non-fiction book, *The Art of Loving* (1956) by philosopher Eric Fromm has been praised and was a best seller. A more recent book, *The Five Love Languages: How to Express Heartfelt Commitment to Your Mate* (1992) by Gary Chapman is more of a self-help book. This book shows us how to appreciate one's love interest and express our appreciation.

Lesson 17

The most complete seems lacking

Lao Tzu Chapter 45

Season 2 Episode 3: The Changeling

Story Summary

After investigating a distress call from the Malurian system, Mr. Spock tries to respond but cannot find any life readings from that part of the galaxy. Soon after his comment, a small object on the view screen fires an energy beam as powerful as ninety photon torpedoes. *Enterprise* fires back, but makes no damage to the item. After a few more attacks, and the *Enterprise* near destruction, Captain Kirk demands to talk with the alien-looking probe. The attack stops after a brief conversation. Wishing to beam aboard to further talk, Kirk has no option but to allow it to come onto the ship.

The mechanical object, named Nomad, comes aboard and talks about its mission: to sterilize all imperfection. Since its creator, Dr. Roykirk, is aboard the vessel, it sees no need to continue the sterilization.

Spock performs a quick data bank test and believes that the object was launched from earth hundred so years ago and thought destroyed. The Vulcan asks to do a mind meld with Nomad, and it agrees. Nomad tells a story when it met a powerful probe, *Tan Ru*, that repaired and reprogramed it. *Tan Ru* was an agricultural probe designed to retrieve and analyze soil samples for its people. According to Spock, Nomad's upgrades made it a destructive and it misinterpreted the mission to seek out *all* life forms and sterilize imperfections.

Since humanity is imperfect, and Nomad will soon find this out aboard the starship, Kirk decides to ask Nomad to go to a holding cell where its investigation will be postponed for a short time and until the captain can come up with a solution to the dangerous situation.

After Nomad easily escapes from the holding cell, it confronts Kirk, who uses logic to challenge the dangerous probe. The captain tells the probe that if sterilization is always the answer to imperfection, it must destroy itself. As Nomad realizes that it made two errors, and cannot understand why, Kirk and Spock carry the stunned mechanical object to the transporter room and beams it out into space. Nomad does what it was transformed to do and ends its existence with a terrific explosion outside of the starship.

Notable Dialogue:

> **Nomad**: You are the creator.
> **Kirk**: But I admit, I am imperfect. How could I have created a perfect being like you?
> **Nomad**: Answer unknown. I shall analyze... Analysis complete: Insufficient data to resolve problem.

> **Kirk**: I am the Kirk, the creator?
> **Nomad**: You are the creator.
> **Kirk**: You're WRONG! Jackson Roykirk, your creator, is DEAD, you have mistaken me for him! You are in error! You did not discover your mistake, you have made TWO errors. You are flawed and IMPERFECT. And you have not corrected by sterilization, you have made THREE errors!
> **Nomad**: Error... Error... Error... Examine...

Character Arcs: Kirk and Nomad

Does Nomad, the wandering space probe, understand the meaning of sterilization applied to alien life forms, and for that matter, human beings? Can computer programs uploaded like Nomad's by the alien probe be programmed to be sensitive to life other than mechanical ones? What motivates an artificial life form to achieve perfection? Is it only programming?

Everyday Reflections

Why are many people obsessed with perfection in so many facets of life? Perfection of the human body, perfect test scores, a perfect game in baseball? As Lao says, true imperfection is perfect, and the recognition of this allows a human being to accept one's fate in life.

Everyday Actions

If you enjoyed this story about a probe that takes its mission too seriously and deadly, you may wish to see *Star Trek I: The Motion Picture* (1979) as well. In that story, V'Ger, once an earth probe named Voyager 6, is found by an alien civilization and goes out into the galaxy to learn about everything and return the information back to the creator. The movie was not critically received and deemed a rehash of this episode. The next movie, *Star Trek II: The Wrath of Khan* (1982), is still considered the best feature length film of the franchise and is credited for saving Roddenberry's creation.

Lesson 18

Between yea and nay, how much difference is there?
Between good and evil, how great is the distance?

Lao Tzu Chapter 20

Season 2 Episode 4: Mirror, Mirror

Mistakenly transported into an alternate, Mirror Universe, Prime Universe Captain Kirk, McCoy, Scotty and Uhura and must find a way to combat their evil doppelgangers and return home before found out by the duplicitous Mirror Spock. While Scotty works to alter the transporter to send them back to their universe, but is caught by Spock. After a mind meld with the engineer, the Vulcan realizes what odd occurrence and what must be done next. Mirror Spock confronts Kirk and agrees that he and his friends must return so he can have his captain back onboard *Enterprise*. James thanks his alternative Spock, but also argues that any empire based on violence will eventually be vanquished as well. Spock agrees. The captain also reveals the powerful weapon, the Tantalus Field, that his counterpart, James Kirk, uses in the mirror universe to ride himself of enemies.

Mirror Spock sends Prime Kirk and his bridge officers back to their universe, and their Mirror Twins return to theirs at the same time.

Notable Dialogue:

Kirk: What I don't understand is how you were able to identify our counterparts so quickly.

Spock: It was far easier for you as civilized men to behave like barbarians, than it was for them as barbarians to behave like civilized men. I assume they returned to their *Enterprise* at the same time you appeared here.

Kirk: Probably. However, that Jim Kirk will find a few changes, if I read my Spocks correctly.

McCoy: Jim, I think I liked him with a beard better. It gave him character. Of course, almost *any* change would be a distinct improvement.

Kirk: What worries me is the easy way his counterpart fitted into that other universe. I always thought Spock was a bit of a pirate at heart.

Spock: Indeed, gentlemen. May I point out that I had an opportunity to observe your counterparts here quite closely. They were brutal, savage, unprincipled, uncivilized, treacherous; in every way, *splendid* examples of *homo sapiens*, the very flower of humanity. I found them quite refreshing. *[he returns to the science station]*

Kirk: I'm not sure, but I think we've just been insulted.

McCoy: *I'm* sure.

Character Arcs: Prime Kirk and Mirror Spock

What are the main differences between the Mirror Universe and the beloved *Star Trek* characters in this story? It would appear to Lao Tzu that the evil in the other universe is something inherent in all of us – and it is by choice we make it real in our present world that defines us as evil or good.

Lao posited that there is little difference between good and evil in the world. The first type of evil is what people do to others that cause them pain (the Agony Booth Chekov was placed in is an example). The second evil are the resulting consequences to those in the world and how humans in power use their will to make others suffer in a broader sense in society (any war is an example). Compassion for others is a good that is most applicable in all situations and interactions with others. This is also one of Lao's major principles of how to conduct oneself in society.

Perhaps the key moment in the morality tale is just before James T. Kirk reasons with Mr. Spock of the other USS *Enterprise*. When he reasons that no empire or power hungry military can hold onto power long, the Vulcan agrees – and in 200 years or so it, too, will cease to exist. Logic, for a Vulcan is most necessary in present actions, and in that moment, it is likely that the doppelganger gave serious thought to changing his selfish, evil ways.

Everyday Reflections

If you gave into your most evil ways, what type of things would you be capable of in today's world? What are your darkest, most hidden desires that you know, if carried out, would hurt others and destroy personal or professional relationships?

Everyday Actions

Keep track in your journal how your fellow co-workers or classmates are unfriendly towards each other. In detail, write down a few incidents where you have observed men and women made a choice to be duplicity or simply hateful towards others. You can include your superior's behavior or even the owner or boss. Do not share this with anyone! Who knows, this might even be beneficial to you down the road if complications arise at the workplace.

Lesson 19

Therefore a weapon that is strong will not vanquish;
A tree that is strong will suffer the axe.
The strong and big takes the lower position,
The supple and weak takes the higher position

Lao Tzu Chapter 76

Season 2 Episode 6: The Doomsday Machine

Captain Kirk and his away party find a dazed Commodore Matt Decker at command on another Starfleet starship adrift in space. With no crewmen aboard, Kirk asks the obvious question: Where did they go?

The Commodore tries to answer, but is in severe anguish, barely making sense. Finally, he gets out the words. Matt beamed the entire crew to a planet they were orbiting because the ship had received heavy damage from a powerful alien creature. Kirk responds, "What planet?" "There – it was there, but not anymore!" The weapon destroyed the entire world. "They were pleading with me to take them back, Jim, but I couldn't, I couldn't do it with the transporters down." Decker begins to whimper and sobs.

Kirk guesses correctly that the machine may have been an ancient doomsday weapon that somehow is now roaming the galaxy, armed, and dangerous to anything, living or not, that it senses needs to be eliminated.

Spock takes Decker back to the USS *Enterprise* with the USS *Constellation* in tow. Scotty remains aboard with a small team try to salvage the other starship by reconfiguring the power system and working with the impulse engines. Captain Kirk works on reactivating the view screen from the Engineering.

Once Spock returns to *Enterprise*, the Doomsday Machine appears and begins to chase the starship. Kirk is warned, and the boarding party must stay aboard Decker's ship until *Enterprise* can return. As senior officer, Decker takes command and orders Spock to fire on the powerful alien machine. Spock reminds him that phasers cannot penetrate its solid neutronium hull. As Scotty restores the viewscreen, Kirk is shocked to see Decker engaging in battle with the planet killer and orders him to stand down. The obsessed commander refuses. As the Doomsday Machine is captured by a tractor beam and slowly is drawn in the mouth of the device, Kirk fires on it from the *Constellation*, distracting it and *Enterprise* retreats to a safe distance.

With communications restored, Kirk orders Decker off the bridge. As the beleaguered commander is escorted to Sickbay, he subdues the guards and goes to the shuttle bay and flies towards the mouth of the alien machine. In the suicide, Spock notices that the machine's power signature decreased in the explosion. The science officer guesses that a larger explosion could deactivate the weapon completely.

Kirk recommends he fly the *Constellation* into the device. Without a moment to spare, the *Enterprise* captain is beamed off and back to his starship. The Doomsday Machine dies and so does the chance of it destroying more planets and taking millions of more lives in the galaxy.

Notable Dialogue:

> **Kirk**: Mr. Spock, relieve Commodore Decker immediately. That's a direct order.
>
> **Decker**: You can't relieve me and you know it, according to regulations...
>
> **Kirk**: BLAST REGULATIONS! Mr. Spock, I order you to assume command on my personal authority as Captain of the *Enterprise*.
>
> **Spock**: Commodore Decker, you are relieved of command.
>
> **Decker**: I don't recognize your authority to relieve me.
>
> **Spock**: You may file a formal protest with Starfleet Command, assuming we survive to reach a Starbase, but you *are* relieved. Commodore, I do not wish to place you under arrest.
>
> **Decker**: You wouldn't dare.
>
> *[Mr. Spock waves two security guards forward, who immediately move to flank Decker.]*
>
> **Decker**: You're bluffing.
>
> **Spock**: Vulcans never bluff.
>
> **Decker**: No. No, I don't suppose that they do. Very well, Mr. Spock, the bridge is yours.

Character Arcs: Kirk, Decker and Spock

As Lao Tzu says, the strong will eventually be vanquished and the weak and soft shall rise up. If that is the truth, is it the doomsday weapon itself that is most important story element or the man who intends to render it useless? Is it man that must be tempered in all actions as to not endanger others with weapons of mass destruction?

Matt Decker's guilt over his poor decision to strand his crewmates on the planet that was ultimately destroyed by the doomsday device drives him insane. At this point in his life, even if he had been on a path of righteous, his blind rage could not be stopped. Any weapon as powerful as the one he pursued with *Enterprise* could not be stopped. It was only logical to work together with James T. Kirk and crew. Together, he could he have disarmed the planet killer. Sadly, Matt gave up his life to defeat a weapon that needed to be stopped with the cooperation of Jim and the destruction of Decker's ship inside the belly of the beast.

Everyday Reflections

Was Commodore Decker's obsessive chase after the 'planet killer' the best path for its destruction? What do you obsess over in your life? Have you ever given up an obsession after seeing the self-destructive path it had taken you down? Are many of us Captain Ahab's searching for the White Whale without consideration of what it does to the life we lead?

Everyday Actions

If you can see the entire movie version, fine, but if you can't, read at least one of these famous books that deal with obsessions gone terribly wrong like *Moby Dick* written by Herman Melville 1851, *Lolita* penned by Valdimir Nabokov in 1955 or *Misery,* composed the prolific American horror author, Stephen King in 1987.

In your journal, answer just one question, perhaps the most important ones of each story: what truly makes the protagonist person go mad? Can it be prevented? Do you see yourself ever becoming such characters in real life?

Lesson 20

One may know how to conquer without being able to do it
Sun Tzu Chapter 4

Season 3 Episode 7: Day of the Dove

Story Summary

The USS *Enterprise* investigates a distress call from an unfamiliar planet, but when they arrive no one is on the surface. Soon though, a band of Klingons beam to the surface as well. As Captain Kirk and Chekov are the only members of *Enterprise* on the planet they are no match to battle the enemy contingent.

Commander Kang accuses Kirk of firing at his vessel and demand they surrender. Chekov, overcome with rage, makes a move to attack Kang but is easily subdued. Kang orders Kirk again to surrender, so the captain calls his ship, and in a coded message, alerts Spock to the situation. Enterprise beams up both Kirk and Chekov first, then the Klingons, who are taken prisoners.

As the Klingons are taken to the brig, a bright energy sphere comes about *Enterprise*. Somehow, the energy ball imprisons 392 members of the ship below decks. Now, the Klingons and the Starfleet crew are of equal numbers – 38, and begin to fight in hand to hand combat, and with crude, dangerous weapons as well.

The ball of energy also programs to ship's computer to warp at an extremely high rate of speed towards the edge of the galaxy. The Klingon and human crews have no means of escape and without help from Starfleet, too, the two groups seem to be in a battle to the death match. Even more oddly, an *Enterprise* crew member is stabbed to death by an assailant, but then comes back to life minutes later to join his Starfleet crew.

Both Kirk and Spock realize that another alien force is controlling this battle – and finally see the strange ball of light move through a bulkhead. Kirk realizes that both his crew and the other is being used as a macabre theater of death for the sheer enjoyment of the vile creature. Even though he risks his life, Kirk tells the wife of Commander Kang, who is in custody, of the true nature of their ordeal. She agrees to meet with her husband and point out the real puppeteer.

Kirk and Kang's wife transport to the Klingon commander's location. At first, Kang disbelieves his wife, thinking that she now must be in league with the humans. As Kirk and Kang battle with short swords, they see the entity grow a brighter red glow the more than strike at the other. At one point, Kirk grabs Kang and points to the floating creature near the ceiling. Then, Kang realizes that he may be play acting for the cruel being's amusement.

Both Kang and Kirk agree to a peace, and order their crews to put down their weapons. Slowly, the warriors put down their swords. Spock suggests that laughter may also be important to drive away the creature. Kang and Kirk begin to laugh at the creature. The bright red glow changes to a clear white glow. It moves up through the *Enterprise's* bulkhead and heads out into open space.

Notable Dialogue:

> **Kirk**: There's another way to survive-- Mutual trust and help.
>
> **Spock**: Those who hate and fight must stop themselves, Doctor, otherwise it is not stopped.
>
> **Kang**: Only a fool fights in a burning house.

Character Arcs: Captain Kirk and Commander Kang

Captain Kirk is drawn into the fierce hand to hand battle by the alien creature, as is his Klingon counterpart, Commander Kang.

Kirk finally realizes what needs to be done, and is helped by his first officer, Spock, to determine the best course of action.

Commander Kang must be convinced of the alien deception, but eventually agrees with his counterpart aboard the *Enterprise*.

Everyday Reflection

As Sun Tzu says, a person may know exactly what to do in war, but not have the ability to complete the task.

In this story, both humans and Klingons were pawns to the evil entity being that thrived on conflict and hate. At first, the creature succeeded in pitting the two groups together and grew stronger. Even when Kirk and Spock put the pieces together and realized that the only action to truly defeat the alien was to end all hostilities, it was incredibly difficult to convince Kang that peace was the only solution to their dilemma.

In your life, when have you tried to solve a problem, known the answer, but have been unable to bring about the appropriate solution? Very likely, it involved personal interactions. No one can make another do what is best for them – and this could be convincing another to stop using illegal drugs, or overeating, or any other addictive behavior that leads to ruin.

Sun Tzu's words, like Lao Tzu's, are applicable in daily life, and with such ideas, we can succeed if we find a way to make the solutions work for us. The difficulty, such as it was with Kirk and Kang, was to fight one's natural tendencies. Humanity, like the Klingons, fight and battle because it is in the DNA. Relearning to go against one's natural tendencies of giving in to anger and hate is the hardest lesson for all, human and Klingon alike.

Everyday Actions

The story touches on the use of propaganda as misinformation but basically starts the path to cooperation between the two races that the Organians predicted in *Errand of Mercy*. Kang is seen once again in the *Star Trek: Deep Space Nine episode, Blood Oath*. You can also see Sulu's interactions with the Klingon Commander in the *Star Trek: Voyager* episode, *Flashback*.

Lesson 21

Those who are right do not argue. Those who argue are not right.
Lao Tzu Chapter 81

Season 2 Episode 10: Journey to Babel

Story Summary

The *Enterprise* is on a diplomatic escort mission to an important conference dealing with the admission of the Coridan System into the Federation. Coridan has a rich supply of dilithium protected neither by civilian nor military personnel – which is exactly the way certain groups want it to remain so they can plunder the mineral.

Captain Kirk is stunned to know that the famous Vulcan Ambassador Sarek is Spock's father as he boards the *Enterprise* with his human wife, Amanda. Kirk learns from Amanda that Spock and Sarek have not spoken for years when the son disobeyed his father by joining Starfleet instead of the Vulcan Science Academy.

At a dinner party thrown for the many delegates onboard, Sarek is confronted by a Tellerite on his position concerning admission of Coridan. The Vulcan sidesteps a direct answer until pressed and agrees with Coridan's approval. The Tellerite shoves Sarek, but Kirk intervenes. Later than night, the combatant is found dead, murdered by a Vulcan death grip according to Dr. McCoy.

During Sarek's interrogation, the elderly ambassador has cardiac event and is rushed into surgery. Spock volunteers to donate plasma for the operation, but when Captain Kirk is stabbed and taken to sickbay as well, the Vulcan first officer leaves the infirmary to command *Enterprise*, thus jeopardizing the life of his father.

> **Spock**: *[about being a Vulcan]* It means to adopt a philosophy, a way of life, which is logical and beneficial. We cannot disregard that philosophy merely for personal gain, no matter how important that gain might be.
>
> **Amanda Grayson**: When you were five years old and came home stiff-lipped, anguished, because the other boys tormented you, saying that you weren't really Vulcan, I watched you knowing that, inside... that the human part of you was crying, and I cried, too. There must be some part of me in you, some part that I still can reach. If being Vulcan is more important to you, then you'll stand there speaking rules and regulations from Starfleet and Vulcan philosophy and... and let your father die, and... then I'll hate you for the rest of my life.

When Kirk hears of Spock's compulsion to command regardless of his father's grave condition, the captain feigns fine health and takes the bridge, convincing the science officer is fit for action. Fending off an attack from a small and maneuverable ship. Later, Spock guesses that the ship or Orion origin, attacked to cause tension between Federation members onboard and for the syndicate to sell dilithium to both sides in a potential war.

Sarek survives surgery, thanks to his son's blood donation, and both have a good chuckle as they make fun of Amanda for worrying so much for both of them.

> **Amanda Grayson**: And you, Sarek. Would you also say thank you to your son?
>
> **Sarek**: I don't understand.
>
> **Amanda Grayson**: For saving your life.
>
> **Sarek**: Spock acted in the only logical manner open to him. One does not thank logic, Amanda.
>
> **Amanda Grayson**: Logic! Logic! I am sick to death of logic! Do you want to know how I feel about your logic?!
>
> **Spock**: Emotional, isn't she?
>
> **Sarek**: She has always been that way.
>
> **Spock**: Indeed? Why did you marry her?
>
> **Sarek**: At the time, it seemed the *logical* thing to do. *[She smiles, realizing they're teasing her]*

Notable Dialogue:

> **Amanda Grayson**: After all these years among humans, you still haven't learned to smile.
>
> **Spock**: Humans smile with so little provocation.

Character Arcs: Spock, Sarek, and Amanda

All three of the major characters of this story – Spock, Sarek and Amanda, have been emotionally estranged for years. Even though Spock and his father are knowledgeable about science, culture, history and so many areas, their wisdom on how parents and children can communicate is lacking. Amanda tries broker peace between father and son, but only after the assassination attempt on Sarek does she find an opportunity.

Everyday Reflections

In the case of Spock and his father, the need to 'remove things everyday' refers to the notion of eliminating long held anger, frustration, and fears from their relationship. Both men had never faced their coolness towards each other because it involved emotional confrontation. It was only when Sarek faced death, and the *Enterprise* was freed from the prospect of destruction, did Spock agree to help his father.

Was the distant relationship between Sarek and Spock due, in part, because of the Vulcan's science officer's struggle with emotions or the father's lack of any emotional embrace of his adult son? Is the metaphor of a father-son relationship portrayed in this story similar to any you have seen in your life? Why is it difficult, for many males, to show emotion? Is this a cultural deficit found in many countries around the world? What was/is your relationship with your father or mother? Do you feel closer to one and not the other? Why is that? If you could repair a distant relationship with either, could you? Would you give a kidney, donate blood, or bone marrow to a cousin, a sibling or a parent – even if your relationship has been strained for years?

Everyday Actions

Take a chance and approach someone close to you and tell them exactly how you feel. The conversation may lead you in an uncomfortable direction at first, but ultimately should shed a light on the darkness you two have built up over the years. Keep track of this action in your journal for later reflection.

Lesson 22

Inward spies make use of officials of the enemy

Sun Tzu Chapter 13

Season 2 Episode 15: The Trouble with Tribbles

Story Summary

The Undersecretary of Agricultural Affairs, Nilz Barris, sends an emergency, priority one call to the USS *Enterprise* from K-7 station. Captain Kirk and crew go to warp speed and arrive at K-7 to only find that Mr. Baris is only concerned about guarding the Federation's shipment of quadrotriticale grain before it is unloaded to Sherman's Planet. Granted, the shipment is a valuable commodity to the planet, and by having it arrive safely will put in play the Organian Peace Treaty, but Kirk is irked that he was summoned for such a mundane chore.

Regardless, the USS *Enterprise* captain agrees to the request, but also scolds Mr. Baris for his rude, arrogant behavior – something the Federation leader ignores and merely pushes stronger for protection of the grain shipment.

Put on the spot, Captain Kirk obliges Mr. Baris and assigns a small contingent of crew to guard the grain in storage compartments of K-7.

Soon, Mr. Baris insists that Kirk place even more guards around the station – especially with Klingon Commander Koloth's Bird of Prey taken orbit around K-7. When the Klingons board the station for shore leave, Mr. Baris complains even louder, and Kirk listens, reluctantly and assigns even more *Enterprise* crewmen to keep the peace on K-7.

Perhaps more an insidious problem to the grain supply comes from the reproduction issues of Tribbles on K-7. At the K-7 bar, Uhura falls for the furry little creatures, and brings one back to Enterprise. Within hours, the Tribbles multiply 100-fold, and begin to fill the hallways, the engine room and even the bridge. When Kirk sits on one in the command chair, then needs to collect many of them from the navigation console, the captain slowly sees the potential for trouble with the beginnings of a Tribble infestation.

Kirk, Spock and McCoy beam over to K-&, meet Mr. Baris at the storage containment area, and open a bin. To no one's surprise, Kirk is overwhelmed with tribbles from the grain bin as hundred fall upon his head. Baris is furious and blamed the Enterprise captain for the problem. Soon in his office, the four, plus his assistant, Mr. Darvin and Koloth discuss the problem of who is to blame. Surprisingly, several tribble in the office die. McCoy exams one and realizes they have been poisoned – undoubtedly by the grain. Disbelieving the claim, Spock supports McCoy's diagnosis.

One remaining tribble turns against Koloth, simply because they do not like Klingons. But when the same tribble makes a horrible noise at Darvin, McCoy scans him and realizes that he, too is a Klingon. Spock shares his belief that the grain must have been poisoned by the Klingon spy, Darvin, to cause tension between the Federation and an important ally. Baris thanks the Starfleet leaders for their help, arrests Darvin, and asks Koloth to leave K-7. Cyranos Jones is ordered to collect all of the tribbles and remove them from K-7 – which should take 17.2 years – or spend time in a Starfleet prison.

Once back on the *Enterprise*, Kirk notices all of the tribbles are gone and ask Scotty what he did to them, worrying that he might have beamed the furry, adorable creatures into space. Scotty takes offense, and admits that he beamed them off the ship, but into Koloth's vessel where they will "no tribble at all."

Notable Dialogue:

> **Kirk**: Where did you transport them? Scott, you didn't transport them into space, did you?
> **Scotty**: Captain Kirk, that'd be inhuman!
> **Kirk**: Well, where *are* they?
> **Scotty**: I gave them a good home, sir.
> **Kirk**: *[exasperated now]* Where?!
> **Scotty**: I gave them to the Klingons, sir.
> **Kirk**: *[whisper]* You gave them to the Klingons?!
> **Scotty**: Aye, sir. Before they went into warp, I transported the whole kit and kaboodle into their engine room, where they'll be no tribble at all.

Character Arcs: Kirk, Baris, Darvin, and Cyrano Jones

James T. Kirk must accomplish a priority Starfleet mission against the Klingons without using violence – which for him is nearly impossible – but he does so with the help of Spock's logic and McCoy's support. Thus, for the captain, he does not need to no boast about his ship and crew, like the Klingon commander Koloth does in the station's bar. Nor does Kirk need to use weapons or force of any kind against the Federation foe. Therefore, James T. Kirk uses his Taoist mastery to remain calm, be reasonable and avoid violence.

Undersecretary of Agricultural Affairs Nilz Baris is a loud, demanding Federation official who pushes Kirk to take action, but is rebuffed repeatedly by the *Enterprise* captain. His assistance, Arne Darvin, is quiet, but his role in the grain problem is much more sinister than the Tribbles.

Cyrano Jones, is an entrepreneur, and a cunning one, and although his pitches for selling his merchandise – the Tribbles – he is harmless, non-aggressive and friendly.

Everyday Reflections

Arrogance and boastfulness, which can be a trait of both Klingons and humans alike, are often characteristics of people who deep down do not believe in themselves. Bragging is simply a way of showing others personal flaws and fears. Thus, in Trek lore, Klingons, like Koloth, are representative of humbleness and quiet confidence that all true Taoists possess or aspire to in their lives.

When looking at your outward actions, are you more like Koloth or James Kirk, who may be confident, but is not cocky to the level of Klingon arrogance? If you could be more like either one, which persona would you want to adopt – or drop?

Everyday Actions

Is Mr. Baris that different than me or you? Would you have reacted as he did with the grain shipment or did he overreact to the extreme?

Consider this: which one of your possessions are you most worried might be stolen or damaged?

Is it your car – are you afraid someone might scratch the new red paint job?

Are you more worried about a treasured item like your photos? What do you do to protect them from being ruined from heat or moisture?

Write about your ten most sacred possessions and what you would do if one or more were stolen.

Lesson 23

What has not yet emerged is easy to prevent

Lao Tzu Chapter 64

Season 2 Episode 18: The Immunity Syndrome

Story Summary

Mr. Spock senses the death of an entire Federation starship when the USS *Intrepid* is destroyed. The crew compliment of 400, manned completely by Vulcans, reached out to Spock, and in emotions of shock and sheer terror. Taken to sickbay, McCoy examines the *Enterprise* science officer, amazed that he could sense the loss of life so far away, but admits he knows little about Vulcan culture.

Enterprise tracks down the last know location of the *Intrepid* and finds only a void, a null space where planets and stars should normally be located. Uhura loses contact with Starfleet, and her and many others on the ship faint. Even though Kirk has Chekov launch a probe, it does nothing to help better understand this energy turbulence.

As Captain Kirk orders *Enterprise* into the null space, the crew grow weaker and the ship's power systems are drained as well. Spock guesses that this area must use biological and mechanical energies for sustenance. As all systems seem to be working in reverse, the captain orders Scotty to take one big thrust of power to free the ship from the void. The effort is minimal and the starship lunges closer to the center of the phenomena.

Enterprise slowly is pulled inside the area and it is revealed to be a multicolored, amoeba made of protoplasm. Spock wants to launch a probe for further analysis. The Vulcan suggests that he alone can deduce the best way to destroy the living creature. Against Kirk's better judgement, he allows Spock to take a shuttle to the center of the giant creature. Shortly afterwards, Spock tells the captain that the living being is about to reproduce and must be stopped at any cost. He suggests a way to do it, but the message is garbled and all contact the science officer is cut off.

With only instincts to guide his next move, McCoy and Kirk determine the amoeba-like creature may best be destroyed by an antimatter bomb. Scotty loads a torpedo and launches it towards the center of the being.

Just after the launch of the antimatter torpedo, and after *Enterprise* slowly starts to back away from the center of the creature, they pick up a signal of the Spock's shuttlecraft. Scott puts a tractor beam on it and both ships barely escape the destructive power of the bomb.

> **Spock**: Do not risk the ship further on my behalf.
> **McCoy**: Shut up, Spock! We're rescuing you!
> **Spock**: Why, thank you, *Captain* McCoy.

The entity explodes. Spock survives and the shuttle is pulled into the bay.

Captain Kirk communicates with Starfleet Command and advises them to stay out of this region of space for the immediate future.

Notable Dialogue:

> **Spock**: I've noticed that about your people, Doctor. You find it easier to understand the death of one than the death of a million. You speak about the objective hardness of the Vulcan heart, yet how little room there seems to be in yours.
> **McCoy**: Suffer the death of thy neighbor, eh, Spock? You wouldn't wish that on us, would you?
> **Spock**: It might have rendered your history a bit less bloody.

Character Arcs: Spock, McCoy and Kirk

Lao Tzu felt that if humans have the ability to prevent something if caught in the early stages. For example, the COVID-19 pandemic, if China, America, Italy, Brazil, and other countries leaders had preached using safety measures, alerted the public to exactly how to fight this (masks and social distancing), the death toll would never had reached the hundreds of thousands in these country.

In this *Star Trek* tale, a giant virus infects the Gamma 7, and it is feared that over a billion inhabitants may already be dead. Only with the brilliance of Spock, McCoy and Kirk do they figure out how to destroy the alien creature with the ship's antimatter. In essence, they find a way to prevent the disease becoming the ultimate pandemic in the galaxy.

Everyday Reflections

In the beginning of the story, Spock senses the death of over 400 Vulcan on the starship Intrepid. In *Star Trek: Discovery*, we see Michael Burnham reach out to Sarek, her adopted father, when the Vulcan is dying on a shuttle. Do you believe that it is possible for humanity to develop this type of emotional acuity in the future?

In your life, how sensitive are you to others to another's pain and suffering?

Everyday Actions

Keep track in your journal on everyone you happened to think about in a reflective way over the course of a day.

Reach out to that person, just using your thoughts, talk to them and tell them that you would like them to call you. For fun, do this for a few days. Does this person pick up the phone to call you – or, perhaps, have you called this friend and he/she says, "I was just thinking of you!"

Lesson 24

There is no greater crime than desire

There is no greater misfortune than greed. To have enough of enough is always enough.

Lao Tzu Chapter 46

Season 2 Episode 16: A Piece of the Action

Story Summary

After an polite invitation from a Lotian named Okmyx, who promised information about a the lost starship USS *Horizon* who was last seen over his planet, Kirk, Spock and McCoy beam down to talk with the Lotian. Concerned that they may be breaking the Prime Directive, Kirk calms Spock and tells him that the crew of the *Horizon* 100 years ago likely did so and their presence will likely not do much more damage to the Lotian society.

The three Starfleet officers arrive to the planet and are hurriedly escorted Okmyx's men to the Boss's office. The style of the buildings, cars and even the clothing is of a 1920's Earth era. The security team has Tommy guns for their protection. As they walk to a building, the party witness a drive-by shooting, and one of Okmyx's men is murdered right in front of Kirk. Regardless, everyone goes about their business as if it is an everyday occurrence to the calm civilians of the neighborhood.

Once in Okmyx's office, the gang leader demands *Enterprise* leave them phasers to use against their rivals. Kirk, of course, refuses. The leader threatens to kill them, but the captain holds his ground.

The three Starfleet officers find out that the Laotian civilization has based its society on an old earth book, Chicago Mobs of the Twenties, one published by in 1992 and left behind by the *Horizon* crew. Distracted by the captain's made up card game of Fizzbin, the guards are overpowered by Spock, who with McCoy flee to a radio station to contact Enterprise. Kirk is once again capture, but this time by Krako's men.

Like Okmyx, Krako demands phasers, but offers Kirk a third of 'the action' in town.

Okmyx uses the communicator and tells Scotty of Kirk's capture, but offers to help if gives them a piece of the action as well.

The kidnapping goes back and forth, between rival gangs, before Kirk finally plays along, and has Scotty stun the entire gang outside on the street. Impressed, all rival gang leaders agree to Kirk's solution to join the Federation for only a 40% cut of all the planet's 'action'.

Back safely aboard *Enterprise*, McCoy sheepishly reveals to Kirk that he may have left his communicator in Okmyx's office. The captain, jokingly playing that he is upset, tells the doctor that if they find a way to make use of the technology, the Federation will be compromised one day the Lotians will demand 'a piece of their action.'

Notable Dialogue:

> **Kirk**: Are you afraid of cars?
> **Spock**: Not at all, Captain. It's your driving that alarms me.

Character Arcs: Okmyx and Grako

Rival gang leaders Okymyx and Grako wish to be the most lauded men on the planet. Why? The Book guided them to a culturally vapid way of life. Greed, guns, and girls are their only desire – besides riches and territory. Their actions reflect that of Chicago in the 1920's Earth and neighborhoods in America and all over the world where drugs and violence often rule the poorest of ghettos.

Without interfering in the culture of the Sigma Lotia II, Kirk and Spock eventually find a way to bring a standstill to the violence and negotiate a peace between the rival gangs and the Federation. Lao Tzu might be pleased with the settlement of hostilities, but would have shaken his head at the mere idea that leaders of any society would be based on gang hierarchy and lack of ethics.

Everyday Reflections

What is it about gang dynamics that creates a need to conquer territory? Can you think of anything similar in your city? Is this need based on cultural inheritance where a disenfranchised ethnic group must possess property, people, or valuables?

Everyday Actions

Take a few minutes, and read a document or go to reference books and look at what Chicago mobs were truly like in the 1930's. Were they as 'cute' as the ones found in this story? I promise you will not like see people like the lovable foils, Okymyx and Grako, of James T. Kirk.

But if you would rather watch fiction about mobs, some fake, others very real, take a look at the following movies or television series:

For the best movies on American mobs/the Mafia, *The Godfather I, II & III* (1972-74), *Good Fellows* (1990) or *Casino* (1995) would be the top three. *Mafioso* (1962) shows the real political and brutal conflict between northern and southern Sicily. *The Road to Perdition* (2002) is a very different movie about a mob boss son who recoils when approached to take over. Tom Hanks give a solid performance as the son. If you have Netflix, take a few hours to look at the real stories about the Columbia and Mexican cartels in *Narcos* (2015-present). *The Irishman* (2019) with Scorsese at the helm leader, Pesci, Pacino and DeNiro is also a winner – though a three and a half hour document about a broken down man and his journey through layers of mob hierarchy. *Black Souls* (2014) is another fine portrayal of Italian men rising to power in Italy. If you can find the movie, *Drunken Angel* (1948), directed by Akira Kurosawa, shows another side to the Japanese Mafia. *Eastern Promises* (2007) is about the Russian mob. And if none of these are enough for you, try *The Sopranos* (1999-2007) or *Ray Dovovan* (2013-2020).

Lesson 25

By seizing something which your opponent holds dear he will be amenable to your will

Sun Tzu Chapter 11

Season 3 Episode 2: The Enterprise Incident

Story Summary

The USS *Enterprise* is captured by a Romulan vessel as it strays into their space. With an hour to decide whether to surrender or fight his way out, Spock joins Captain James T. Kirk on the Romulan starship. At one point, Kirk boils in rage, and is thrown in the brig. As he feigns an emotional breakdown, Kirk is injured when he throws himself against the cell door. McCoy is called to assist Kirk. When he awakens, James attacks Spock, calling him a traitor. The Vulcan protects himself against Kirk's attack by administering an alleged 'death grip'. McCoy pronounces the *Enterprise* captain dead.

Back on board *Enterprise*, Kirk awakens from his self-induced sleep from the Vulcan knockout grip – not a death grip. Surprised, McCoy is informed that Kirk and crew are in Romulan space to steal a cloaking device from their enemy. Starfleet has authorized the secretive bold move to even the odds against their current mortal enemy.

As Spock shares a dinner with the female Romulan commander, the Vulcan secretly calls Kirk to tell him where the cloaking system is located on the ship. Caught by the Romulans, Spock surrenders but not before the cloak is beamed aboard Enterprise.

Scotty connects the Romulan device as Chekov finds Spock's life sign on the enemy ship. As soon as the cloak is activated, Spock is beamed back to *Enterprise*, but also with the female commander who clung to him as he transported. The Vulcan admits to her that he did have feeling toward her, but nothing that could turn him against his Starfleet oath of loyalty.

Notable Dialogue:

> **Spock**: It is not a lie to keep the truth to oneself.

> **Spock**: Military secrets are the most fleeting of all.

Character Arcs: Spock, Kirk, and Romulan commander

Spying on enemies – even in the Federation – is performed by Section 31 operatives, and rarely by Starfleet officers. In this story though, Kirk, Spock and McCoy are involved in a covert operation to steal a cloaking device.

Are their actions against Starfleet policies, or is spying to maintain a balance of power most important?

Are Captain James T. Kirk and his friends doing the dirty work so as to give Starfleet generals and admirals plausible excuses to the enemy and the public?

Everyday Reflections

As Sun Tzu notes, stealing something the enemy deems valuable should lead to compromise between two warring groups. In this case, a Romulan cloaking device is the prize. Still, as Spock surmises, the Romulans will simply improve their current model in a short amount of time and render the stolen one obsolete.

Thus, if this is the case, why does the military always spy on their opponents and do their best to steal secrets? Is it only the plans leaders wish to know in advance so they can mobilize their forces?

In the case of the development of atom bomb, the US was alerted to the underwater experiments by the Nazi scientists without spying. The military did not try to steal the weapon prototype, but hurried the testing of their own version.

Everyday Actions

In your journal, answer a few of these questions honestly:

In your youth, did you ever steal a toy from your kid brother or sister? Why did you do it? What was the end result of this act? Did your relationship sour from then on, or did you learn that stealing from a family member is an unwritten rule that no one can ever get away with for long?

Lesson 26

Return animosity with virtue

Lao Tzu Chapter 63

Season 3 Episode 9: The Tholian Web

Story Summary

While searching for the USS *Defiant*, *Enterprise* and its crew experiences intermittent power failure due fractures in space to the region of the galaxy. Mr. Spock locates the ship, and wearing environmentally protect suits, Chekov, Kirk, McCoy and Spock investigate the newly discover *Defiant*.

Kirk and the others find the *Defiant* crew dead, seemingly at their own hands. As McCoy reaches over to a examine crewman, his hand passes through the body and the table it rests on. Spock determines that the space fracture is pulling the *Defiant* into another dimension of space, and the starship will be lost to known space momentarily.

Kirk calls for emergency transport, but Scotty can only beam a few of them due to the power drain on the system. Spock and McCoy beam back to Enterprise, then Chekov, but Kirk does not. Captain Kirk and the *Defiant* are last seen as they disappear into another dimension.

Back onboard *Enterprise*, Spock hypothesizes that both the ship and the captain will rematerialize in their dimension within the next two hours.

As they wait, a ship hails *Enterprise* and demands they leave their territory. Spock asks them for two hours so they may rescue their captain. The Loskene allows his request but say they will not wait a second longer.

Two hours pass, but Kirk does not reappear – only the Loskene.

Spock surmises that their first appearance must have disrupted the interphase. The first officer asks for more time, but the Loskene deny this request and fire at the *Enterprise*. Spock has to fire back and disables their vessel. Scotty tells Spock that the *Enterprise* cannot maintain their position if they continue in a battle with the Loskene.

Another alien ship approaches, and now both ships begin to weave energy strings around *Enterprise*. After careful analysis, Spock determines the Loskene are building a cage around *Enterprise*, and once completed, will be impossible to break.

After Mr. Spock conducts a memorial service for their captain, yet another crewman loses his sanity. After he is restrained, Spock and McCoy go to his quarters and listen to their captain's tape recording imploring them to work together in the event of his death. When Uhura and Scotty see ghostly visions of Kirk in his environmental suit, Spock surmises that the interphase is about to end but also bring the captain into their reality for a short while. McCoy prepares an antidote for the captain as Spock times the next interphase.

Spock orders *Enterprise* out of the Tholian's nearly completed cage, but not before locking onto Kirk's probable coordinates. Miraculously, Kirk is transported back to the ship just as his oxygen runs out. Later on the bridge, the captain asks if Spock and McCoy had time to watch his final words, but both lie to the disbelieving, but ever-knowing captain.

Notable Dialogue:

Kirk: *[speaking to Spock and McCoy on a taped message]* Bones. Spock. Since you are playing this tape, we will assume that I am dead. And the tactical situation is critical, and both of you are locked in mortal combat. It means, Spock, you have control of the ship and are probably making the most difficult decisions of your career. I can offer only one small piece of advice, for whatever it's worth: use every scrap of knowledge and logic you have to save the ship. But temper your judgement with intuitive insight. I believe you have those qualities, but if you can't find them in yourself... seek out McCoy. Ask his advice. And if you find it sound... take it. Bones. You've heard what I've just told Spock. Help him if you can. But remember, *he is the Captain*. His decisions *must* be followed, without question. You might find that he is capable of human insight and human error. They are most difficult to defend. But you will find he is deserving of the same loyalty and confidence each of you... have given me, Take care.

Character Arcs: Spock and McCoy

The first major plot point of contention are the Loskene who demand that the *Enterprise* leave their space. When Spock does not leave, but asks for more time, the aliens fire at the ship. When disabled, after they fire back, Spock still chooses to stay and wait for an interphase to occur and likely bring back his friend and commanding officer, Captain Kirk.

Another major plot point driving this story Spock stubbornness towards McCoy and other bridge officers who want to leave Tholian space before they are caged in the web. Thus, Spock must act intelligently as others around him act unintelligently – in fear that they will lose their lives due to Spock's lack of judgement.

Everyday Reflections

When did you last time act stubbornly, but did so to study your opponent's next move? Was this at work, or in a game, like chess, where you refused to concede the match? Watch the mini-series, *The Queen's Gambit* (2020) on Netflix to understand the importance of working with others to achieve your biggest dream.

Everyday Actions

The next time someone you may not know well, or at all, treats you poorly – or even threatens you, take a few seconds before reacting in a similar way. Consider where this person is coming from – consider their age, their socioeconomic status (if possible), and gender, to guess where their anger may be coming from and why it is aimed at you.

A typical situation could be a teacher at school treating you like a stupid, disrespectful kid. Was the teacher's angry totally out of line? Did you do anything to provoke the negative reaction? Do you walk away or try to talk it out afterwards? Was there a coming together later that day where apologies were exchanged or offered?

Keep track of your actions in your journal.

Lesson 27

The sage has no concern for himself, but makes the concerns of others his own

Lao Tzu Chapter 49

Season 3 Episode 20: The Empath

Story Summary

Enterprise warps to Manara II to recover a research team on the planet before the nearby sun goes supernova. Kirk, Spock and McCoy beam down to the station but find it abandoned. As Mr. Scott moves the ship to a safe distance from the planet as solar flares erupt from the sun, the landing party is kidnapped and brought to an underground cavern. All three *Enterprise* crewmen are held in a cyclical force field.

Kirk, Spock and McCoy meet a beautiful mute humanoid, they name, Gem. At first they think she is their captor, but soon realize that she, too, is a prisoner in this laboratory.

In the cavern, two Vians, proceed to torture all three men with near life threatening injuries to their internal organs as well as superficial cuts and bruises.

After each man is brought back to the holding area, Gem treats their serious wounds with empathy. She absorbs their punishment, channeling their deep physical trauma to her own body.

Eventually, Spock is able to move through the force field, disable the guard and free his friends. Kirk pleads with the Vians that Gem has passed her test and no other innocent lives should be lost to their deadly test. The capturers admit that the test was to see if her people were worthy of being saved by their technology from an impending supernova. As they watch Gem pushed away from a dying McCoy, the Vians call off the test, restore the physician to full health and say their goodbyes – taking Gem away with them on a mission to save her people as well.

Notable Dialogue:

> Scott: She must have been a pearl of great price.

Character Arcs: Kirk, Spock, McCoy, Gem and the Vians

After murdering several Federation citizens in a macabre psychological experiment, Captain Kirk accuses the Vians for lacking the same trait – empathy – that they hope to nurture in Gem.

Compassion is one of the three major character strengths Taoism promotes in their philosophical treatise. But can compassion be taught? Gem seemed to possess it – without any instructor showing her the way to develop it.

Everyday Reflections

If Lao Tzu were to look at this story, he would undoubtedly shake his head and say that the Vian's test of character went too far for any civilized race.

As a child, did your parents encourage you to be empathetic?

If anything, human development is all about its ability to understand the need to show caring, love and sympathy for others who do not possess basics.

Do you believe you are empathetic? Can you, or anyone become empathetic towards others or is it an intuitive characteristic that one is born with (the common nature or nurture question)? What are the advantages and disadvantages of being compassionate to others in time of need? Do we need more people like this in the world, especially those who rule and hold political power in high office at a local, state or national level?

Everyday Actions

In your journal, jot down the times you show kindness and compassion to others over one week's time. Your acts should be targeted to people you do not know. At the end of thirty days, look over the acts of kindness. Could you have done more?

Lesson 28

When equal armies battle, the grieving one will be victorious

Lao Tzu Chapter 19

Season 3 Episode 15: Let This Be Your Last Battlefield

Story Summary

While *Enterprise* is carrying out its mission to decontaminate the planet Arannus, they come across a stolen shuttle craft. Kirk moves to intercept the craft and take in the thief, Lokai, a political dissident of the planet Cheron. Lokai's facial features are unique: one side is black while the other is white. The dissident complains loudly about his capture and demands to be released. Kirk will have none of it, but promises him a fair trial back at a Starfleet base.

Soon, another small alien vessel pursues *Enterprise*. As it reaches the starship, it self-destructs, but not before its captain beams to the Kirk's bridge. Bele, another citizen of the planet Cheron, argues that he has traced his enemy, Loaki, to their ship and demand that Kirk turns him over. The captain tries to remain calm, telling Bele that it is not in his authority to release a known thief.

As Lokai is escorted to the Bridge, he and Bele begin to immediately argue and nearly come to blows. Bele informs Kirk that he has pursed this political dissident for nearly 50,000 earth years and will not let him slip away again – no matter the crime he may have committed. Finally, Bele, whose face is also black and white but on different sides than Loaki, agrees to wait for Starfleet's answer to his request to extradite his political prisoner.

For the next few hours, both Cheron citizens are free to move about the ship. Lokai tries to drum up support to his cause with the crew as Bele stays with the Bridge officers, trying to persuade them of his just cause. When Starfleet answers, and tells Kirk to bring Lokai back to the nearest base, but will consider Bele's request after the trial, the Cheron becomes infuriated and forces his will on the computer's directional control to turn the ship towards his home planet.

Neither Spock nor Kirk can change the ship's navigational control. Bele, smug, tells him he has it in his power to do this earlier but hesitated in the name of good relations with Kirk. Now that he has no choice, he is forced to take command of the vessel.

Knowing that he has only one option, the captain puts the self-destruct order into the computer. Bele believes Kirk is bluffing and does not return control of the ship. Step by step, Spock, Mr. Scott and Kirk give their unique command codes to *Enterprise*. The computer accepts the codes and starts the two minute countdown.

Kirk tells Bele that when the ship counts down to five seconds, there is no force in the universe that can change the outcome. Bele scoffs, and tells Kirk that his ruse will not deter him. As the countdown continues, Bele become more concerned that the bluff may indeed be carried out. When the clock ticks to ten second, Bele tries to negotiate, but Kirk stays firm. At seven seconds, Bele concedes control of the ship to Kirk and the captain calls off the self-destruct order. Humbled, Bele leaves the Bridge.

Soon, *Enterprise* reaches Cheron – but no life is found on the planet. Lokai and Bele finally realize that they are the only survivors of the world, a planet that destroyed itself over hate in a civil war. Both beam to the planet and Lokai runs from Bele in the rubble. As Kirk and crew see the hatred run its course, they return to their stations and prepare for their next mission

Notable Dialogue:

> **Kirk**: The cause you fought about no longer exists... Give up your hate.
> **Lokai**: You're an idealistic dreamer.

> **Sulu**: Their planet is dead. Does it matter now which of them was right?
> **Spock**: Not to Lokai and Bele. All that matters to them... is their hate.
> **Uhura**: Do you suppose that's all they had, sir?
> **Kirk**: No. But it's all they have left.

Character Arcs: Loaki, Bele, Kirk and Spock

From the final scene of Cheron, a planet devastated by troops from both sides of the battle it appears that both Loaki's and Bele's fight were lost with an equal amount of supporting troops.

Regardless, both men beam down to the planet, looking to gain revenge on the other for the loss of families and friends.

Did either side win? Spock and Kirk think not, and neither would anyone who followed the story closely.

As Lao Tzu would likely have seen this war as one where both sides grieve, and through the horrors felt, may have learned that their causes were unjust. If neither side learned anything from the death of the world, then no one learned anything from the death struggle.

Everyday Reflections

> "For the record, suspicion can kill, and prejudice can destroy. And a thoughtless, frightened search for a scapegoat has a fallout all its own, for the children and the children yet unborn." - Rod Serling – *Twilight Zone,* 1963

If people on Earth had mark on their skin like the inhabitants on Cheron, would we likely take the same type of action towards our fellow men and women? Just because we do not have exactly similar markings, are we a more advanced civilization than that of Cheron? Not surprisingly, dark skinned individuals and groups are discriminated against without doubt not only in America, but throughout the world. Loaki and Bele's struggle is, once again, a metaphor for the worst of traits that mark so many human beings. Apartheid in South Africa is perhaps the most striking example in the world. Slavery in the southern states of America until 1864 is yet another stain on the country. But beyond the obvious examples, remember the Jim Crow Laws that existed in the United States for well over a century – and still exists, in hidden and not so secretive way throughout the country even in 2021.

Everyday Actions

Have you ever worked for an organization that specifically dealt with race or race relations? This could be a school, a social service, or a community or state-level government agency Volunteer to be a tutor/reader for second language children in a recreation center after-school program.

Lesson 29

See others as yourself. See families as your family.

See towns as your town. See countries as your country.

See worlds as your world.

Lao Tzu Chapter 54

Season 3 Episode 21: The Cloud Minders

Story Summary

The *Enterprise* arrives at Ardana, a planet rich in zenite, a mineral needed to combat a plague on a nearby world. Kirk and Spock beam directly to the mines to close a deal for a supply of zenite but the miners try to take them hostage. When High Advisor Plasus and his security team arrives, the miners scatter, but capture Vanna who led the assault. For further negotiations, Plasus invites the two Starfleet officers to Stratus, his society in the clouds, as his team tries to locate the promised zenite on the planet.

Kirk and Spock learn that Ardana is separated into two distinct civilizations: the Troglytles, who mine the zenite and live in the caves of the planet, and the cloud people, who live in luxury miles high above their workers.

When Kirk and Spock return their ship, McCoy alerts them that zenite produces invisible and odorless gas that, overtime, highly diminishes cognitive ability and brings out strong emotions. Kirk contacts Plasus and recommends that all miners wear special masks to prevent such problems. The leader balks at the notion that the miners are in any danger and warns the captain of interfering in their society. Kirk disregards the minister and tells Vanna of the zenite problem. She hears him out, then escapes to return to the mines with the Starfleet officer. Once there, Kirk is recaptured.

Vanna forces Kirk to dig in the mine, but soon the captain attacks his capture, fires at the ceiling and traps them both inside. He next calls *Enterprise* to beam an unsuspecting Plasus to the location. There, Kirk forces the minister to dig for zenite. Soon, Plasus becomes emotional and attacks Kirk. Vanna finally believes the story of the odorless gas and calls Enterprise to beam the two men up to the ship before they murder each other.

Back in the cloud city, Plasus orders the distribution of masks to the miners. Vanna thanks Kirk as pledges to continue her push for equal rights for her people on the planet's surface.

Notable Dialogue:

> **Vanna**: It's hard to believe that something which is neither seen nor felt can do so much harm.
>
> **Kirk**: That's true. But an idea can't be seen or felt. And that's what's kept the Troglytes in the mines all these centuries – a mistaken idea.

Character Arcs: Kirk, Plagus, Spock, McCoy and the Troglytes

Captain Kirk and Spock act as arbiters between the Troglytes and Plasus to secure a valuable mineral, zenite, for transport to another planet fighting a botanical plague. In their negotiation, both men find a serious conflict between the miners and their fellow brothers and sisters in Stratos, a city in the clouds.

The problem is that Plasus only sees their counterparts in the mines as Disruptors and rebels, people who challenge them for power. His view is not unlike so many civilizations who see differences in people based on birth heritage (Still in 2020, India is one prime example of severe class distinction).

At the end of the story, Kirk has Plagus beamed down the mines to force him work in the mine, to breathe the toxic air, to experience the enhanced emotions the gas from the zeinite creates for the miners. Taking a walk in their shoes, as the saying goes, the Stratos leader feels their pain and anguish. Kirk's actions forces Plagus to see the Troglytes as equals, as potential fellow citizens among the cloud city of Stratos.

Lao Tzu would be pleased with James T. Kirk. The captain's leadership in the potentially deadly problem for the miners and insurrection potential brought about a fundamental agreement with the powerful and the powerless.

Everyday Reflections

Can you think of any time in American society – before the Civil War eventually gave freedom to Africans enslaved in the states - that people were treated as poorly as they were in this Star Trek story? What type of rationale was done by the more powerful people in the clouds? Can this type of behavior from humanity ever be changed? Will more education be the answer or is something more needed?

Everyday Actions

Next time you are walking through your city, be sensitive to how others are treated in public places. For example, how are the homeless regarded at a subway, trolley or bus stop? Do people keep their social distance? What subtle actions are taken to ensure no contact is made from such men and women, even if, in your opinion, a homeless person seems safe and non-threatening?

Lesson 30

He who acts recklessly shall lose the essence of Tao.
He who is agitated with lust and desires shall lose his true nature.

Lao Tzu Chapter 26

Season 3 Episode 23: All Our Yesterdays

Story Summary

The *Enterprise* crew prepares to help a civilization of a planet whose sun is about to go supernova. When Kirk, Spock and McCoy arrive they find no one on Sarpedion except an elderly librarian names Mr. Atoz. Not answering any of their questions directly, Atoz mistakes the trio as natives and chides them to hurriedly pick a disc and prepare to go through a portal. When Kirk hears a woman scream, in runs towards the portal and disappears even though Atoz warns him he is not 'prepared'. Spock and McCoy follow their friend into the portal as well – but in a different time period of the planet's past.

One in the time period similar to 17th century Earth, Kirk is accused as a witch – by the very woman he risked his life for moments earlier. The captain is jailed, but when the judge walks back and hears Kirk's story about the portal, speaks with him privately. When he hears James was not prepared, the legal advocate warns him he must return or die. Kirk breaks out of the cell, and with his friend, finds the spot in the alley wat, passes through a wall and returns to the library.

For Spock and McCoy, they end up in a frozen tundra, devoid of any shelter. McCoy begins to feel the pain of exposure and frostbite, and although Spock cannot help, the Vulcan tries and carries him towards the mountains. Soon, Zarabeth, a former political dissident who was sentenced to life in Sarpedion's past of 5,000 years ago, brings the two to a cave. Although McCoy is weak and exhausted, Spock's Vulcan heritage protects him from the cold. He and Zarabeth talk, even laugh, and counter to the Vulcan's way of life today, he begins to have feeling for the female. Within minutes, the two kiss.

Back at the library, Mr. Atoz's clone continue to harass Kirk to prepare to go to the past, no matter James' refusal to do so. One clone manages to knock the captain out, but he awakes in time to avoid being sent to the past through the portal. Kirk forces the original Atoz to help him find his friends. Atoz tells Kirk to call for them as he puts one disc after the other on the Atvachron until the captain nearly gives up.

Mr. Scott warns his captain that the sun is about to go supernova in a matter of minutes – and his tells him to stand by with the transporter.

After Leonard McCoy wakes up, stronger from his exposure, berates Spock for his desire to remain in the past. The insults soon bother the Vulcan so much that he grabs his friend and threatens him.

> **McCoy**: Think, Spock – what's happening on your planet right now?
> **Spock**: My people are barbarians... warlike barbarians.
> **McCoy**: Who nearly killed themselves off with their own passions. Spock – you're reverting back to the ways of your ancestors... five thousand years before you were born!

McCoy reasons with him that he is reverting to the time of his ancestors when emotions were high and dangerous to all. Spock sees the logic, and lets his friend loose from his grasp. Zarabeth admits that she does not know what would happen to the two if they go back to the library, but that they will surely die there if they had not been prepared by Atoz before their trip to the past. Spock and McCoy head out of the cave to try to locate the portal.

Kirk continues to call for his two friends, and finally, they hear him. Spock still does not want to go and tells McCoy to go ahead, but he cannot pass through the rock to the portal. Atoz deduces that the two must have gone together – so must do the same if they are to return. Still, Spock does not wish to leave, but does so after a final kiss with Zarabeth. He and McCoy pass through the portal and back to the library.

Mr. Atoz hurriedly puts in his personal disc, pushes through the two, and runs through the portal to his past destination.

Mr. Scott beams the away party back to *Enterprise* and the starship moves clear of the sun as it explodes and quickly envelopes Sarpedion in a bright yellow glow.

Notable Dialogue:

> **Spock**: There's no further need to observe me, Doctor. As you can see, I've returned to the present in every sense.
> **McCoy**: But it did happen, Spock.
> **Spock**: Yes, it happened. But that was five thousand years ago. And she is dead now. Dead and buried. Long ago.

Character Arcs: Spock, McCoy and Kirk

Mr. Spock is out of character as he shows lust, anger and agitation in the icy environment with a woman he has just met, who unlike him, has been sentenced to life in the past.

In this story, we see Spock succumb to the base urges of former Vulcans of 5,000 years ago. He is passionate, affectionate and even violent. This is not the Vulcan we have grown accustomed to throughout the series.

Smartly, Leonard McCoy challenges his friend, firmly telling him off in front of his lover. Angered, Spock throws Bones up against the wall for the insult, then, slowly, realizes that he is not the same Vulcan he was on the *Enterprise*. Logic, finally, catches up to the enraged bridge officer, lets McCoy go, and reflects on how his emotions have overwhelmed him.

Captain Kirk finds his way back to the library after his escape from the prison. Mr. Atos finds the correct portal disc, and tells James that his friends must leave the past or die within the hour. With Kirk's voice leading the two to the mountain entrance to the library, Spock kisses his lover, and steps back to the present with the half-frozen McCoy.

Everyday Reflections

We have all seen how drugs have destroyed the lives of celebrities and even the people next door. Are they the exceptions to the rules or are they people just examples of what do many others go through each and every day of their lives?

As a young man, I remember neighbors in our modestly wealthy neighborhood who had severe drinking problems. Alongside these poor souls were others who dealt with social anxiety, domestic violence and rage problems. In my own way, I tried to help, but no one can direct others to take a path towards redemption unless they wish to take the first step.

Can you remember a time when your desires led you down the wrong path? If you are a true Taoist, and can control how certain self-created needs have led you down the worst path possible, what can you do to change your behavior?

Everyday Actions

In your journal, ask yourself these important questions:

What should you do if you feel overwhelmed with anger, stress and frustration over a simple or difficult scenario playing out in your daily life?

The most important of Taoist practices is to feel emotions but not to let them take over our daily actions. A true Taoist needs to focus on the strongest of emotions and allow them to dissipate. In a counseling session, a hypnotherapist may ask the client to remember a time in childhood to mediate the anger or sadness into a more relaxed, soothing state of mind. In psychotherapy the act of 'smiling' into all parts of the body brings a calm, something that a child could do in his/her imagination.

Lesson 31

Things exalted then decay.

This is going against the Way.

What goes against the Way meets an early end.

Lao Tzu Chapter 55

Feature-length Movie: Star Trek II: The Wrath of Kahn

Story Summary

The starship, USS *Reliant*, is on a search for a lifeless planet to test the new Genesis Project. Created by scientist, Dr, Carrol Marcus, former lover of James T. Kirk, Genesis is a can create the beginning of microorganisms that will induce plant life where none existed. She and her son, David, with the *Reliant's* help, are ready for the test run of the life-giving project.

Currently stationed on the *Reliant* is Commander Chekov, the former navigations officer on *Enterprise*. Pavel and *Reliant's* Captain Terrell beam down to investigate Ceti Alpha VI as a possible selection for Genesis. Soon, they are captured by a small band of heavily armed men.

Tied up, Chekov and Terrell are brought back to a settlement on the inhospitable planet. There, young officer is shocked to see Khan Noonien Singh, the genetically engineered human who nearly murdered Captain Kirk and captured *Enterprise* fifteen years earlier, in charge. The hateful enemy tells Chekov of the explosion of his world that killed many of his people, including his wife. Khan blames Kirk for his misery and swears revenge on his mortal enemy.

Knowing that this is his one chance to escape the barren world, Khan puts an indigenous eel larvae in the ears of both men, using it as a mind control device. As both Chekov and Terrill beam back to the Reliant, the two act as sleeper agents and murder the transporter officer. Khan and his group beam up and they hastily take over the starship.

As Kirk takes command of *Enterprise*, now deployed on a training mission, he receives a distress call from Regula 1. As they travel to the planet, the ship is ambushed by the Reliant. Khan offers to spare their lives if Kirk gives him all information the Genesis Project. The captain remotely lowers the Reliant's shields and counterattacks. Khan must retreat. Kirk continues to Regula 1, though at a slow pace.

When *Enterprise* arrives, Kirk, McCoy and Saavik beam to the station to find Terrell and Chekov alive, but seriously under control of the ill. Although both resist Khan's suggestion to murder Kirk, Terrell must kill himself to prevent the murder. Chekov collapses under the stress.

Khan discovers Genesis aboard the *Reliant* and challenges Kirk to a battle. Both ships are evenly matched, but Spock advises Kirk that three-dimensional combat is a strategy unfamiliar to the Augment. Fighting in the nebula, Kirk finally delivers the death blow to Khan, but not before the superhuman activates the Genesis.

With *Enterprise* heavily damaged and unable to go use warp drive, Spock surmises that their ship and all matter nearby will be affected by the Genesis. McCoy figures out Spock's plan and tries to prevent him from giving up his life for the crew. Spock pretends to agree with his friend, but gives him a Vulcan nerve pinch to disable him. Spock also transfers his *katra* to McCoy with a mindmeld and tells him to *remember*.

The Vulcan sacrifices himself and manually repairs power to the ship and *Enterprise* is saved.

After a touching death scene between Spock and Kirk, the science officer dies. Spock is memorialized and his coffin shot out into space, landing softly on the surface of the new Genesis planet nearby.

Notable Dialogue:

> Kirk: [eulogizing Spock] We are assembled here today to pay final respects to our honored dead. And yet it should be noted, in the midst of our sorrow, this death takes place in the shadow of new life, the sunrise of a new world; a world that our beloved comrade gave his life to protect and nourish. He did not feel this sacrifice a vain or empty one, and we will not debate his profound wisdom at these proceedings. Of my friend, I can only say this: Of all the souls I have encountered in my travels, his was the most.... *[voice breaks]* human.

Character Arcs: Captain James T. Kirk, Mr. Spock and Kahn Noonien Singh

According to Lao Tzu, when people go against the Way, they meet an early end. This covers behavior, intentions and perception of what the Way is actually about and how it can lead the virtuous to a better relationship with nature and society.

James T. Kirk and Mr. Spock may demonstrate different way of expressing themselves to the crew and even their friends. Kirk is more charming, friendly and outgoing where Spock is closed off emotionally. Yet different styles in interactions with other does not mean they do not care deeply for their friends, family nor the general welfare of their crew and all other life forms they meet in their adventures across the galaxy. Neither one seeks status or power but only equality and fair play.

Khann Noonien Singh is quite different, and perhaps, it is comes from his life in the Eugenics War. In a real sense, Khan was raised to be the best, in whatever it was, be it physical strength, leadership qualities or intellectual prowess. Supermen, like Khan, were not meant to be subservient or equal to any other – but only to be a leader or oppressor if others opposed him and his ideals for a better world. Khan's life ended as it was lived – in pursuit of glory and revenge for all those who challenged his authority, such as Captain Kirk. The warrior that once was Khan could have given so much to Earth, but simply was not meant to kind, helpful or selfless. For all his flaws, his life ended earlier than it should have – something Lao Tzu could have predicted.

Everyday Reflections

We are born, age, and die. Life is cyclical and cannot be changed. Yet, in this *Star Trek* movie, life can be terraformed and made anew, by a scientific invention – the Genesis Project. And in a sense, this is what scientists and researchers strive for in the 21st century – to create chemical formulas that can rekindle life in dead soil so that plant life can thrive and feed humanity across the world. What makes the movie so unique is the sequel, when Spock, who gives his life for his crew, comes alive again, thanks to Genesis.

The question posed to you is this: Should life be finite? Does having a term limit to life create more of an urgency to life it to its fullest, and as so, do the best we can while on this plane of existence?

Everyday Actions

Once again, play screenwriter for this story. In your journal, change the final act – before Khan is outplayed by Kirk. Would you keep the ending as is, with Spock giving his life to the crew, or would you make it Kirk, or McCoy, or Scotty, who give everything to save their friends. In other words, why is it poignant and so important for the Vulcan to sacrifice himself and not another? Do we even need to have anyone die in the final act – besides Khan?

Lesson 32

All things arise in unison.

Thereby we see their return.

All things flourish,

And each returns to its source

Lao Tzu Chapter 16

Feature-Length Movie: Star Trek III: The Search for Spock

Story Summary

After *Enterprise* returns to Earth after winning the battle with Khan, but losing first officer Mr. Spock, Dr. McCoy acts very strange, and is held for observation. Admiral Morrow, commander of Starfleet, tells Kirk to keep all knowledge of the Genesis Project to himself, and decommissions *Enterprise*.

While onboard the science vessel, the USS *Grissom*, Kirk's son, David, and Lieutenant Saavik, investigate the Genesis planet. Quite surprisingly, they find a child – Spock, who was resurrected through the device. Genesis affects young Spock, and the child begins to age rapidly, also proving that the planet will self-destruct due to the unstable protomatter within hours.

A Klingon Bird of Prey commander by Kruge intercepts communication of the Genesis and warps to the planet, destroys the USS *Grissom* and investigates the surface for survivors.

Back at Starfleet Headquarters, Sarek talks with Kirk about his son's death. Discussing McCoy's unusual behavior, Sarek surmises that Spock put his *katra* in his friend. The Vulcan advises Kirk to help him free his katra to Vulcan before too long passes or McCoy will die. James agrees to help his friend and Sarek. Kirk rescues the doctor from imprisonment and steals *Enterprise* to find Spock's body on the Genesis planet.

At the same time, Kruge takes Marcus, Saavik and Spock back to his ship for interrogation. When Captain Kirk reaches the planet, both ships battle. Kruge orders the death of one of the three hostages to show Kirk he has the upper hand. Marcus sacrifices his life for Saavik and Spock. Kirk agrees to surrender his ship to Kruge and beams to the planet, but before doing so, engages the self-destruct sequence.

Both captains fight to the death, with Kirk winning and gaining revenge on his son's brutal murder by the Klingon. Kirk, and his crew of Uhura, Sulu, McCoy and Scotty, take over the bird of prey and head towards Vulcan. Once there, Spock's *katra* is reunited with his body. The Vulcan begins to remember his life, and his friends, and all rejoice.

Notable Dialogue:

> **Spock**: My father says that you have been my friend. You came back for me.
> **James T. Kirk**: You would have done the same for me.
> **Spock**: Why would you do this?
> **James T. Kirk**: Because the needs of the one... outweigh the needs of the many.
> **Spock**: (Spock begins to remember) I have been and ever shall be your friend.
> **James T. Kirk**: Yes. Yes, Spock.
> **Spock**: The ship .... out of danger?
> **James T. Kirk**: You saved the ship. You saved us all. Don't you remember?
> **Spock**: Jim .... your name is Jim.
> **James T. Kirk**: Yes.

Character Arcs: Captain James T. Kirk, Dr. McCoy and Mr. Spock

As Lao Tzu says, all things return to their source eventually. For Mr. Spock, when his *katra* is returned to its source, his soul, his memories, and his intellect are once again reunited with his body. If not for his closest of friends, James Kirk and Leonard McCoy, Spock would have been lost and alone, without essence even though he was one again a mortal being.

Everyday Reflections

For Vulcans, the *katra* is the name for the spirit in each of us and exists well after death. We see it transferred to McCoy, then brought back to the reborn Spock. In *Star Trek: Enterprise*, Captain Johnathan Archer carries with him Surak's *katra ark*, too, until a Vulcan priest can remove it safely from the human. In a sense, in Vulcan mythology, the spirit never dies.

What are your thoughts on human spirit? Does it live on in your children and future generations? Do we pass on our finest or worst personal characteristics in spirit as well as in our DNA?

Everyday Actions

In case you have not watched, *Star Trek IV: The Voyage Home*, the third of three movies that are companion stories, please do, and look for what make it the most different and unique of the feature-length movies.

Does it work for you? Is the humor dated? Is the issue on saving all life, no matter the species, still an important message for humanity?

Write in your journal, as you watch this film, what issues are still important for us today as it was back over 35 years ago.

Lesson 33

Therefore the sage takes care of all people, forsaking no one.

He takes care of all things, forsaking nothing.

This is called following the light

Lao Tzu Chapter 27

Feature-Length Movie: Star Trek IV: The Voyage Home (1986)

Story Summary

After living in exile on Vulcan for several months, the Captain James T. Kirk, Dr. McCoy, Chekov, Sulu, Uhura and a resurrected Mr. Spock, travel back to earth in a Bird of Prey to stand trial for their actions.

When they near their home world, a Starfleet general distress warning goes out to all ship not to land. Kirk and the others can see a large, cylindrical shape buoy hovering above Earth. The buoy is making sounds loud enough to create hurricanes, earthquakes and other catastrophes on Earth. Mr. Spock, still recovering from his death experience, surmises that the machine is calling out to humpback whales – a species of aquatic mammal that no longer exists in the modern day. Without an answer to its greetings, the Vulcan assumes that it will simply continue to send the repeated message until it ultimately destroys Earth.

The only solution to the problem is to find a humpback whale somewhere in earth's past, return it to the present, and hope it sends the right message back to the alien machine.

Using a slingshot approach towards the sun from earth – a successful method similar to one done years earlier in another time travel adventure, Captain Kirk and his bridge crew return to Earth in the past, 1986, to locate a humpback. Their Bird of Prey lands in Golden Gate Park, cloaks, and Kirk assigns tasks to several teams to solve the problem on present day Earth. Sulu and Mr. Scott must build a tank big enough to hold one or two whales while Uhura and Chekov need to find a nuclear reactor to recharge their Klingon vessel. Lastly, Spock and Kirk must locate a humpback whale and safely return it to their time to communicate with the alien probe and hopefully save earth.

With help from Gillian from the Monterey Aquarium, Kirk and Spock locate two humpback whales releases from captivity and transport them to the Brid of Prey. With Gillian, the crew returns to their time, release the whales, and they signal the alien space probe with their language that all is well. The probe leaves Earth, the disaster is averted, and Kirk is demoted to the rank of captain from admiral and returned to command once again. The USS *Enterprise* NCC-1701-A takes off for her maiden voyage with the familiar crew aboard.

Notable Dialogue:

> *[while traveling over the Golden Gate Bridge in a passenger bus]*
>
> **Spock**: Admiral, may I ask you a question?
>
> **James T. Kirk**: Spock, don't call me Admiral. You used to call me Jim. Don't you remember "Jim"? What's your question?
>
> **Spock**: Your use of language has altered since our arrival. It is currently laced with, shall I say, more colorful metaphors-- "Double dumb-ass on you" and so forth.
>
> **Kirk**: You mean the profanity?
>
> **Spock**: Yes.
>
> **Kirk**: That's simply the way they talk here. Nobody pays any attention to you unless you swear every other word. You'll find it in all the literature of the period.
>
> **Spock**: For example?
>
> **Kirk**: *[thinks]* Oh, the complete works of Jacqueline Susann, the novels of Harold Robbins....
>
> **Spock**: Ah... The giants.

Character Arcs: James T. Kirk and Spock

Lao Tzu believed that a sage should take care of all people, not just those of the Chinese royal court. Educators and those with wisdom were a valued commodity in China, but were not shared with commoners. In Lao's world, a sage understands his value to the community and the society at large – and that goes for anyone in the 21st century, too.

Mr. Spock always shared his particular type of Vulcan logic with James T. Kirk and Leonard McCoy during their time on the *Enterprise*. Although the good doctor often found his attitude patronizing, Spock never meant to show up his colleagues.

Captain Kirk demonstrated his wisdom more as a military tactician than as an intellectual. Still, his personal skills always rallied the crew together against unspeakable evil aliens and dangerous humanoids in their travels. Regardless of his lack of intellectual brilliance, the captain always sacrificed himself for the betterment of the crew, the Federation, and the galaxy at large. Going back in time to retrieve the humpback whales was a dangerous plan, but teamed with his sage friend, Spock, they found a way to bring back the prized mammals and save the world – once again.

Everyday Reflections

This *Star Trek* movie is over 35 years old – has it aged well, compared to *Star Trek II: The Wrath of Khan*? What makes it one of the critically successful feature length movies in the Trek franchise? Which social themes are most important in this story? Would this movie be as successful in 2020?

Everyday Actions

Though shunned by Starfleet, Captain James T. Kirk and crew go back in time to retrieve humpback whales to prevent a worldwide disaster.

In your journal, trace back to major events your life when you sacrificed yourself entirely for family, friends, sports teams, or coworkers. Why did you put so much effort into the betterment of others or an important project? If you were to do it all over again, would you? Write down at least five reasons that seem linked to your behavior. Are you the same, giving and loving person today?

Lesson 34

He who can modify his tactics in relation to his opponent
and thereby succeed in winning,
may be called a heaven-born captain
Sun Tzu Chapter 4

Feature–length Movie: Star Trek (2009)

Story Summary

In a series re-boot, the *Kelvin timeline* starts with Nero, a Romulan, destroys the planet Vulcan, as a way of vengeance against Mr. Spock and his people. Although the *Enterprise* first officer had tried to save Romulus, Nero's home world, he inadvertently exploded the world, and it was now time for payback from his sworn enemy who lost his family in the death of the accidental explosion.

In this prequel, the audience witnesses the backstory of James T. Kirk's father on the USS *Narnada* to Nero from the future, who saves his pregnant wife and crew but sacrifices himself in the process.

After a bar fight on Earth, Captain Pike sees potential in the bright young man, and recommends he enlist in Starfleet Academy and focus his energies in a positive manner. Kirk meets Uhura in the academy, and later Leonard McCoy on a transport. After passing the final exam in a highly unorthodox way, Along with McCoy, Kirk joins Starfleet, accepting a commission on the USS *Enterprise* with Pike.

While on *Enterprise,* Kirk recognizes a lightning storm near Vulcan, which reminds him of the one that happened before he was born and when his father sacrificed his life for him and his mother. Pike is convinced of the importance of the event and investigates the distress call that is a trap set by Nero, the Romulan who holds Spock responsible for the destruction of the home world.

As Nero's ship attacks *Enterprise* and kidnaps the captain, Kirk takes command. Although Kirk, Sulu, and at the time Chief Engineer Olson, try to prevent a potentially dangerous drilling of Vulcan itself by the enemy, their efforts are useless. Olson dies in the attempt to destroy the platform and Nero launches red matter into the world causing an artificial black hole that ultimately destroys Vulcan. Kirk does save Spock's father, Sarek, but is unable to save his mother who dies before a transporter can lock on her signal.

Next, Nero plans his revenge on Earth as well and speeds towards it on the *Narada*. Pike is tortured for Earth's special defense codes. Spock strands Kirk on Delta Vega after the young man's mutiny attempt. On Delta Vega, Kirk meets the future Spock from 129 years later who explains why Nero destroyed his planet as revenge for the Vulcan's inadvertent destruction of

Romulus years earlier. Both Spock's and Nero's ships were caught in the black hole and flung back in time.

On Delta Vega, Spock and Kirk meet Mr. Scott. Scotty helps Kirk to beam back onto *Enterprise* even with the ship travelling at warp speed. Once on the bridge, James provokes the Vulcan to attack him – thus proving Spock is emotionally unfit to serve as captain. After speaking with his father later, Spock is convinced to help Kirk to defeat Nero before he can destroy Earth, too.

While hidden in the Titan gas clouds, Spock and Kirk beam aboard Nero's ship. Pike is recused and Spock uses his future self's ship to destroy Nero's planet drill. Though Kirk shows mercy for Nero, the Romulan takes none of it and dies with his ship in the black hole.

In the end of the story, Christopher Pike promotes Kirk to captain of his former ship as he is promoted to admiral. Present Spock meets his future self and the elder one tells him to work with James T. Kirk for the good of the galaxy and for the friendship that will endure the rest of their lives.

Notable Dialogue:

[Spock notices an elder Vulcan walking in the docking bay]

Spock: Father...

Spock Prime: *[turns around to face him]* I am not our father. There are so few Vulcans left. We cannot afford to ignore each other.

Spock: *[gets closer]* Then why did you send Kirk aboard, when you alone could have explained the truth?

Spock Prime: Because you needed each other. I could not deprive you of the revelation of all that you could accomplish together, of a friendship that will define you both in ways you cannot yet realize.

Spock: How did you persuade him to keep your secret?

Spock Prime: He inferred that universe-ending paradoxes would ensue should he break his promise...

Spock: You lied?

Spock Prime: Ah... I - I implied.

Spock: A gamble.

Spock Prime: An act of faith. One I hope that you will repeat in your future in Starfleet.

Spock: In the face of extinction, it is only logical that I resign my Starfleet commission and help rebuild our race...

Spock Prime: And yet, you can be in two places at once. I urge you to remain in Starfleet. I have already located a suitable planet in which to establish a Vulcan colony. Spock, in this case, do yourself a favor: Put aside logic. Do what feels right. *[turns to leave]* Since my customary farewell would appear oddly self-serving, I shall simply say... *[shows Vulcan hand salute]* Good luck.

Character Arcs: James T. Kirk, Spock Prime, Spock and Nero

Although word interpretations are always a tricky thing in translations, Sun Tzu is believed to have compared a natural born leader, a *captain*, as someone who can modify tactics to win in any situation.

In this story, we see James T. Kirk as a man born of guile, intelligence and strength of conviction and physical prowess who can always find ways to defeat the enemy.

Spock, and his future self, work together with Kirk to defeat Nero and save *Enterprise* – although Amanda, their mother is lost as is their home world.

Motivated by vengeance and hatred, Nero is eventually defeated by Spock, Kirk, and his loyal crew of Uhura, McCoy, Scotty, and the others who lead Starfleet's finest starship.

Everyday Reflections

Have you ever felt you were born to succeed at a certain craft, hobby or professional activity? For example, have you always found a way to win, more often than not, in sport contests due to your understanding of the game? Have you found ways to ace exams in school? Do you figure out ways to succeed in projects at work while others fail? What gives you the edge? Is it your passion or your smarts or a something unquantifiable?

Everyday Actions

In your journal, keep track of your *wins* for one month. How did you achieve success? Try to figure out what makes you a winner – like James T. Kirk!

Chapter Three

Star Trek: The Animated Series

The Original Adventures Continue!

When the *Enterprise* Crew Travelled *only* on Saturday Mornings

Back in 1971, NBC negotiated a deal with Gene Roddenberry to continue the original series – but this time, one focused on children in their Saturday morning line-up. With a chance to renew interest in his television show, Gene took the chance and produced an initial season of sixteen episodes, which was standard for original kid's programming at that time. The second season only had six episodes, and the twenty-two were shown as reruns for several years. According to D.C. Fontana, Gene's executive producer, this *Star Trek* series failed to reach the desired demographic audience desired by the NBC rating system. More adults and teens were attracted to the show than children. Although the stories were tailored for a more mature audience, and created more as a continuation of the original series, this was not translated into higher ratings nor audience appeal on a nationwide level. Thus, once again *Enterprise's* five year mission was once again cut short, this time to only a season and a half.

Regardless of the lack of an audience, this Trek series was the first one to achieve a high water mark for television critics: it won its first Emmy Award – for Best Children's Programming for Under 30 minutes. Subsequent *Star Trek* series, such as Next Generation, was nominated for Best Dramatic Series (like the original series), and also received Hugo and Golden Globes Awards, and even Emmys, but the animated version was the first big winner.

> On June 27, 2007, *Star Trek*'s official site incorporated information from *The Animated Series* into its library section, with many pointing to this as evidence that the animated series is canon, though this has not been officially confirmed. Both David Gerrold and D. C. Fontana have stated that the animated series is essentially the fourth season that fans wanted originally. (Wikipedia, 2020)

Let's examine the very best of this limited series, and take notice to the Taoist messages created in the most noteworthy of adventures with Kirk, Spock, and McCoy and the friends and enemies they meet along the way.

Lesson 35

To a surrounded enemy, you must leave a way of escape

Sun Tzu Chapter 7

Season 1 Episode 1: Beyond the Farthest Star

Story Summary

As the USS *Enterprise* explores the outer rim of the known galaxy, it is pulled towards a dead star. As the starship maintains orbit, Mr. Spock finds a 300,000,000 million year old ship also trapped along with them.

Kirk, Spock, McCoy and Scotty investigate the ancient ship that was once the home of an insectoid race. As they explore further in the various sections of the ship they find a taped warning from the ship's captain telling them of a dangerous creature captured within their vessel. The captain had wanted to self-destruct, but the monster would not allow it. By all costs, the malevolent being must not reach any other world, warned the insectoid captain.

As the creature finds the small contingent, Kirk calls for an emergency beam-out, but too late – the entity is transferred with them onboard *Enterprise*. Once there, it takes over the computer system, forcing the captain to seek options on how to prevent it from travelling with them to other worlds. Threatening to kill each one of them, the being demands it takes them to the nearest populated planet.

Working in secret with Scotty and Spock, Kirk bypasses the normal ship control system and implements an emergency back-up approach. Kirk directs the ship for a suicide run into the dead star. Although the creature continues to threaten the crew, Captain Kirk tells it nothing can stop *Enterprise's* destination. Frightened, the creature beams off the ship.

Kirk uses a sling-shot approach and uses the gravity of the dead star to speed away and leave the sentient, malevolent creature all alone to ponder its fate.

Notable Dialogue:

>**Uhura**: It's beautiful. What kind of people could have built it? To touch even a starship with grace and beauty?
>**Kirk**: A civilization that advanced 300 million years ago before life even emerged on Earth.
>**McCoy**: Barely an instant in eternity, Jim.

Character Arcs: Captain Kirk, Mr. Spock and the Alien

With nowhere to go for hundreds of millions of years, an entity who desperately wishes to leave the insectoid ship, tries to force James T. Kirk and crew to take it with them to other worlds so it can seek lives to torture. No matter the ability to take over the *Enterprise's* computer system, Kirk and Spock, with Scotty's help, keep the malevolent entity from flying the ship to a nearby planetary system where it could thrive off their life forces. Only when the captain flies towards a sun, in what appears to be a suicide run, does the entity leave the ship.

Sun Tzu would be proud of the *Enterprise* crew for giving the enemy a place to flee to – it saved them and countless others.

Everyday Reflections

When has Sun Tzu's recommendation been an effective strategy in the history of warfare? Have you read about significant battles in world history where the enemies were allowed to flee to prevent massive bloodshed and secure territories?

Everyday Actions

If you have not watched the 1979 movie, *Alien*, give it a try. This movie is a full-length version of this *Star Trek* adventure – with a powerful creature that must be fought with guile and intelligence. The alien in this *Star Trek* story gives up too easily, but with a limited time, the character fulfills its role.

Lesson 36

The Wise are quiet – follow them.

You may not see them, though they are present.

Like water, reflecting sky.

Lao Tzu chapter 15

Season 1 Episode 2: Yesteryear

While doing research for Starfleet in conjunction with the Guardian of Forever, Mr. Spock changes his destiny, and dies as a young child of seven. The science officer must use the Guardian to go back in time and save his younger self from death on his home planet of Vulcan. During this journey to the past, Spock relieves the pain of self-doubt, the death of a beloved family pet, and begins his adult-like transformation in Vulcan philosophy. The bravery of allowing I Chaya to die honorable and in peace allows the younger boy to develop self-empowerment with his adult-like decision. Spock returns to the present with a renewed appreciation of the child he once was and the adult he is today.

Notable Dialogue:

> **Sarek**: My apologies, visitor. I regret you were witness to that unfortunate display of emotion on the part of my son.
> **Spock**: In the family, all is silence. No more will be said of it. Live long and prosper, Sarek of Vulcan.

Character Arcs: Spock (adult and child), Sarek and his wife, Amanda

After young Spock goes to the desert in search of a way to control his emotions, his anger and fear, he searches for a 'stillness' and calmness that eludes him in his normal days at school and even with his family. The dishonor of being a 'half-breed' product of a human and Vulcan haunts him. To reconcile this emotional tumult, he thinks that he can create a new persona, one that does not allow others to hurt him with insults.

Like young Spock, children are taught in many families, due to culture and social norms, that strong emotions must be repressed if they are to become adults. To be emotional is not a strength and is strongly under-valued in certain ethnic groups across the world even today. For example, adults must be strong-willed and not allow fear control them. It was this way for seven year old Spock, who decided to allow his pet, I Chaya, to die with dignity. Is this the way you wish to raise a child? Do you want your children not to confront their emotions and simply do the 'logical' thing each and every time they face a tough life choice?

Everyday Reflections

Even though Spock wishes to understand the ways of Vulcan philosophy, he does not always abide by them. This is, in part, due to his more emotional side, due to his human mother's DNA. Therefore, Spock, even as a young child, always fought to be the emotionless Vulcan – something impossible for anyone not born of pure Vulcan blood.

What we do each day ultimately decides what we become as adults. Do you remember ever being bullied at school? Do you believe its effects formed your personality well beyond your younger years?

Everyday Actions

Based on a belief system, a racial profile, or a religious leaning, children and adults are too often shunned in life in the academic, work, or social setting. Although this is sometimes very easy to see, even people of good conscience walk away from this problem. Why is this? Why is bullying accepted in the 21st century?

When you see people bullied or intimidated at school or at work, or in the community, how do you react? Do you weigh in and try intervene or do you walk away from the uncomfortable situation? If you walk away, does that ultimately help the person/people who are treating badly and unfairly?

> The episode was nominated for a **Daytime Emmy Award** in the category Outstanding Entertainment Children's Series "Yesteryear" is noted as one of the most celebrated episodes of the animated series. The episode content has influence on later productions, and the fictional Vulcan city of ShiKahr, which is featured in *Star Trek: Enterprise.*
>
> The 2008 book *Star Trek 101: A Practical Guide to Who, What, Where, and Why* notes writer D.C. Fontana's contributions to the Vulcan story, and that she also wrote the "Journey to Babel" episode, which also further established this species. They also note that despite being planned for presentation as a children's cartoon, it has a sci-fi plot and emotional impact that ranks among the best of live-action *Star Trek* episodes.
>
> (Wikipedia, 2020)

Lesson 37

A virtuous person is like water which adapts itself to the perfect place.
His mind is like the deep water that is calm and peaceful.
His heart is kind like water that benefits all.
His words are sincere like the constant flow of water.

Lao Tzu Chapter 8

Season 1 Episode 3: One of our Planets is Missing

Story Summary

The USS *Enterprise* must prevent a cloud-like being from consuming Mantilles, a Federation world. With only a hand full of starships to evacuate the colony, Captain Kirk must find a way to communicate with the creature before it takes the lives of tens of thousands on Mantilles.

Weapons cannot stop the cloud, so Kirk takes *Enterprise* inside it. Mr. Spock determines that the life form has a brain center. Using a Vulcan mind meld, Spock convinces the creature that it will kill other sentient beings if it consumes an upcoming world. The entity understands Spock, and since it does not wish to kill living creatures, even tiny ones like humans, it agrees to change course and return to where it first was born.

Notable Dialogue: None

Character Arcs: Spock and the Cloud Creature

Mr. Spock has always had a way with words, and in this story, the ideas stem from compassion and love for all beings in the universe – even the deadly Cloud creature that has consumed planets in its wake and course towards a planet with hundreds of Federation colonists.

Spock's mind meld with Cloud comes from a place of peace and serenity. The Vulcan's logic reaches the Cloud's sense of moral laws. Surprisingly, the Cloud accepts that the small beings on planets, and on the ship inside its belly, are sentient and should not be destroyed and consumed.

Everyday Reflections

Can you reach friends or strangers in ways that is enriching to their lives? Do you have the ability to talk to others, reason with them, and help them steer to a course of action beneficial to their lives? If you are a teacher, a parent, a community leader, you seem to already have this important human quality.

Everyday Actions

Find a seemingly impossible scenario you have recently become aware of and try to solve it with logic and persistence. Can you simply talk your way out of it or do you need to prepare for the confrontation?

Lesson 38

Searching for precious goods leads us astray

Lao Tzu Chapter 12

Season 1 Episode 5: More Troubles with Tribbles

Story Summary

Kirk and crew escort robotic carriers loaded with quinto-triticale to Sherman's Planet amidst rumors the Klingons have a new weapon. On their way to the planet, Klingons attack a small scout ship. The *Enterprise* rescues trader Cyrano Jones – who, of course, has more tribbles. Captain Koloth says why they want Cyrano, but go into no further detail. It seems that Jones escaped his sentence on Station K-7 by finding a Tribble predator (a Glommer) on a Klingon claimed world. Koloth tells Kirk that the Klingons created it to eradicate the species that was an ecological nightmare for his world.

During the battle to save Cyrano, Captain Kirk finds out the Klingons new weapon is an energy beam that leaves both ships powerless.

Once aboard *Enterprise*, McCoy examines Jones' tribbles. Bones discovers these tribbles don't reproduce – but just get bigger and bigger. Later we find that the tribbles simple gather together in a bigger ball to produce a giant tribble. At the end of the story, Kirk beams the giant-sized tribbles aboard the Klingon ship. Koloth rages at his nemesis as the *Enterprise* flies off with Cyrano and to deliver the grain shipment to Sherman's planet – what's left of it after the tribbles nibble most of it!

Notable Dialogue:

> **Cyrano Jones**: Under space salvage laws, (the Glommer's) mine!
> **Scotty**: A planetary surface isn't covered under space salvage laws. But, if you want the little beastie that bad, Mr. Jones, we'll transport you over with it.
> **Cyrano Jones**: I withdraw my claim!

Character Arcs: Cyrano Jones

A bit like his counterpart in *Star Trek* lore, Harry Mudd, Cyrano Jones is a get-rich-quick entrepreneur. Cyrano's actions, though, typically put others at risk – which, for the crew of the Enterprise, means putting their lives at stake several times to the Klingons. Although the rescue attempt does bring tactical information to the Federation when the Klingons reveal their energy status ray, Mr. Jones's remains a self-centered man in pursuit of money – a path that true Taoists avoid.

Everyday Reflections

Cyrano Jones is an entrepreneur – and one who goes to any lengths to create a gimmick to ring-in the client base. Stealing a Glommer from the Klingons is just another example of his conniving ways. And why does Cyrano do this? Greed.

What in your life do you pursue the most – is it money, success, social status, love?

Everyday Actions

Pick one of your most non-Taoist desires to examine. Who in your life represents the exact opposite of your most ardent desires? Pretend you are him for one week, and go against everything you have learned in pursuit of this goal. After seven days, do you feel better about your obsession, or must you continue it into the future? Your choice may well determine the life you may lead and a path to *The Way* Lao Tzu would not approve of for anyone.

Lesson 39

What has not yet emerged is easy to prevent

Lao Tzu Chapter 64

Season 2 Episode 4: Albatross

Story Summary

Ordered by Starfleet Command, Captain Kirk, Spock and Dr. Leonard McCoy beam to Dramia II to meet with planet representatives to discuss the current state of affairs. After their meeting and just before they are about to leave, McCoy is arrested on charges of murdering hundreds of innocent citizens. The reason: a mass inoculation program gone wrong. Kirk and Spock must find a way to prove their friend innocent or he will serve the rest of his life in a Dramia II prison.

Notable Dialogue:

> **Kirk**: Now, now, Demos. You're hardly in a position to take on an entire crew.
> **Demos**: And you are not in authority to conduct an investigation in our star system.
> **Kirk**: You will remind me to report my conduct to the Federation, won't you, Mr. Spock?
> **Spock**: Of course, Captain.

Character Arcs: Dr. McCoy and Demos

For physicians like McCoy, taking precautions to vaccinate a population from a known disease was a simple and routine act. In the 24th century, science is considered sacred. In the 21st century, amidst the COVID-19 pandemic, top scientific organizations like the WHO, CDC and other respected medical experts have been challenged to find a vaccine for the deadly virus. Thus, what McCoy experienced may have seemed far-fetched in a Trek story is not so unbelievable today in 2020.

Everyday Reflection

Leaders of Dramia II thought McCoy started a plague with the inoculations, but it the effects of an aurora that caused the problem.

In today's world, there are many people (anti-vacers) who believe that inoculations can cause illness in a child or an adult. Even scientists believe this is a possible side-effect. As of August 25, 2020, Dr. Faucci, and American spokesperson for the CDC and Dept. of Health and Welfare, warned the American public not to expect a vaccine for the COVID-19 virus soon until it a mass testing trail is passed.

Everyday Actions

Read about the anti-vaccination campaign against COVID-19 in a prominent newspapers – like the Washington Post or New York Times (September 2, 2020). What does it say about teachers and other workers view on the vaccine? Will a rushed trial of the anticipated vaccine cause even more damage in countries such as Russia, China or the United States?

Lesson 40

People fail at the threshold of success. Be as cautious at the end as at the beginning.

Then there will be no failure

Lao Tzu Chapter 64

Season 1 Episode 12: The Time Trap

Story Summary

When *Enterprise* investigates a section of space known for strange disappearances of starships and other vessels, three Klingon Birds of Prey force them into the area. *Enterprise* and the Klingon Bird of Preys reappear in a strange null space. Immediately, both Kirk and Kor are beamed to a meeting with the Council – a group of aliens, who like them, have been trapped in this area for centuries. Although Kor and Kirk are told that they have no way out, the two decide to work together to escape.

Before Kirk and Kor star their unlikely escape, the Klingon captain plants a bomb onboard *Enterprise*. The two ships work together, and as they near completion of their daring plan, Scotty finds the bomb and jettisons it before it explodes. Kor vows to destroy Kirk in a future battle as both ships leave null space.

Notable Dialogue:

> **Xerius**: You will fail.
> **Kirk**: We must try, Xerius. Elysia is, in many respects, a perfect society. But with all its virtues, it is not home. And home with all its faults... is where we prefer to be.

Character Arcs: Kirk, Kor and Xerius

Kirk reluctantly must trust Kor so both ships can escape the temporal time pocket. The plan for both ships to work in unison seemed an effective one, but only with the help of the Elyians does Kirk find out the Kor has set a deadly trap. Kirk's trust was guarded, and due to the Elysians warning, his quick actions saves the *Enterprise*. As is the condition in any military encounter with the enemy, one must be cautious for trust is something that must be earned rather than be given.

Everyday Reflections

Would you say that you too easily trust others? What type of troubles will you run into if you assume another is honest and forthright? Although Lao Tzu believes that trust is essential in every relationship, one must use caution upon meeting others and making friendships. If, as Lao Tzu suggests, you use your instincts when judging others, you will likely have long lasting friendships instead of short-lived ones.

Everyday Actions

In your journal, keep track of the times your trust in a friend or family member is honored. You may even wish to test this trust by sharing a *fake* secret to see if it comes back to you.
Also, make a point of working with someone you normally would not, and see if your joint effort actually is a winning move for both of you.

Lesson 41

We go from birth to death. Three out of ten follow life. Three out of ten follow death. People who rush from birth to death are also three out of ten. Why is that so?

Because they want to make too much of life.

Lao Tzu Chapter 50

Season 2 Episode 6: The Counter-Clock Incident

Story Summary

With a special guests onboard the *Enterprise*, Commodore Robert April and his wife, Captain Kirk attempts to rescue an alien ship that has fallen into a supernova. As Kirk's ship is also sucked into the gravity well of the dangerous spatial event, he and all others on the ship begin to age backwards. Time in this supernova runs backwards, and Commodore April and his aged wife return to a more vibrant age, but Spock reverts to a child. After Kirk and April manage save the alien vessel and themselves, the commodore must decide if he wants to return to his youth or live out his remaining days as the man he was before.

Notable Dialogue:

> **Robert April**: No matter where I've traveled in the galaxy, Jim, this bridge is more like home than anywhere else.
> **Kirk**: Yes, Commodore, I know the feeling.
> **Robert April**: To me she was always like my child. I was there in the San Francisco navy yards when her unit components were built.

Sarah April: But what about us? We don't have to use the transporter. We can remain young, live our lives over again. You could command a starship once more.

Robert April: What a blessing to be able to live one's life over again. If the life you've lived has left you unfulfilled. No, Sarah, I don't want to live it all over again. I couldn't improve one bit on what we've had together.

Character Arcs: Commodore Robert April

Living life in the richest of ways is not to rush it through – so Lao Tzu would say to anyone in the past or present day. Moreover, Lao would say three of ten people follow life's evil path, and death comes too early. To live life in the way it is presented, without a need to hurry and accumulate wealth, power or status is the best path for a Taoist.

For Commodore Robert April, even though he and his life now have chance to live their lives again, from an early exciting period, is not a wise choice. The Starfleet officer realizes that he and Sarah should savor the fruits of the past and move on to the end of their lives without regrets.

For this, Robert April is a Taoist in the most necessary way – and illustrates that he very likely followed the path of life at just the right pace.

Everyday Reflections

Commodore April and his wife had a chance to remain young and restart their lives again, but chose not to because of their gratitude for what shaped their existence from the start. They lived their lives without fear of death or selfishness. Can you say the same about your life today? If you had an opportunity to start at a certain point in your life and continue on without the health, economic or social problems plaguing you, would you? Why? Would it truly change the person you are today?

Everyday Actions

If possible, look at a few clips, or the entire 2008 movie featuring Kate Blanchet and Brad Pitt, *The Curious Case of Benjamin Button*. The movie is based on the 1922 short story by F. Scott Fitzgerald about a baby who is born an old man, and as he ages, becomes younger, until he is actually a newborn. The implications for this sort of life experience is strange. Still, a man like Benjamin Button may have normal interactions with others when reaching middle-age or a bit younger.

Lesson 42

The valley spirit never dies. It is called the mystical female

Lao Tzu Chapter 6

Season 1 Episode 4: The Lorelei Signal

Story Summary

Communications Officer Uhura and Nurse Chapel must take command of *Enterprise* when the male crewmen are enraptured by a Lorelei Song of alien women.

As Kirk, Spock and McCoy cannot resist the signal as well, they beam down to a planet, greeted by alien females, and given headsets that drain their life energies. They eventually do escape, but no barely alive as feeble old men, nearly die in a giant bucket of rainwater.

Once Uhura and Chapel rescue the men, Kirk promises to take the women to a planet with livable conditions for females like them. Scotty uses the transporter to restore Kirk, Spock, McCoy and other males to their original selves.

Notable Dialogue:

> **Spock**: The form is humanoid. There are many internal differences. Their bodies appear to function on an unusual psychokinesis level.
> **McCoy**: First time I ever admired a body function.

Character Arcs: Uhura and Nurse Chapel

The female in Taoism is the birth of all goodness and strength. The Ying and Yang are an important concept in Tao, but the female is the one who soothes, comforts, and raises the quality of life through her gender and sexual nature.

Both *Enterprise* officers save their ship and crew when female aliens capture and drain the life force out of the captain, first officer, and other prominent bridge crew. Uhura's and Chapel's inner strength and mental abilities uplift the men and rescue them from a hideous death.

Everyday Reflections

In American society in 2020, both men and women have incrementally moved the needle to include females into politics and other leadership positions. Still, the glass ceiling is still in place. How can America change this systematic problem in society?

Everyday Actions

Perform a quick research task: find out how many females are in Congress and the Senate. Compare the current day numbers to, say, what it was 50 years earlier. Are you pleased with the percentage increase or does America have a long way to go before women reach any type of equal status in the political ranks?

Lesson 43

Those who advise the ruler on the Way, do not want the world subdued with weapons

Lao Tzu Chapter 30

Season 1 Episode 14: The Slaver Weapon

Story Summary

When Spock, Uhura and Sulu travel to a nearby star base in a shuttlecraft with a unique, ancient weapon developed the highly sophisticate Slavers, they find indications that yet another such artifact my indeed be close. As they fly towards a planet, they are attacked and captured by the Kzinti, a cat-like race bent on dominating their enemies by any means possible. The signal Spock's crew had received was manufactured by the aliens to obtain the real Slaver super weapon. Armed with their prized toy, the Kzinti must figure out how to use it so they can rule the galaxy.

Notable Dialogue:

> **Spock**: Consider. Chuft Captain has been attacked by an herbivorous pacifist, an eater of leaves and roots, one who traditionally does not fight. And the ultimate insult, I left him alive. Chuft Captain's honor is at stake. He must seek personal revenge before he can call for help.
> **Sulu**: That gives us some time. You did plan it that way?
> **Spock**: Of course.

Character Arcs: Spock, Uhura and Sulu

As Lao Tzu suggested, rulers are advised to not use weapons to suppress their population – or that of the world in general. Violence is not the way to rule, but using compassion and kindness towards others is the best way of leading a nation.

Therefore, in this story, the main protagonists and Trek characters of Spock, Sulu and Uhura are an afterthought to the focus on the alien race who invented the ultimate weapon. Even the antagonists are merely a prop to show that if evil intent, one of ruling the world or others through violence, will ultimately return to you.

The changeable weapon settings is a unique thought, as is the idea of a smart one that will destroy the enemy – something that even Sun Tzu would be amazed at, too. If weapons were used in war, and if they had an intelligence about them (which the slaver weapons to not technically have in this story), that would be interesting.

What if only weapons would turn off when anyone tried to use them? That truly would be their best use.

Everyday Reflections

If weapons had a sentience power control, could they prevent wars and needless violence? Are all weapons simply extensions of humanity's need to control overs and take their most precious possessions? If we as people could create a philosophy of kindness, one that everyone would believe in, would that not serve best in our culture?

Everyday Actions

Armed with only a pencil and paper, design your own Slaver weapon. Create a handgun that is even more powerful than the one in the episode, but also insert a way to turn it on based on threat, not as an aggressive tool, but as a defensive one.

Lesson 44

Being a model to the world, eternal virtue will never falter in you,

as you return to the boundless

Lao Tzu Chapter 28

Season 1 Episode 7: The Infinite Vulcan

Story Summary

Captain Kirk and crew discovers a planet inhabited by a race of plants, the Phylosians, they also find a giant humanoid named Dr. Kenicius 5 – a fugitive from the Eugenics War on earth centuries earlier. Impressed with Mr. Spock's mind, the evil doctor captures and clones him to serve as his right hand Vulcan to rule over the protect every living creature in the universe. As the real Spock lay dying on a medical table, Kirk argues with the giant Spock to save the smaller, original version. The captain is successful, and giant Spock mind melds with the real Vulcan, saving his life. Dr. Keniclius 5, the fifth generation of his kind, takes a gentler approach now with Kirk, Bones and Spock, and decides that staying behind and reviving the Phylosians' culture is most important after all.

Notable Dialogue:

> **Kirk:** Mr. Sulu – you're the most scrutable person I know.

Character Arcs: Spock, Spock Clone, Sulu, Kirk and McCoy

The original eugenics scientist, Keniculus had virtuous intentions – to create a master race to bring peace to the galaxy, but to impose a master race's will on civilizations throughout the Federation would have been in violation of intergalactic laws throughout the quadrant. Kirk convinced him of his flaws, as did the Spock clone.

Everyday Reflections

Eugenics may be a crime in *Star Trek* lore, but in world history it is steeped in racism and hate. Plato suggested selected breeding back in 400 BC, but in the 20th century it was associated with white supremacy and scientific racism. Even though the Nazi's promoted this agenda, American Charles Lindberg, the first person to fly from New York to London, also believed in in a creating master race of Germanic roots.

Cloning itself is governed by world laws to prevent this type scientific research from ever becoming reality – in part, due to the World War II.

If you could change the laws, would you? Could cloning, like we will see in perhaps the best Star Trek: Enterprise episode titled, Similitude, help humanity?

In the original Khan episode of *Space Seed*, we see how the Eugenics War spun out of control quickly.

Everyday Actions

Watch or re-watch your favorite clone movie, like *Star Wars: Attack of the Clones* (2002), *Replicas* (2015), or, *The 6th Day* (2000). Which one did you like the best? Why?

Lesson 45

The whole secret lies in confusing the enemy, so that he cannot fathom our real intent

Sun Tzu Chapter 5

Season 1 Episode 16: The Jihad

Story Summary

Captain James T. Kirk leads a Special Forces team to recover a unique religious artifact. If Kirk cannot find the item within 24 hours, an intergalactic jihad is likely to begin with horrible consequences for millions across the known universe.

Notable Dialogue:

> **Kirk**: That's it. End of a long hard journey.
> **Lara**: We still have to go back, James. I'd tell you true, I find you an attractive man. If we were...together, the trip'd be easier. And if anything happened, why... we'd have some green memories.
> **Kirk**: I already have... a lot of green memories.

Character Arcs: Skorr

Early on, we believe that Skorr is leading the way to recovering the lost artifact, but he was only trying to mislead the others. By confounding the efforts of Kirk and crew he tried to put an end to their quest. Like any good military leader, Skorr took the road most likely to bring success to his campaign.

Everyday Reflections

When did you last see a person mislead another, whether on a television show, a movie, or read about this in a short story or novel? Is this a sound strategy? In the end, does this prove to be the winning decision?

Everyday Actions

Choose one of these popular books to acquaint yourself the reality (though fiction) of what a religious Jihad may look like in the world today: *A Fury of God* (2002) by Malise Ruthven, *Jihad in Saudi Arabia* (2010) by Thomas Hegghammer or *The Secret Agent* (1907) by Joseph Conrad. Read a thumbnail sketch of the text. If you find one fascinating, as Mr. Spock would say, purchase it and take a serious look at what it means to believe in something so fiercely that you can not only lose yourself in the religion, but take actions against others who may not.

Lesson 46

A faithful Tao cultivator does not use force

Lao Tzu Chapter 68

Season 2 Episode 2: The Pirates of Orion

Story Summary

Captain Kirk is torn between saving Mr. Spock's life and rendezvousing with a Starfleet freighter, the SS *Huron*, to deliver much needed medical supplies for an entire world suffering from a deadly virus.

When Orion pirates capture the *Huron*, they inadvertently steal Spock's curative. Kirk negotiates with the Orion captain on an unstable asteroid (by threat of self-destruction of the Orion ship), save Mr. Spock, and deliver the medicine on time to save innocent lives on Deneb V.

Notable Dialogue:

> **McCoy**: What's the use of being a doctor anyway? We're only as good as our drugs and technology make us. Underneath all the tricks, I might as well be practicing in the Middle Ages.
> **Kirk**: If you really believed that, Bones, you wouldn't still be a doctor after 25 years.

Character Arcs: Spock, Kirk, Bones and Orion captain

With Spock dying due to an illness that is fatal Vulcans, Kirk must negotiate with an Orion pirate to obtain stolen medicine. His negotiating skills, rather than a military strategy of strike first, works. Force should never be the first option, and as a faithful Tao follower, Kirk obtains the cure and saves Mr. Spock.

Everyday Reflections

Is your first instinct to fight through problems with others – whether at work, with friends or family or on playgrounds? Have you changed your method of confrontation the older you became or are you still act on instinct and fight to win, no matter the cost?

Everyday Actions

In your journal, discuss any recent moments when you had to negotiate a truce between two co-workers or family members. What tactics did you use to bring the two parties together? Could you do it again with others if you needed to at work or at home?

Lesson 47

The one who does not honor the teacher and the one who does not honor the task,

although ever so knowledgeable, they are confused.

Lao Tzu Chapter 27

Season 2 Episode 5: How Shaper the Serpents Teeth?

Story Summary

As James T. Kirk follows a strange probe's signal, *Enterprise* is attacked by an energy field that looks like a serpent and has a hold of the starship. The alien claims to be Kulkukan, a Mayan-Aztec warrior legend. Kulkukan beams Kirk, Spock, McCoy, Scotty and Ensign Walking Bear to its ship to solve a puzzle. As they figure out questions to the riddle, Mr. Spock finds a way to break the tractor beam's hold on *Enterprise*. When the puzzle is solved by Kirk, very old being that once helped young races across the universe is revealed to be behind the energy field. McCoy harkens back to Shakespeare and recite the verse, "How sharper than the serpent's teeth than an ungrateful child."

Notable Dialogue:

> (Kirk is trying to reason with the Kulkukan)
> **Kirk**: If children are made totally dependent on the teachers, they'll never be anything but children.

Character Arcs: Kulkukan

The ancient being, one who brought mystery to the Mayans and other cultures, did so to cultivate peace and curiosity for all those on earth. Although none of the civilizations figured out his puzzles, he still considered them as children to be loved. Upon his recent return to Federation space, he still found hatred and rage.

A Taoist could see the alien Kulkukan as a being who simply wished to be quiet and peaceful like water, teaching his children the Way. But as Captain Kirk said to the being, you cannot treat humans like children all their lives; you must allow them to grow and change at their own pace, without interference. This lesson was not lost on the intelligent being, as he left to allow earth and the Federation to learn, through mistakes, what it takes to take the path of the Way.

Everyday Reflections

Over the long course of your life, can you remember the best teachers – where they in elementary school, high school, in college? Perhaps the ones who helped you learn about life were your parents, or friends, or even religious mentors?

What type or critical literacy skills did your academic instructors teach you and have you used them throughout life to examine the problematic nature of the world today?

Everyday Actions

If possible, take a few minutes from your busy schedule to call or email a former teacher. Thank him/her for the guidance they gave you in class, in your studies, and how they impacted your current life. Be kind, loving and grateful to a mentor who taught life skills in addition to course content. Whether it was a K-12 teacher, a college professor or a music instructor, there must be a few that you owe a friendly thank you, right?

Chapter Four

The Next Generation:

Challenges to Ethical Behavior a Century Later

The Baton Handoff to Picard's Enterprising Crew

In the 24th century, well beyond the early voyages of the starship USS *Enterprise* NC 1701-A, Captain Jean-Luc Picard takes command with the same mission: to boldly go where no one has gone before. Surrounded by a diverse crew that includes a Betazoid, an sentient android, and even a Klingon, the starship meets a variety of alien civilizations, both kind and cruel, and even an omnipresent being called Q from the Continuum. Captain Picard, Commander Will Riker, Mr. Data, Chief Security Officer Mr. Wolf, Counselor Deanna Troi, Chief Engineer Geordi La Forge, and Dr. Beverly Crusher explore the galaxy, and although threatened by hostile and deadly foes such as the Borg, the Romulans, and others, still manage to maintain peace in the Alpha Quadrant.

Lesson 48

A good wanderer leaves no trace

Lao Tzu Chapter 27

Season 1 Episode 1: Encounter at Farpoint Station

Story Summary

In the year 2364, Captain Jean-Luc Picard takes control of the new flagship of the Federation of Planets: the USS *Enterprise*. The USS *Enterprise's* NCC 1701-D maiden journey is to Deneb IV; Picard's first mission is to develop a friendly relationship with the Bandi people. Why Deneb IV? The Bandi have created a powerful energy source that has allowed them to build Farpoint Station, but have kept the method for this construction a secret. Starfleet would like to know – as would the rest of the galaxy, how this new form of energy was designed so they can replicate it as well.

On their important mission to Farpoint, Picard and crew meet Q from the Q Continuum – an all-powerful being that can master time and space. At first, Q forbids *Enterprise* to explore the far reaches of the galaxy – and traps them behind a grid, a cage, like an animal in a zoo. The *Enterprise* captain argues with Q, who is now on the bridge with him, that it is not the right of the Continuum to prevent travel, or even try to stop the natural evolvement of any species in its quest to explore and discover new civilizations across the universe.

Hesitant at first. Q agrees to let *Enterprise* go on, but on one condition: Picard must figure out how the Bandi have created an unlimited power source on their planet. IF they fail to solve this puzzle, Q will not allow their further exploration of the galaxy.

Without much of a choice, Jean-Luc agrees to the deal.

The power grid is removed and *Enterprise* is allowed to fly to Deneb IV – with Q in close proximity to judge humanity in its quest to be more than it already is in the universe.

When *Enterprise* arrives at Deneb IV, the bridge crew beams down to the planet and meet the Bandi governor, Groppler Zorn. When their simple wishes for food come out of nowhere, suspicious are aroused. Counselor Troi senses a powerful and sad emotion nearby. As Troi and others move through a labyrinth beneath Farpoint Station, no explanation is given for its complex structure. Suddenly, a large ship enters Bandi orbit and start to fire near the station, then kidnaps Zorn.

Before Picard can fire on the craft, Q reappears and suggest that he board the alien ship – which the captain does instead. Once inside the ship, the away team finds similar passages as found on the Farpoint Station. They find and free Zorn who was being tortured by something – a being that *was* the ship itself.

The Bandi leader tells Picard that they learned that the creature could create objects, and due to this amazing quality, his people decided to capture and use it for their own selfish benefit. Zorn admits his complicity in holding the creature's mate on his planet was wrong and promises to release it. Soon, both creatures below turn into jelly fish-like beings, reuniting in a loving embrace above Bandi.

Q congratulates Picard on figuring out the riddle of the Farpoint Station – but warns him that he and his crew will continue to be observed on their journeys across the galaxy.

Notable Dialogue:

> **Admiral McCoy**: Have you got some of a reason my atoms scattered all over space, boy?
> **Data**: No, sir. But at your age, sir, I thought you shouldn't have to put up with the time, and trouble of a shuttlecraft.
> **Admiral McCoy**: Hold it right there, boy?
> **Data**: Sir?
> **Admiral McCoy**: What about my age?
> **Data**: Sorry, sir. If that subject troubles you...
> **Admiral McCoy**: Troubles me? What's so damn troublesome about not havin' died? How old you think I am anyway?
> **Data**: 137 years, Admiral, according to Starfleet records.
> **Admiral McCoy**: Explain how you remembered that so exactly.
> **Data**: I remember every fact I am exposed to, sir.
> **Admiral McCoy**: I don't see no points on your ears boy, but you sound like a Vulcan.

Data: No, sir, I am an android.

Admiral McCoy: Almost as bad.

Data: I thought it was generally accepted, sir, that Vulcans are an advanced, and most honorable race.

Admiral McCoy: They are, they are, and damn annoying at times.

Character Arcs: Captain Jean-Luc Picard, Q, Commander Will Riker, Counselor Diana Troi, Data and Wesley Crusher

The newest adventures of the starship USS *Enterprise* 1701-D poses interesting challenges to the crew and alien beings encountered before and at Farpoint Station.

Q, an eternal being of power over space and time, is the biggest obstacle for Captain Picard and his crew. Nearly denied space travel entirely, Q allows Jean-Luc to show his intelligence in the first mission – or be denied warp travel anywhere in the galaxy.

Captain Jean-Luc Picard must figure out the riddle posed by Q or his very trip among the stars may be jeopardized by the omnipresent being.

Commander Will Riker has to balance a failed relationship with his duty as first officer.

Counselor Diana Troi, like Will, must find a way to deal with her feeling for him while counseling the crew compliment. In Diana's first significant role helping Picard, she struggles to understand the mystery of Farpoint. Still, when powerful creatures reach out to her, she puts the pieces together and alerts Jean-Luc to the caged, but intelligent beings providing power to the planet.

Data, a singular lifeform, and sentient android and only one of his kind, is also the put in the command position aboard the starship. His role, beyond acting as a science officer and navigator on the bridge, is one of self-exploration. Data's continual search for his humanity is his biggest challenge.

For Wesley Crusher, a teenage son of Dr. Beverly Crusher, the ship's chief physician, his desire to learn and one day be a Starfleet officer may irk Captain Picard at first, but because of his friendship Beverly, he appoints the young man an acting cadet. Wesley's brilliance combined with a natural curiosity gains respect and admiration from Jean-Luc and all the senior officers.

Everyday Reflection

As Lao Tzu states, a good traveler leaves no traces of his/her stay in a strange land. The Prime Directive of Starfleet is not to interfere with any culture – although in this instance, Captain Picard decides to save the lives of sentient creatures imprisoned by the ruler of a planet intent on acceptance by the Federation. In this case, the traveler to a distant land leaves his mark – that of compassion for all creatures taken captive by greedy beings intent to exploit the weak and helpless.

If you travelled into an unknown part of the world, would you be discouraged by others who told you via a blogsite that you shouldn't go because of the dangers awaiting you (muggings, hygiene, lack of food, etc.)? Would you change plans and take the safest journey to a more touristic spot in the world? What was the last daring adventure you took in your life? Would you take it again? What do you most wish to take with out of any trip you take today? A better skill for language? Meeting foreign residents who may become lifelong pen pals? The taste of a great meal? A piece of art? In essence, what motivates you to begin any journey in life and push aside the mere notion of failure or uncomfortableness?

Everyday Action

Plan a detailed trip somewhere exotic– even one merely in theory – and afterwards take notice to the most important aspects of it that come out. What did you most wish to achieve on this adventure? Then, plan a trip that you can point towards, even if its someone in the near future, but one you can eventually take if nothing horrific happens to you or the world in the days leading up to the departure date.

Lesson 49

The separate parts make no carriage

Lao Tzu Chapter 39

Season 2 Episode 6: The Measure of a Man

Story Summary

While at Starbase 173 for maintenance, Commander Bruce Maddox asks to visit with Lieutenant Commander Data so he can learn more about his unusually designed positronic network. Data agrees to meet Maddox, but it becomes clear quickly that the commander is more interested in downloading Data's network into a computer mainframe before disassembling the android to determine how it/he was created. Although Data is reassured that his memories and personality will be reconstructed after the procedure, he cannot guarantee these results. Therefore, Mr. Data refuse to participate in the science experiment.

As Commander Maddox appeals to the Judge Advocate General, Captain Picard must come to Data's defense. The judge, a former friend of Jean-Luc listens, but realizes she cannot play favorites with Picard. A trial must proceed to determine Data's rights.

Commander Will Riker acts as the prosecutor in the trail and Captain Picard as Data's advocate. Up first, Riker argues that Data is simply a machine constructed by and is merely the sum of its parts. As Riker turns off Data from a small switch in the back, Picard is devastated. He asks and is given a recess to reassess his tactics moving forward with the defense.

Back on *Enterprise*, Guinan reminds her friend that if Maddox is allowed to disassemble Data there will be thousands made in his likeness – which will likely lead to slavery of the sentient creatures. Picard uses her basic argument in court. Using Maddox's own definition of sentience,

Picard provides logic to show that Data is intelligence and self-aware, and has also just began to exhibit emotion and sentimentality – which in this case leads him to pronounce that his client possesses consciousness measuring that of humanity itself.

Judge Louvois says plainly that neither she nor anyone can truly measure the rules for Data and that he has the right to choose. After the court's ruling, Data formally refuses to be taken apart by Maddox, but also adds that his work is intriguing. As Maddox refers to Data as 'he' rather than 'it', the judge notes that even he accepts her verdict as the right one.

Later, Riker apologies for his participation in the court proceeding. Data thanks him for doing what he needed to do to preserve his right of choice, reminding him that his act was selfless and gave him the chance to win in the eyes of the court.

Notable Dialogue:

Guinan: Consider that in the history of many worlds there have always been disposable creatures. They do the dirty work. They do the work that no one else wants to do, because it's too difficult and too hazardous. With an army of Datas, all disposable, you don't have to think about their welfare, or you don't think about how they feel. Whole generations of disposable people.

Jean-Luc Picard: You're talking about slavery.

Guinan: I think that's a little harsh.

Jean-Luc Picard: I don't think that's a little harsh, I think that's the truth. That's the truth that we have obscured behind...a comfortable, easy euphemism. 'Property.' But that's not the issue at all, is it?

Character Arcs: Data, Picard, Riker and Maddox

If Lao Tzu is correct, and separate parts do not make the carriage, do all the parts put together in a highly sophisticated manner make a 'man'?

If Maddox had taken Data apart, he would have destroyed the essence of the new life form. Since Data is unique, his being must have rights as well as any other creature or human being. To take him apart, in essence, is to destroy the life inside the machine/life. To treat Data like a toaster, you can then enslave him and treat others like him, if made, without respect or rights.

Everyday Reflections

What makes Data so unique? Is he/it a machine, a person, a sentient being? Can this life form ever take the Taoist path to a peaceful existence? Can Data ever show compassion, humility and patience – three basic principles of Tao? If so, will that show his humanity?

What are the rights of artificial intelligence lifeforms? Are there moral and ethical dilemmas when considering the rights of any sentient life form like Mr. Data? Can we put human qualities on Data or are the ethics far beyond such simplistic forms?

In essence, is the legal system of Starfleet Command, and the Federation at large, equipped to judge an A.I., and will their actions to enslave it or tear one apart, like Mr. Data, simply for the advancement of science, a fair and equitable way of making law in the 24th century?

Everyday Actions

How did this early TNG episode resonate with the cast and executives of the *Star Trek* universe?

Brent Spiner, who played Lieutenant Commander Data, called this story his favorite of the TNG episodes. Michael Pillar, who later went on to co-create *Star Trek: Deep Space Nine*, chose this in his top three episodes. Marina Sirtis, Counselor Troi, picked this story as her favorite of the series.

In your journal, write down your favorite TNG stories – ones that contain a clear moral compass that embraces Gene Roddenberry's philosophy for the *Star Trek* franchise. After you list your top five or ten, write down a few reasons why each story embraces the best of *Star Trek* concepts that intertwined with humanity's challenges in the future as well as the ones that we still struggle with in 2020.

Lesson 50

The clever combatant imposes his will on the enemy,

but does not allow the enemy's will to be imposed on him

Sun Tzu Chapter 6

Season 2 Episode 8: Q Who

Story Summary

Q returns to *Enterprise* and wishes to join the bridge crew as it explores the farthest regions of know space. Captain Picard is reluctant to have the all-knowing being part of his crew because of his trickery and cunning that has already caused him and his crew problems in the recent past. Q, faking hurt feelings, calls this an insult. Taking a moment to assess the situation, Q once again decides to pose an even greater challenge to Picard – and flings them across known space to soon meet a fierce race: the Borg.

Guinan, who is very familiar with Q's behavior, warns Picard to set a course back immediately, but Picard disregards her advice. Soon, Jean-Luc and his crew discovers a world that has been totally stripped of all industrial and mechanical parts, one similar to another found by Federation posts near the Neutral Zone months earlier. Soon after the discovery, a cube-shaped vessel appears but refuses to answer hails. Guinan explains that the ship belongs to the Borg, a cyborg race that devastated her people many years ago.

The captain raises shields, but Borg beam aboard their ship and probe the computer system on the bridge. Though Worf incapacitates one, the others adapt their shielding and cannot be stopped. Once they beam off the ship, a voice from the Borg's cube demands that *Enterprise* surrender itself. Immediately, the Borg stops the ship with a tractor beam and beings to cut into the ship's saucer section, killing eighteen crewmen.

After the *Enterprise* disables the cube momentarily, Riker and Data transport aboard the Borg shop to investigate. They find a Borg nursery, and a fortress of cyborgs attached to walls, and notice the cube regenerating itself. The two crewmen beam back and Picard orders the ship to maximum warp to flee the enemy. Within moments, the Borg begin the chase, and there is nothing to stop them when they intercept *Enterprise.*

Though it leaves a bad taste in his mouth, Picard knows what to do: he asks Q for his help. Q accepts Picard's plea, snaps his fingers and returns *Enterprise* to its last know position, hundreds of light years away from Borg space. The powerful being confirms the deaths of the crew members and reminds Picard that what awaits them in further adventures in space will be more than challenging.

Later on, Guinan warns Picard that the Borg are now aware of the Federation and will be coming for them soon. Jean-Luc replies that Q may have done the right thing for the wrong reason, but at least Starfleet could better prepare for this strong enemy in the near future.

Notable Dialogue:

> **Q**: You judge yourselves against the pitiful adversaries you've encountered so far: the *Romulans*, the *Klingons*... They're **nothing** compared to what's waiting. Picard, you are about to move into areas of the galaxy containing wonders more incredible than you can *possibly* imagine... and terrors to freeze your soul. I offer myself as a guide -- only to be rejected out of hand.

> **Q**: **It's not safe out here. It's wondrous, with treasures to satiate desires both subtle and gross; but it's not for the timid**.

Character Arcs: Picard, Q and the Borg

In this encounter, Q said he wished to be a part of the *Enterprise* crew. Is he there to continually bother Picard, to get his goat as the old expression goes, or has he visited once again to see how his favorite human will react to meeting an overwhelming foe?

Picard is overwhelmed by the Borg, and must ask his nemesis for help. The captain may hate to ask for help, but the prudent act was to defer to his enemy – one not as vicious or all-consuming as the Borg.

The Borg reflect everything Sun Tzu saw in an all supreme military leader – one that can overwhelm with forces and strength.

Everyday Reflections

When you take chances in life, do you consider all the possible roads that may lead to failure? If so, do you try to minimize the potential for problems? Have you ever given up on a road to success, personal or professional, because the challenge seemed too arduous and challenging, and that you might fail in your quest?

Everyday Actions

In your journal, write about your current life choices and how safe they seem to you today. What factors have brought you to the place you are today? Are you satisfied with who you are today and where you are headed into the near future?

Take a chance – and if possible, throw yourself into a new job, a new friendship, a new hobby. Challenge yourself – perhaps not as in a deadly way as Q did to Captain Picard and the *Enterprise*, but anything that will broaden your mind and make you work harder at life. We are not here to place it safe – a lesson that Picard quickly understood from his mission.

Lessons 51

The onrush of a conquering force is like the bursting of pent-up waters

into a chasm a thousand fathoms deep.

Sun Tzu Chapter 4

Season 3 Episode 3: The Survivors

Story Summary

Captain Picard and crew respond to a distress call from Delta Rana IV. When they arrive, the entire colony is destroyed, as is their world – except for a very small patch of land where two colonists still live in peace. A married couple, Rishon and Kevin Uxbridge, tell Jean-Luc that they saw the attack by the Husnock but did not realize that they were the only survivors of the attack.

When the Uxbridge's invite Picard, Riker and Troi into their home, they find nothing extraordinary about the house. Deanna finds a lovely music box, but it offers only beauty to counterbalance the destruction surrounding their small piece of heaven among the hell around them. Picard insists that the Rishon and Kevin join them aboard *Enterprise* for their protection, but Keven resists. Soon, a strange spaceship appears and destroys the Uxbridge's home, apparently killing both husband and wife. Yet, when Picard takes the ship to a higher orbit, their home miraculously reappears. This time, Jean-Luc orders Kevin and Rishon to come aboard so he may question them both.

Soon, persuaded by Picard's insightful questions, the image of Rishon vanishes. Kevin admits that his house, and his wife, were lost in an unprovoked attack by the Husnock. He also reveals himself to be a Douwd, an immortal being with powers unknown to humanity. After he had fallen in love with Rishon, he lived happily with her for years until the attack. Keven removes the music box sound that had been torturing Troi – something he had done to prevent her from telepathically learning the truth about him.

The Douwd, after the attack to his adopted world, lashed out, and in a moment, murdered 50 billion Husnock across the galaxy. Keven stayed on with his imaginary wife and home as a way of exiling himself from the rest of the universe so not to ever do such a hideous act ever again.

Picard, resigned to the fact that he is powerless to render judgement or act against such a being, allows Kevin to leave peaceably and return to his planet and his illusions.

Notable Dialogue:

> **Kevin Uxbridge:** No, no, no, no, no — you, you don't understand the scope of my crime. I didn't kill just one Husnock, or a hundred, or a thousand. *I killed them all*. All Husnock, everywhere. Are 11,000 people worth... 50 billion? Is the love of a woman worth the destruction of an entire species?

Character Arcs: Kevin (the Douwd)

As an all-powerful, eternal being, Kevin's raged upon the death of his wife and partner, Rishon, causing the obliteration of the entire Husnock civilization. In the *Art of War*, Sun Tzu comparing an all-powerful army to that of rushing water, falling into a thousand foot chasm. In this case, the water released drowned all of the Husnock, and for that, Kevin feels unrepentant remorse, guilt and shame. IF he had acted as a Taoist instead, accepting the death of his wife would not have been as unrelenting or murderous.

Everyday Reflections

Has anyone ever done something so horrible to you that you struck back immediately without a second thought? Did you feel shame and remorse afterwards for your crime? Today, if a similar incident were to occur, would you strike with forceful violence (physical or emotional) or would you stop yourself and reflect upon the hurtful action?

Everyday Actions

If you have ever severely emotionally hurt someone, could you summon the courage to apologize?

Reach out to someone this month, spend an hour or more with that person on a Zoom call or in person, and be honest about your feelings. Even if the person refuses to accept your apology, you may still feel better for letting of the anger you've felt for so many years.

Lesson 52

It is only the enlightened ruler and the wise general who will use the highest intelligence of the army for purposes of spying and thereby they achieve great results. Spies are a most important element in water, because on them depends an army's ability to move.

Sun Tzu Chapter 13

Season 3 Episode 10: The Defector

Story Summary

The *Enterprise* is near the Neutral Zone when it meets a small scout vessel pursued and fired upon by a cloaked Romulan Warbird. The scout ship makes a run for Federation space, and Captain Picard comes to its assistance. As the tiny ship crosses into Federation territory, it uncloaks, pauses for a few moments, then turns back toward the Neutral Zone. A Romulan officer claiming to be Sub-Lieutenant Setal asks for asylum. Picard grants the request and allows him to beam his ship into *Enterprise*.

While meeting with Picard, Setal tells him that the Romulans are building a secret installation on Nelvana III. Jean-Luc asks for more evidence of this claim, but Setal offers nothing more, but begs Picard to take him at his word. Picard decides to investigate the Romulan's ship to confirm his words, but Setal has it self-destruct. After this incident, Picard, Riker, Data and others believe that the defector may have been sent by the Romulans to entice *Enterprise* to cross over to the Neutral Zone to provoke a war or at minimum, their capture.

Regardless of their concern, Picard orders the ship to Nelvana III. Once there, they do not find military installations. Immediately, two Romulan warbirds decloak and fire on *Enterprise*. Picard guesses that the Romulans used Jarok to feed disinformation to entice Starfleet into the Neutral zone and expose their own as a spy. As Commander Tomalak demands *Enterprise's* surrender, Picard calmly refuses. Three Klingon Birds of Prey decloak and surround the Romulan ships, creating a stalemate. Tomalak nods, almost jokingly, and warns Picard that the next time they meet will be different.

As the starship leave the Neutral Zone, Jarok is found dead by suicide in his quarters – but as left a note for his family. Data, his only friend on the ship says that he must have known it could not be delivered. Picard, now in a solemn mood, applauds Admiral Jarok's courage and conviction, hoping that one day they can deliver the letter to his family.

Notable Dialogue:

> **Admiral Jarok:** There comes a time in a man's life that you cannot know. When he looks down at the first smile of his baby girl and realizes he must change the world for her, for all children. It is for her I am here. Not to destroy the Romulan Empire, but to save it.

Character Arcs: Admiral Jarok

Even military leader who turn against their leaders and become enemies of the State can be used for the nation – and are especially useful when manipulated by the secret police. Sun Tzu understood this just as well as the Romulans.

When Jarok realized, too late, that he was targeted to lure *Enterprise* into their territory, he committed suicide because that was the last honorable act he could perform. Smartly, the Romulans used one of their best military minds against the enemy, and the plan nearly worked if Picard had not planned for the contingency and alliance with the Klingons.

Spying is never a clear case for either the ones observed or the ones doing the observations. In this instance, a double cross served no useful purpose other than a Romulan family to lose their father, husband and honor.

Everyday Reflections

Have you ever been used, without your knowledge, by a superior in a job? What did the person have you do – and did your action truly help your boss or the organization?

On a personal level, have you ever felt emotionally manipulated by a friend, lover or family member? How did you react? Can you honestly say that you will never be used like that again? Is trust something that must be earned over a long period of time?

Everyday Actions

In your journal, consider these questions:

Do military men and women defect in the 21st century, and if so, what happens to them?

In the past, it is well-known that Nazi scientists defected after WWII to the United States. These men and women were given asylum and put to work in the development of weapon projects in America to combat enemy nations.

But what about today, in 2021? Are there still defectors in the world of espionage?

If North Koreans defect to China in 2021, for example, they will be sent back to their home country. After they arrive, they are put through severe interrogations and torture, with many of them dying in their prison cells. If they survive this ordeal, they will go to years of reeducation camps in either Chungsan, Chongori or Pukch'ang.

After being set-up by his Romulan superiors, Admiral Jarok's suicide was the only way out of shame and separation from his family. Is it likely that if defectors in today's world would take a similar path eventually as well?

Lesson 53

Those who are unswerving have resolve

Lao Tzu Chapter 33

Season 3 Episode 15: Yesterday's Enterprise

Story Summary

While the USS *Enterprise* NX 1701-D investigates a spatial rift in the space-time continuum, another Starfleet vessel slowly comes out of it – the USS *Enterprise* 1701-C. Instantaneously, the current *Enterprise* changes from a starship of exploration with families to a vessel of war, engaged in a fierce and prolonged war with the Klingons and Romulans. There is no Lieutenant Commander Worf or Counselor Troi on the Bridge – but there is Tasha Yar, head of security, back from the dead in a former timeline. No one is aware of this change in personnel – certainly not Tasha.

Captain Picard moves to intercept the other starship, but hesitates, now aware that the other *Enterprise* has come from an earlier time. Captain Rachel Garret messages Jean-Luc and pleads for assistance for her injured and dying crew and badly damaged ship. Reluctant, but resolved to help a comrade in arms, Picard order Riker and others to board the ship, but not reveal any details of their ship or the year.

Most importantly, one member of *Enterprise* 1701-D has intuitively perceived the drastic change in timeline and events: Guinan.

While tending to her station in Ten Forward, the perceptive alien knows something has changed a ship of peace to a ship of war. Although it takes a few moments for the changed timeline to settle in, Guinan knows that her existence, and all of those around her, has changed for the worse. Soon, she walks onto the bridge and asks to meet with Picard in private. Guinan explains the situation and the discussion becomes heated:

> **Jean-Luc Picard**: How can I ask them to sacrifice themselves based solely on your intuition?
>
> **Guinan**: I don't know. But I do know that this is a mistake. Every fiber in my being says this is a mistake. I can't explain it to myself, so I can't explain it to you. I only know that I'm right.
>
> **Jean-Luc Picard**: Who is to say that this history is any less proper than the other?
>
> **Guinan**: I suppose I am.
>
> **Jean-Luc Picard**: Not good enough, damn it, not good enough! I will not ask them to die!
>
> **Guinan**: 40 billion people have already died. This war is not supposed to be happening. You've got to send those people back to correct this.
>
> **Jean-Luc Picard**: And what is to guarantee that if they go back, they will succeed? Every instinct is telling me this is wrong, it is dangerous, it is futile!
>
> **Guinan**: We've known each other a long time. You have never known me to impose myself on anyone, or take a stance based on trivial or whimsical perceptions. This timeline must not be allowed to continue. Now, I've told you what you must do. You have only your trust in me to help you decide to do it.

Captain Picard asks Captain Rachel Garret in sickbay. Garret tells her counterpart that they were responding to a hail from the Klingons on Narendra III when the Romulans attacked her ship. Suddenly, a spatial rift appeared, and soon they were in another time with Picard. Rachel says that she wants to go back to her time, but if it means staying here, now, she will fight the enemy.

In the Ready Room, Riker is adamant about keeping the former crew and ship in the current timeline. On the other hand, according to Mr. Data, if *Enterprise* 1701-C had defended the Klingon outpost in the past, it would have been seen as an honorable act and the current war may not exist in the present day. Picard decides to take Data's advice over Will's and goes to meet with Captain Garret.

In their meeting, Jean-Luc reveals that the war is going very badly and it is likely that the Federation will be surrendering in the near future. Her crew and her ship may be more valuable defending the Klingon outpost in the past, and perhaps that alone will prevent the present conflict. Rachel accepts her role, and tells Jean-Luc that her ship should be repaired in about two hours.

Soon afterwards, two Klingon ships appear near the time rift and attack Garret's *Enterprise*, killing the captain and leaving Helmsman Richard Castillo in command. Picard chases off the Klingon ship but now must face the fact that others will return to battle both *Enterprises* in several hours.

During the final shakedown of Garret's *Enterprise*, Tash Yar realizes her affection for Castillo. Tasha is aware that she will not exist in the other time line asks for a transfer.

Tasha Yar: Captain, I request a transfer to the *Enterprise*-C.

Jean-Luc Picard: For what reason?

Tasha Yar: They need someone at Tactical.

Jean-Luc Picard: We need you here.

Tasha Yar: I'm not supposed to *be* here, sir.

Jean-Luc Picard: Sit down, Lieutenant. What did she say to you?

Tasha Yar: I don't belong here, sir. I'm supposed to be...dead.

Jean-Luc Picard: She felt it necessary to reveal that to you?

Tasha Yar: *I* felt it was necessary.

Jean-Luc Picard: I see. You realize that it is very possible the *Enterprise*-C will fail. We will continue in this time line, in which case your life, hopefully, will continue for a long while.

Tasha Yar: I know how important it is that they don't fail, Captain. That's why I'm requesting this transfer.

Jean-Luc Picard: You don't belong on that ship, Lieutenant.

Tasha Yar: No, Captain Garrett belongs on that ship. But she's dead. And I think there's a certain logic in this request.

Jean-Luc Picard: There's no logic in this at all! Whether they succeed or not, the *Enterprise*-C will be destroyed!

Tasha Yar: But Captain, at least with someone at Tactical they will have a chance to defend themselves well. It may be a matter of seconds or minutes, but those could be the minutes that change history. Guinan says I died a senseless death in the other time line. I didn't like the sound of that, Captain. I've always known the risks that come with a Starfleet uniform. If I'm to die in one, I'd like my death to count for something.

Jean-Luc Picard *(after a thoughtful pause)*: Lieutenant...permission granted.

Tasha Yar: Thank you, sir.

As *Enterprise*-C prepares to go through the anomaly, three Klingon war ships return. Picard orders his ship to cover the other and *Enterprise*-D suffers major damage and loss of life.

Jean-Luc Picard: *(prior to battle)* Attention all hands! As you know, we could outrun the Klingon vessels, but we must protect the *Enterprise*-C until she re-enters the temporal rift. And we must succeed. Let's make sure that history never forgets the name *Enterprise.*

Enterprise-C crosses into their time through the rift just as her counterpart is about to explode. Suddenly, with the timeline resolved, all is calm on *Enterprise*-D. Guinan calls Picard and asks if everything is okay – and is the only one who recalls what happened the past 24 hours.

Notable Dialogue:

Guinan: Geordi, tell me about Tasha Yar.

Character Arcs: Guinan, Tasha Yar and Jean-Luc Picard

Fortunately for USS *Enterprise* 1701-D, and millions of innocent lives in the Alpha Quadrant, Guinan's intuitive instincts convinces Captain Picard to force the other *Enterprise* back into the spatial rift to fight with the Klingons against the Romulans on the Nerendra III outpost. By this gallant and self-sacrifice action, the war between the Klingons and the Federation never existed in the proper timeline.

Ms. Guinan simply uses her instincts in the best possible way to save her friend's lives, the Federation of Planets from a deadly battle with the Klingons and Romulans, and helps to reset the normal timeline.

For Chief of Security, Tasha Yar, she exhibits resolve in doing whatever is necessary to save her friends and helps to prevent war that was never meant to be in the true timeline. Her selflessness and strength of will makes her death a meaningful one. Although latter on we find that Tasha did not die on USS *Enterprise* 1701-C, her efforts were still meaningful.

Captain Picard, always a man of strength and resolve as well, fights until his ship is about to explode from enemy fire. His bravery is apparent in any timeline thrown at him.

Everyday Reflections

In what ways has your intuition saved you from making crucial mistakes in your life? On the other hand, how many times have you wished you had gone with your first instinct in a personal or professional scenario? Can a 'gut reaction' to a problem lead you to making the right move that eventually solves a problem of small or big consequences?

Everyday Actions

Is the plot of this story believable – can one event bring about a war?

Over the course of world history, key events have triggered wars across the globe. In 1914, the Austrian-Hungarian war started by the double shooting of Archduke Ferdinand and his wife, Sophia; which also put into play the beginnings of World War I, based on alliances and enemies of the states.

Take a few minutes, or a few day or a week, to examine the causes of armed conflicts around the world. You may use video, too, in your investigations. Consider the American Civil War, the Vietnam War and Korean War and World War II in your research.

As you do this, take your journal with you and take copious notes. Compare and contrast reasons for wars in the historical records. Are there patterns? What are they? Thus, in the end, ask yourself this one major question: what pivotal events, if avoided, could have prevented these wars? Or, as Q of the Continuum said, is humanity a violent, childlike race?

Lesson 54

Cultivate virtue in the family and it will be overflowing

Lao Tzu Chapter 54

Season 3 Episode 16: The Offspring

Story Summary

Commander Data invites Deana Troi, Wesley Crusher and Geordi La Forge to his lab to unveil his most recent, but certainly most unexpected creation: a new life form - an android based on his neural net system. His child, named Lal – Hindi for Beloved - was born out of an inspiration from a recent Federation Cybernetics conference.

With Troi's assistance, Lal chooses what gender and race she most prefers. After nearly choosing to inhabit the outer shell of a male Klingon or Andorian, Lal chooses to adopt a human female appearance. The choice pleases her father, Data, and her new friend, Deanna.

Captain Picard is furious at Data at first for not telling him about his newest creation. When Data counters the argument with the proposition that no one on *Enterprise* has ever asked the captain about their procreation activities, Jean-Luc is disarmed, but also sees the android's logic.

When news of Data's child is supposed to be sent to Starfleet, Admiral Haftel immediately demands that Lal be immediately transferred to the nearest star base for examination. In fact, Haftel soon joins *Enterprise* and questions Data and Lal to assess the value the newest life form could bring to Starfleet. Soon, Haftel orders Data to release his creation to him for further study. Picard supports his officer and claims that Lal is a sentient life form like her creator and thus, refuses the order.

Lal, knowing that she may be separated from Data, shows an emotional outburst, which is a symptom of a cascade failure in her positronic brain. Haftel works with Data to repair the damage, but neither can save her. Left alone with his daughter, Data apologizes that he could not save her. Lal tells her father that she loves him as she is about to experience total systems failure.

Back on the bridge, the crew commiserates with Data, but he tells them that Lal's memories will always be a part of him as he has downloaded her program into his; and as such, Lal will live on through his experiences.

Notable Dialogue:

> **Data**: Lal is my child. You ask that I volunteer to give her up. I cannot. It would violate every lesson I have learned about human parenting. I have brought a new life into this world, and it is my duty, not Starfleet's, to guide her through these difficult steps to maturity. To support her as she learns. To prepare her to be a contributing member of society. No one can relieve me from that obligation. And I cannot ignore it. I am...her father.

> _____

> **Jean-Luc Picard**: There are times, sir, when men of good conscience cannot blindly follow orders. You acknowledge their sentience, but ignore their personal liberties and freedom. Order a man to turn his child over to the state? Not while I'm his captain.

Character Arcs: Data, Picard and Lal

Same situation as Data's day in court, but this time, Starfleet summarily decides to take Data's child back to a Federation station to examine it – ultimately killing it in the name of science.

Lao Tzu noted that by cultivating value in the family, but parents and children would benefit. In this story, Data shows his ferocious parenting demeanor as he protects Lal from Starfleet – although, the stress eventually overwhelms his child.

Captain Picard sides with Data and Lal, and disallows Starfleet to take Lal for further study. Jean-Luc's demonstrates virtue by protecting Data and Lal's civil liberties.

Everyday Reflections

Do you believe you are over-protective person for a child, sibling, or even a pet? Why do you feel this way? What is it about parenting that automatically makes a person fearful of losing the one he/she loves? Have you ever tried to ensure that a child you have raised – yours or another – develop strong values? If so, what social rules have you tried your best to instill in the conscience of the youngster or teenager? Is virtue over-rated?

Everyday Actions

In your journal, take a few minutes to remember the times of your early life when your parent(s) were over-protective. What did your parents do, you feel today, was unfair or over-protective? Were their actions out of love or insecurity? Did their actions stifle your emotional growth?

Lesson 55

The more laws and commands there are, the more thieves and robbers there will be

Lao Tzu Chapter 57

Season 3 Episode 17: Sins of the Father

Story Summary

Commander Kurn, as part of a Klingon-Federation Officer Exchange Program, requests to be placed on the *Enterprise*. Once there, he shadows Lieutenant Worf, but soon repeatedly irritates the Starship's Chief Security Officer. Worf confronts Kurn in private. It is then when Kurn reveals to be Worf's brother – separated when their parents moved to the Kitimor colony. It was only recently that his adopted father, Lorgh, told him of his true identity.

Kurn goes on to tell Worf that the Duras family has accused Mogh, their father, as a traitor, one that sided with the Romalans when they massacred Klingons decades ago on Kitimor. If this claim goes unchallenged, the House of Mogh will be shamed, stripped of land and wealth by the High Council. Worf understands and agrees that both should immediately go to their home world – but that Kurn keep his identity secret in case their challenge is lost.

Captain Picard agrees with Worf decision to defend his family's honor and directs *Enterprise* to the Qo'Nos.

At the High Council, Duras brings with him falsified evidence to prove that Mogh passed along the Kitimor planetary defense codes the day of the attack. Worf challenges this evidence. In private, Kempec, the ailing head of the High Council, begs Worf to go home and drop the challenge. The Starfleet officer protests and tells Kempec that the truth about his father must come out.

Back on board *Enterprise*, Date investigates the Duras claim. During this time, Duras tries to bribe Kurn, Worf's second for the challenge, knowing that he is next in line in Mogh's bloodline. Kurn calls the bribe insulting, a fight occurs, and Worf's brother is seriously injured.

Due to the injury, Captain Picard decides to fills in as Worf's second, his *Cha Dich,* in the trial the next day.

Although Data cannot prove that Mogh did or did not transmit the codes to the Rumulans, the android does find a single survivor from the massacre, Kahlest. With this new information, Jean Luc plans a strategy to reveal the true traitor in the final day of the trial.

The next morning, Picard presents Kalest to the High Council. Once presented, she says she knows the identity of the traitor, but before she is allowed to speak, Kempec calls Worf, Picard and Kahlest into his private chamber. The elder leaders admits that he and the other council members know that Duras's family were the treacherous ones who betrayed their brothers on Kitimor, but due to their political clout on the home world, this cannot be admitted to the public. If this information were disseminated, the entire planet may fall into a bloody civil war that the High Council needs to avoid to retain their high ranking position on Qo'Nos.

Picard, like his client is outraged – and will not stand by as his officer is executed for the crimes of his father. Worf intercedes, and suggests that he receive a discommendation, which essentially means that he accepts the Council's decision, and that his brother's true heritage remain unknown.

Kempec agrees to the deal, as does Picard. The Klingon-Federation peace remains intact, his first officer spared from death, with Kurn living a full life apart from his true brother.

As the sentence is accepted in court, each Klingon High Council member turn their backs towards Worf – even Kurn.

Captain Picard and Lieutenant Worf walk out of the Great Hall disgraced, but the Federation alliance with Klingons preserved – the best solution to an impossible situation.

Notable Dialogue:

> **K'mpek**: (high-ranking Klingon) This is not the Federation, Picard. If you defy an order of the High Council, the alliance with the Federation could fall to dust.
>
> **Jean-Luc Picard**: The alliance with the Federation is not based on lies, K'mpec. Protect your secrets if you must, but you will not sacrifice these men.
>
> _____
>
> **Duras** (Klingon): This is not your world, human. You do not command here.
>
> **Jean-Luc Picard**: I'm not here to command.
>
> **Duras**: Then you must be ready to fight. Something Starfleet does not teach you.
>
> **Jean-Luc Picard**: You may test that assumption at your convenience.

Character Arcs: Worf, Picard, Duras and Kurn

As Lao Tzu noted, the more laws and commands there are, the more thieves take over to disrupt the very standards the people must abide to in society. This happened in China centuries ago, and it still occurs in nations across the world today. Rules are made for commoners and the poor to adhere to, but for the very wealthy and well connected, laws will always be broken. No penalties will be levied, often due to well-paid lawyers, corrupt judges and leniency towards the upper economic class.

For the Klingons, honor is everything. Yet, why does the High Council protect the Duras family? Picard tries to navigate a rocky road for Worf, but in the end, it is only by a discommendation that his life is saved. Duras, like the very rich and privileged of today's 21st society – able to cover-up his family's dishonor by a corrupt system that prides itself on honor. The corrupt are always above the law if they are well-placed in the richest of families on the Klingon home world.

Everyday Reflections

What is it about the Klingon High Counsel that reminds you of politics in the world today? Do you believe that the true often blinds those in power, and people simply do which is convenient of what serves their best personal interest? Was Worf wrong in accepting the judgement about his father?

Everyday Actions

Watch the TNG episode, *Redemption (Parts 1 & 2)*, to see how the resolution of Worf's discommendation plays out. Captain Picard, Data, and Starfleet will play a much bigger role in a Klingon and Romulan confrontation in this story – as well as a former USS *Enterprise* Security Chief, Tasha Yar.

Lesson 56

The sturdiest of virtues at times seems fragile

Lao Tzu Chapter 41

Season 3 Episode 23: Sarek

Story Summary

In a crucially important diplomatic mission for Starfleet, highly decorated Ambassador Sarek from Vulcan boards *Enterprise* to meet with the Legarans to help form a trade agreement between them and the Federation. Although the aged Vulcan is still treated with the respect he has earned with over seventy five years of service, no one but his wife and assistant know that Sarek cannot keep his emotions under control.

While watching a concert, the ambassador, his wife and associate listen to the emotionally intense piece. Amazingly, Ambassador Sarek sheds a tear, one that his wife quickly wipes away with her finger. Shortly afterwards, the three leave the concert, but not before Captain Picard's had captured the unbelievably emotionally charged moment coming from Sarek.

Soon, *Enterprise* crew members start acting hostile towards each other for no reason. After Jean-Luc confides in Beverley what he saw at the concert, Dr. Crusher deduces that it could be Sarek's strong projections of anger and frustration affecting many of the crew.

Captain Picard is forced to confront Sarek's associate to ask about his leader's condition. The underling denies Sarek's condition as anything but weariness. Yet later in Jean-Luc's quarters, Amanda, Sarek's wife visits the captain and admits that Sarek is in no condition to hold a peace agreement with the Lagarans, but hopes Jean-Luc can help him complete his final mission with dignity.

Captain Picard meets with Sarek and shares with him his concern for the upcoming negotiations. Sarek claims he is well, but when Picard presses him with evidence to the contrary, the Vulcan calm venire gradually turns into a loud rage. Jean-Luc offers this reaction as proof that Sarek is not fit to conduct the trade agreement.

Seeing the error in behavior, Sarek offers a solution to the problem at hand: A Vulcan mind meld.

Dr. Crusher is hesitant to allow a mind meld between the captain and the ambassador. Vulcans emotions, repressed for decades, can cascade through a human and destroy their mind. Sarek. Regardless of the possible deadly consequences, Picard undergoes the mindmeld. It proves successful. Sarek finishes his negotiations with the Legarans as Jean-Luc is comforted by Beverly Crusher in his quarters as he goes through a near emotional breakdown.

Before departing, Sarek thanks his friend for his invaluable assistance. Jean-Luc replies that they both will always retain the best of them – a gift for both human and Vulcan alike.

Notable Dialogue:

Jean-Luc Picard: NOOOOOOOOOOOOOOOOOOO!!!! It is... it is... wrong! IT IS WRONG!! A lifetime of discipline washed away, and in its place... *[laughs awkwardly, then grunts]* Bedlam. BEDLAM! I'm so old. There is nothing left but dry bones, and dead friends. Oh... tired. Oh, so tired.

Beverly Crusher: It will pass, all of it. Just another hour or so, you're doing fine, just hold on.

Jean-Luc Picard: *NO!* This weakness disgusts me! I HATE IT! Where is my logic? I'm betrayed by... desires. Oh, I want to feel, I want to feel... everything. But I am... a Vulcan. I must feel nothing! Give me back my control! *[he sobs uncontrollably]*

Beverly Crusher: Jean-Luc!

Jean-Luc Picard: Pe- Perrin... Amanda... I - wanted - to give you - so much more. I wanted to show you such... t- t- tenderness. But that is not our way. Spock... Amanda... Did you know? P-Perrin, can you - know... how - much I - love - you? I - do - *LOVE YOU!*

[Picard weeps heavily, then manages to compose himself]

Jean-Luc Picard: Beverly...

Beverly Crusher: I'm here, Jean-Luc. I'm not going anywhere.

Jean-Luc Picard: It's... quite difficult. The anguish of the man. The despair... pouring out of him, all those feelings. The regrets. *[sobs]* I c- I can't... stop them! I can't stop them, I can't. I can't...! *[breaks down crying]*
Beverly Crusher: *[comforting him]* Don't even try.

Character Arcs: Sarek and Picard

Even Vulcans age poorly – and with it goes their most important of virtues: logic. Sarek loses his control over emotions before a critical diplomatic conference, but it takes a human, Jean-Luc Picard, to hold him together. Ironically, Picard is an emotional creature like all of his race, but it must be the captain to reinforce the Vulcan with a mind meld. The meld works, and the connection between the two remains. Taoist virtues of kindness, compassion and patience works in this case for Sarek, thanks to Picard's generosity, though at a cost of painful experiences of the Vulcan's most guarded fears. Picard bore his pain, but the negotiation were successful and Sarek was able to end his career on a high note.

Everyday Reflections

Have you experienced a family member or close older friend experience the loss of his mental skills through a disease or traumatic brain injury? How did this person deal with the impending loss of even more mental acuity? Were you able to communicate with him/her in a way that allowed you both to share strong emotions? How did you feel after encounters with the person? Did you breakdown in tears, or were you grateful to have meaningful moments with him/her?

Everyday Actions

Take a few moments, and if you feel you have the strength to do so, watch a few, short online reports on patients with mentally challenging, old age related diseases.

After my father had his first stroke, it was very hard for me to spend a lot of time with him. Of course, I did make the time, and visited, performed chores around the family house and garden, but it was not an easy task. In time, I learned to accept the heartache of being with someone who was suddenly less a person than he was before the health incident.

Life is always a challenge, at best, but when those you love are no longer the person you grew up with – strong, funny and resilient, it is up to us to accept their diminished capacity and love them regardless.

Lesson 57

Heaven and Earth are not kind.

They regard all things as offerings

Lao Tzu Chapter 5

Season 3 Episode 26; Season 4 Episode 1: The Best of Both Worlds (Parts 1 & 2)

Story Summary

Part 1

After the battle at Wolf 359, the Borg hail the *Enterprise*. The enemy demands Captain Picard surrender himself. Of course the request is refused, and although *Enterprise* initially can resist the Borg's attempt to break through its shielding, the enemy locks a tractor beam on the ship, and start to cut away at the hull. Commander Shelby, a newly received addition to the crew due to her expertise in fighting the Borg, recommends to randomly modulate the shielding. The plan works, and *Enterprise* takes off, fleeing from the Borg cube.

Back in Engineering, La Forge and Wesley Crusher work on modifications to the deflector dish to send an energy surge able to destroy the pursuing Borg. Momentarily hiding in a nebula, Enterprise is found by the Borg and start their run to freedom once more. Regardless of their attempts to protect their captain, the Borg finally adapt their systems to the starship. Several Borg beam to the ship, and Jean-Luc is captured and brought back to the cube. The enemy goes to high warp and proceeds towards Earth, with Riker at command and chasing it.

On the bridge, Deanna Troi reminds her friend, Will, that he is now the commander of the ship and should not lead an away team to rescue Jean-Luc. Though angered by her words, Riker sees the reason in it and assigns Shelby to lead the mission.

Soon, *Enterprise* catches up to the Borg cube and beam over the team. Shelby finds Picard, but cannot return the assimilated human the ship. Instead, Picard, now calling himself, Locutus of Borg, speaks with the words of the enemy to his former friends.

Knowing what must be done, Commander Riker orders Worf to fire the deflector dish at the Borg cube.

Part 2

The story beings with Jean-Luc Picard is about to be retrofitted into a Borg. Captain Picard shouts that he will not relegate himself to their subjugation – no matter their demands. The Borg tell him his individual strength is irrelevant; the strength of the Federation is irrelevant as is their death. Resistance to the Borg is common throughout the universe, yet only through the assimilation of everyone and everything it touches to the Borg believe will bring them one step closer to perfection. Picard, despite his resistance, is transformed into a Borg spokesperson to the Federation and Earth itself. He becomes part of the Borg Collective, and as such, finds way to attack those who oppose him and his new family.

Back in real time, we see the deflector dish fired at the Borg cube – but with no affect. Locutus tells Riker and the others that the Borg had prepared for the attack, using Picard's knowledge of the plan. The Borg cube goes off, once again, at high warp with *Enterprise* badly damaged from their encounter and left behind to ponder their next move.

While working on repairs, Admiral Hanson promotes Riker to captain of *Enterprise*, with Shelby promoted to his first officer. When available, the ship is ordered to meet at Wolf 359 to stop the Borg.

Privately, Guinan advises Will to let Picard go – and that he is now the enemy. Riker takes the advice to heart. Since he is aware that Jean-Luc knows traditional strategic moves against the Borg, he plans an unorthodox approach to rescue his friend from the deadly foe.

When *Enterprise* finally reaches Wolf 359 they find the entire fleet has been destroyed by the Borg. Following the warp trail, Riker soon catches up to the Borg. After negotiations with Locutus fail, Picard's location inside the cube is ascertained. Immediately, *Enterprise* engages with the enemy, separating the saucer and main sections of the ship to engage the enemy. Firing an antimatter attack on the cube with the main section of the ship, the Borg sensors are disrupted. A shuttlecraft leave *Enterprise*, and flying through the fight, stops just outside the cube and transports Lieutenant Worf and Data through the shielding and into the main section of the Borg vessel. The Borg ignore the two, and both Starfleet officers grab Locutus, beam back to their shuttle and then immediately transport back *Enterprise*.

After rescuing Borg Picard, Dr. Crusher, Data and Geordi find a way to communicate with him as a human – not the Borg mouthpiece.

Through a veiled statement of brilliant strategy, Jean-Luc utters the most important of lines that saves humanity: "sleep, Data, sleep". By literally placing the Borg to sleep, *Enterprise* is able to deactivate the cube. The sleep cycle soon cascades through the system and builds a feedback loop that destroys the cube.

Back on the starship, Dr. Crusher works on removing Borg implants from Jean-Luc.

With the battle over, *Enterprise* returns to a nearby shipyard for repairs.

Although Riker is offered command of any ship in Starfleet, he remains as second in command on Enterprise. Shelby leave to lead a task force on rebuilding the fleet.

As Jean-Luc recovers, Counselor Troi helps him talk through the traumatizing experiences.

Notable Dialogue:

> **The Borg**: Captain Jean-Luc Picard. You lead the strongest ship of the Federation Starfleet. You speak for your people.
>
> **Picard**: I have nothing to say to you. And I will resist you with my last ounce of strength!
>
> **The Borg**: Strength is irrelevant. Resistance is futile. We wish to improve ourselves. We will add your biological and technological distinctiveness to our own. Your culture will adapt to service ours.
>
> **Picard**: Impossible! My culture is based on freedom and self-determination!
>
> **The Borg**: Freedom is irrelevant. Self-determination is irrelevant. You must comply.
>
> **Picard**: We would rather die.

The Borg: Death is irrelevant. Your archaic cultures are authority driven. To facilitate our introduction into your societies, it has been decided that a human voice will speak for us in all communications. You have been chosen to be that voice.

Character Arcs: Picard, Riker, the Borg and Commander Shelby

Lao Tzu believed both Heaven and Earth were not kind to humanity. They demanded sacrifices. Just like straw dogs thrown into a fire pit of a Chinese religious ceremony, the symbolism of the individual for the greater good is evident.

If we apply this notion to any *Star Trek* storyline, the Borg can be seen as the enemy from the heavens, demanding everyone's sacrifice for its own uniqueness and perfection in the universe.

For Lao Tzu, the sage knows the truest path to the Way, but could be unkind too. If he needed to sacrifice others for the betterment and safety of all, the sage would do this without question. As Spock said in *Star Trek II: The Wrath of Khan*, "The needs of the many outweigh the needs of the few." Metaphorically speaking, a handful of lives given in battle so the many of society can survive is exactly what military and national leaders say in a call to arms.

Yet somehow, the sage in our story finds a way to battle his enslavers.

Thus, Commander Riker saves Picard, the sage, who does not sacrifice Earth or the Federation for the Borg Collective. His individual strength, courage and intelligence saves human, Vulcan, Klingon and other society from death.

Everyday Reflections

Due to acts taken earlier in life, have you ever felt that you were heading into a troubling situation no matter the direction you had taken? What do you do when you find yourself headed into a no-win situation? Do you fight or back off, hoping to evade the consequences?

Could Captain Picard have done anything to prevent the Borg from using him as their mouthpiece to the Federation? How long do you think he felt shame and anger over what the enemy made him do to his comrades in arms?

Everyday Actions

In the battle with the Borg, Picard's friends helped him win the battle – much like an intervention. In the latest installment in the long line of *Star Trek* series, *Star Trek: Picard*, Seven of Nine asks Jean-Luc in the story, *Stardust Memories*, if he believes that he ever recovered his humanity since the kidnapping. Seven admits she never has – Picard is a bit evasive, but admits he is a work in progress towards reclaiming all he was before the horrid kidnapping and conversion.

In your journal, write down the most significant of times when you went up against impossible odds but succeeded.

What personal attributes brought you out of a disturbing, frightening or highly uncomfortable situation?

Who helped you recognize the battle could be won?

Lesson 58

Abandon benevolence, discard duty, and people will return to the family ties
Lao Tzu Chapter 19

Season 4 Episode 2: Family

Story Summary

After the deadly battle with the Borg, *Enterprise* goes to McKinley Station for much needed repairs. While dry docked, members of the crew are allowed a well-deserved vacation from their duties. Captain Picard, Lieutenant Worf, Dr. Crusher, and her son Wesley, meet with family or just take time to recover from the recent horrors inflicted by their mortal enemy. Their individual journeys home are not simple, as each one meets new challenges from their traumatic experiences.

Notable Dialogue:

> **Jean-Luc Picard**: They took everything I was. They used me to kill and to destroy and I couldn't stop them. I should have been able to stop them. I tried. I tried so hard. But I wasn't strong enough. I wasn't good enough! I should have been able to stop them. I should... I should...
>
> **Robert Picard**: So... my brother is a human being after all. This is going to be with you a long time, Jean-Luc. A long time.

Character Arcs: Picard, Rene, Robert, Worf and his family, Beverly, Jack and Wesley Crusher

In each separate story, *Enterprise* family members have different and difficult journeys to take back to their families after the Borg attack. In their own ways, the return to their families represents a more intense, emotional challenge then even fighting against their deadly enemy.

But as Lao Tzu says, if we let go of our duty to job and state, we realize that the family unit is much more important. For Jean-Luc, Worf, Beverley and Wesley, each encounter was a significant one to ground them in the most valuable assets of their lives: family

For Worf, he spent time with his parents – but of more significance was accepting his son back into his life. As a Klingon, parenting rests on the mighty shoulders of the female, the mother. To consider taking a Klingon child aboard the *Enterprise* is almost laughable, but it is a ship of exploration, not of war. Worf's human mother convinces him Alexander needs his father more than his grandparents at this stage of his young life.

For Wesley Crusher, playing a holographic recording his father made for him when he was only 10 weeks old uplifts his spirits. Since Wesley and Beverly have only recently comes to terms with Jack's death, the message resonates in their hearts. Both find a way to communicate their love for each other, too, which is what always makes a family stronger.

For Jean-Luc, returning to France to visit his brother's family is also comforting. After his transformation into a Borg, the *Enterprise* captain feared returning to space. Jean-Luc nearly takes a job in his hometown, out of shame for losing control as the *Enterprise* leader and Starfleet officer. His brother, Robert, convinces him that he must let go of his pride, of his ego, and accept that he is 'human', and not infallible as the Borg captures. After an emotional breakdown in the vineyard, Jean-Luc admits his pain, and temporary loss of his humanity as a Borg. Regardless of their long time feud over leaving the family business, Jean-Luc sees his true course is the one in the stars and not hiding underwater for the France government.

As he is about to leave earth, Jean-Luc encourages his nephew, Rene, to live his dream among the stars one day, too, if that is where his ambitions take him.

Everyday Reflections

Which family had the most difficult of problems in this story? How did Robert Picard, Jean-Luc's older brother, find a way to lure the *Enterprise* leader into self-admission of weakness and guilt? Have you ever learned an important life lesson through a brother, sister or other family member without noticing it? Years later, when you realized what you were taught, how did it change you? Have you ever tried to do the same for others close to you?

Everyday Actions

As an educator, family member or co-worker, plant a seed of courage in the mind and heart of another. In that life lesson, do not worry if it blossoms into a larger than life character trait. Your job is not to push another into the light, but only to illuminate the power of the journey in front of them today.

Lesson 59

When family ties are disturbed, devoted children arise

Lao Tzu Chapter 18

Season 4 Episode 3: Brothers

Story Summary

In this story, Dr. Soong is dying. To give his favorite creation, Data, one more gift before he passes, he attempts to pass along an emotion chip. Unbeknownst to the father, the beacon calls his other son, Lore, and soon after Data arrives, so does he.

Both sons reunite, and although the good son, Data, is robbed of a precious program enhancement, he wakens in time to spend time with his near dear father. Data grieves in his own way, though a more sterile, unemotional one.

Notable Dialogue: None

Character Arcs: Data, Lore and Dr. Noonien Soong

In many close families, brothers and sisters unite and help when parents are in dire trouble. Lao Tzu saw this trend and noted that this behavior was laudable.

In Data's world, he had never seen his creator, nor even knew where he last lived. Fortunately, Dr. Soong implanted a homing beacon to call him in case of emergency. The android senses it, takes a shuttle and leaves *Enterprise* to meet his father.

Everyday Reflections

Have you ever competed with a sibling for attention, status, or monetary rewards or gifts from a parent? If so, what, exactly, and did you win the ultimate prize? Looking back on the contest entered, did you play fairly? If you were play this part over in your life today, would you approach the scenario differently?

Everyday Actions

Lore and Data are not the only siblings with problems.

Many families raise children in a loving environment, but when teen or young adult year hit, they grow apart. Jobs, colleges, love, and different factors push people apart from their parents and their siblings,

If you have estranged brothers or sisters, try to make contact with them. This may be easy – or it may be the roughest thing you'll ever do. Push any resentment, or pettiness aside. But make the effort for everyone's sake.

Lesson 60

Therefore, good leaders reach solutions,

And then stop.

They do not dare to rely on force

Lao Tzu Chapter 30

Season 4 Episode 26 & Season 5 Episode 1: Redemption (Parts 1 & 2)

Story Summary

Part 1

As Arbiter of Succession for K'mpek, Captain Jean-Luc Picard is asked to attend the installation of Gowron as new Klingon leader. On his way there, Gowron intercepts *Enterprise* and tells Picard he expects the Duras family to challenge him during the ceremony and are already on the home world inciting civil unrest. This prediction comes to be and the High Counsel turn their back on Gowron when the Duras sister present the teenage son of their brother. The ceremony ends without an installation.

Lieutenant Worf later meets with Gowron and promises his brother's fleet to back him if he returns his family name. Gowron grudgingly accepts the offer. Since the Federation cannot become involved with any civil problems on the Klingon home world, Worf decides to resign his Starfleet commission and join forces with his brother and Gowron. Captain Picard accepts his decision and watches him transport to a Klingon battle cruiser nearby.

As the Duras sister mock Picard and call him a coward, a Romulan female emergences from a shadow and warns both women that Jean-Luc is not to be underestimated. The Romulan resembles long dead Tasha Yar, the *Enterprise* Security Chief from not so long ago.

Part 2

Since Captain Jean-Luc Picard knows he cannot become intertwined in a civil war, he clearly understands that the Romulans will see it as a chance to install a puppet regime in the society if they can and use it against the Federation. Starfleet Command agrees with Picard, and allows him to lead a fleet of starships to block any and all Romulan aid in terms of troops, weapons, or other supplies to the warring factions.

Though he does not assign Commander Data to any ship, he sees this mistake and assigns his senior officer the captaincy of the USS *Sutherland*.

Back on Qo-Nos, Commander Sela orders her Romulan scientists to find a way to attack the Starfleet's network of ships so that her people can send aid to the Duras sisters.

Contacting Captain Picard, Sela tells Jean-Luc that Tasha Yar was her mother, and it was him that sent her back on the *Enterprise*-C twenty-four years earlier. She goes on to say the ship was destroyed by her people, but that a Romulan captain took a liking to her and mated, producing her as their child. Jean-Luc takes this story lightly. Sela goes on to warn her enemy that if Starfleet does not break off their blockade in 20 hours, the entire fleet will be destroyed by her forces. After discussing the news of Sela's existence with his bridge crew, Jean-Luc says it does not matter what the truth is, but only that *Enterprise* and the others must be ready for battle.

Captain Picard urges Gowron to attack Duras immediately so that it will force the hands of the Romulans. Gowron agrees to act, hopeful that without Romulan support, the Duras family will fail and he would be installed as the next Klingon Chancellor.

Romulan Commander Sela's experts believe that they can disrupt the Federation grid detection net if they send out an energy burst. Sela picks the burst to be directed at the Sutherland. The Romulans do as told and disrupt the net, and Picard decides to reform the fleet until the net can be repaired. Commander Data refuses, against the urging of his first officer. The android decides that it is a ruse and if they fire torpedoes at certain coordinates, the Romulan fleet will be seen if though they are cloaked. The plan works, and the Romulans retreat from their journey towards Qo'Nos.

The Duras sisters learn the news of the failed attempt to resupply them and decide to run away – but not before killing Worf, who had been captured in battle earlier. The Klingon fights back, and defeats the security team, captured Toral, the son of Duras.

Once ordained as Chancellor, Worf is given a chance to kill Toral in his Rite of Vengeance, but declines, and prevents his brother, Kurn from doing so either. Worf gives back Toral's life and returns to *Enterprise* and Starfleet.

Notable Dialogue:

> **B'Etor**: Defeat.
> **Toral**: How? Where are the Romulans?
> **Lursa**: They never came.
> *[Worf is dragged in by his Romulan guard]*
> **Lursa**: Kill him.
> *[Worf fights the Romulan as Lursa and B'Etor beam themselves to safety]*
> **Toral**: *NO!*
> *[Worf defeats the Romulan as his brother arrives]*
> **Kurn**: Toral, the next Leader of the Empire. Gowron is looking forward to seeing you again.

Character Arcs: Picard, Worf, Kurn, Gowron, the Duras Sisters and Commander Sela

As Lao Tzu emphasizes, the best of rulers do not initiate wars. As Klingon Arbiter, Picard will not involve his ship or commit Starfleet's resources to Gowron's side in a civil war. Yet when he finds out that the Romulans, guided by Sela, the child of Tasha Yar from years past in an alternate future (*Yesterday's Enterprise*), Jean-Luc reluctantly agrees to keep the peace between the two Klingons houses.

With help from Starfleet's, Commander Data and Chief Engineer Geordi La Forge and the rest of the bridge officers design a plan to block any Romulan's aid to the Duras family.

In particular, Data shows superb leadership skills when he receives his own command of a starship. It is the astute android who best understands Romulan strategy and reveals their scheme in the asteroid belt near the Klingon home world.

Due, in great part to Data's display of gamesmanship, the Duras sister's allies retreat and Gowron is installed as the new Klingon Chancellor.

Commander Worf and his brother Kurn's family name is reinstated and are accepted back into their culture as respected warriors of a great house.

And all of this was done without firing a single starship photon blast or hand phaser shot.

Lao Tzu, if he had been a *Star Trek: The Next Generation* fan, would be proud of Captain Picard and Data actions in this tricky political and military conflict.

Everyday Reflections

Seemingly in every major battle or war, nations use civil unrest to stoke battles with a nation to destabilize the current government. Why is this strategy used so effectively?

Spend a few minutes reviewing the website, Defense Web: An Africa's Leading Defense Portal, to review which nations in the continent is experiencing serious civilian problems that undermines government leaders.

The website is: https://www.defenceweb.co.za/featured/civil-unrest-on-the-rise-globally/#:~:text=In%20South%20Africa%2C%20there%20was,of%20the%20country's%20top%20universities.

Granted, not all civil unrest is a bad thing for a nation – the civil protests in Portland, Oregon, for example to promote Black Lives Matter and point a spotlight on police brutality against the African American community has, for the most part been a peaceful demonstration of individual rights guaranteed under the U.S. Constitution.

Everyday Actions

If you have not watched the episode, *Sins of the Father*, please watch it before you see this story. Also, you should watch the story, *Yesterday's Enterprise*, to better understand the background of Sela, the Romulan commander in league with the Duras sisters.

Lesson 61

My words are very easy to understand

And very easy to practice.

Still, no one in the world

Can understand or practice them

Lao Tzu Chapter 70

Season 5 Episode 2: Darmok

Story Summary

After a diplomatic venture with a new alien species goes sideways, Captain Picard is beamed down to a planet - against his will, and meets his counterpart. Dathon, the Tamarian captain, who believes that a shared experience in battle will better bond the two and draw their civilizations into a peaceful alliance. Left alone without a weapon to defend himself, Jean-Luc feels quite threatened at first, but comes to realize that the maneuver was meant to bond them over a common foe, a deadly beast that appears and attacks them. Immediately, the *Enterprise* captain is forced to piece together a language he cannot understand with an ally who he must work with to have any chance of surviving against a hostile predator.

As Picard and Dathon try to make each other understand each other's language, the Tamarian continues to use the phrase, 'Darmok and Jalad at Tanagra'. Eventually, the *Enterprise* captain recognizes the allegory as a battle strategy to fight the planet's beast. In the morning, the enemy reappears and although both fight it cleverly, Riker's attempt to beam his captain up to the ship prevents him from working with Dathon at a critical moment in the battle. As the attempt to rescue Jean Luc fails, the captain rushes over to his severely hurt companion.

At last, Picard figures out the metaphor of Darmok and Jalad that night as the two stand watch for the beast. Jean-Luc tells the story of the Epic of Gilgamesh which is a parallel to that of Darmok and Jalad – and finally, Dathon understands his friend.

Jean-Luc Picard: *[paraphrasing* The Epic of Gilgamesh*]* Gilgamesh, a king. Gilgamesh, a king at Uruk. *[metaphor about ancient Babylonian legends from Earth]* He tormented his subjects. He made them angry. They cried out aloud: "Send us a companion for our king! Spare us from his madness!" Enkidu, a wild man from the forest, entered the city. They fought in the temple. They fought in the streets. Gilgamesh defeated Enkidu. They became great friends. Gilgamesh and Enkidu at Uruk.

Dathon: At Uruk.

Jean-Luc Picard: The... the new friends went out into the desert together, where the Great Bull of Heaven was killing men by the hundreds. Enkidu caught the bull by the tail, Gilgamesh struck him with his sword.

Dathon: Gilgamesh.

Jean-Luc Picard: They were victorious. But... Enkidu fell to the ground, struck down by the gods; and Gilgamesh wept bitter tears, saying, "He who was my companion through adventure and hardship, *[as Dathon dies]* is gone forever."

Later that night, the Tamarian dies from his wounds, but knowing that he gave his people, and those of the stranger, a chance to become future allies.

Riker tries yet again to penetrate the planetary shield the Tamarian ship has used to keep both captains on the planet. Once again, the beast appears and goes to attack the knife wielding Picard. Finally, Will's tactics work and the captain is beamed to the ship. Angered and on the edge of a fierce battle, Picard enters the bridge and talks with the Tamarians in their special language.

Tamarian 1st Officer: Zinda! His face black, his eyes red!

Jean-Luc Picard: Temarc! The river Temarc! In winter!

Tamarian 1st Officer: Darmok...

Jean-Luc Picard: And Jalad. At Tanagra. Darmok and Jalad... on the ocean.

Tamarian 1st Officer: Sokath! His eyes opened!

Jean-Luc Picard: The beast at Tanagra? Uzani. His army. Shaka, when the walls fell. *[The First Officer bows his head and the other Tamarian crew members make gestures of tribute. Picard holds up Dathon's notebook, which the First Officer transports to his hand.]*

Tamarian 1st Officer: Picard and Dathon at El-Adrel. *[a new metaphor added to the language]*

Tamarian 1st Officer: *[to the crew]* Mirab with sails unfurled.

Jean-Luc Picard: *[offering Dathon's knife]* Temba. His arms wide.

Tamarian 1st Officer: Temba. At rest. *[You may keep it.]*

Jean-Luc Picard: Thank you.

Later in his office, Jean-Luc reads a Homeric Hymn to Riker and says that his own study of those myths enabled him to finally relate linguistically to the Tamarian. Picard also wonders aloud that if he would have sacrificed his life, like Dathon, just to have a chance to make friends.

Notable Dialogue: None

Character Arcs: Captain Jean-Luc Picard and Dathon (Tamarian captain)

How did Jean-Luc eventually realize that his companion was not a threat, but a comrade in arms pitted against a dangerous opponent?

In the overall lesson for this *Star Trek: Next Generation* story, this author uses a Lao Tzu quote that speaks about the Way and how better to understand it (*Tao Te Ching*; chapter 70 - first stanza). I argue that this quote can also be attributed to any language in general. To understand each other in a written or oral fashion, we base language on five components of the structure: phonemes, morphemes, lexemes, syntax, and the context it is delivered. Piecing this together, we create meaningful communication.

The Tamarian language structure is created by the sociocultural history of their people. Phrases are spoken that represent metaphors and allegories that transfer powerful emotions in conversations. When Dathon spoke, "Tempa, his arms wide", the expression was used to show his embrace of Picard as a friend. With the phrase, "Darmok on the ocean, Darmok and Jalad at Tanagra on the ocean," Dathon is trying to convey a powerful story of two people who meet on an island and had a common opponent – one they defeat.

On El-Adrel, one known to have a dangerous and deadly beast, Dathon hopes Picard will join him in battle. By winning a contest together, Dathon hoped that he and the human would become allies in the future, Sadly, Dathon loses his life before Jean-Luc can save him. When the story ends, and he Tamarian second in command demands to know what happened to his captain, Picard can tell his in the language his is familiar with among his people. "Picard and Dathon at El-Adrel" is added to their lexicon and a new piece of Tamarian history is created.

Everyday Reflections

How are all languages used to express emotions, stories and relationships? Is it merely the words or the understanding of the metaphors in the tales crucial to comprehending the intricacies of perspectives of another person's culture?

Everyday Actions

Two tasks – pick one.

One: Take a few minutes to read an academic article on sociolinguistics – a short one, of course, and examine the way how language represents a culture more than mere words.

Two: Write a poem. Tell a story without being too obvious in the tale. Use metaphors as much as possible. Share it with a friend. Can the friend grasp the main idea of the symbolism you used in it?

Lesson 62

People take death lightly. They expect too much of life.

That is why people take death lightly.

Lao Tzu Chapter 75

Season 4 Episode 5: Remember Me

Story Summary

At Starbase 143, Dr. Beverly Crusher meets a longtime friend, Dr. Dalen Quaice. They reminisce about friends who have passed away and how life is too short. Beverly leaves him in his quarters to check in on her son in Engineering. She finds Wesley is working the creation of a static warp bubble. When the experience seems to fail, Beverly walks back to visit with her friend, Dr. Quaice, but cannot locate him. This bothers her, but she assumes he left *Enterprise* before the ship left base.

As she is helping Chief O'Brien in Sickbay, the physician notices that her nurses are missing, too. Miles looks at her puzzled. After O'Brien leaves, Dr. Crusher looks on her database and finds no mention of any personnel to ever have worked in Sickbay. Soon, Crusher finds that more and more crew members are missing.

As she goes to speak with Captain Picard about the mystery, a vortex suddenly appears and nearly envelopes her. Beverly avoid this fate and goes to Jean-Luc on the bridge. Soon, it is only she and Picard on the bridge, with the captain laughing saying that they have never needed anyone else to run the ship.

Soon, Beverly realizes that it is not her ship that is losing personnel, but that it is her perception of them and the ship itself that is changing rapidly. Crusher remembers her son had experimented on a warp bubble in engineering. After earlier running away from a vortex on the ship, Beverly puts the pieces together and rushes towards engineering in hopes that it will send her back home to the real *Enterprise*.

As Dr. Crusher makes it to Engineering, the ship continues to collapse around her. Taking a chance, Beverly jumps through the intermittent phasing warp bubble vortex and returns to reality. There to greet her is Wesley and The Traveler, a friend from the past who had seen great potential in her son. Picard is also there to greet her back home with a full complement of crew, too.

Notable Dialogue:

> **Doctor Crusher:** Here's a question you shouldn't be able to answer: Computer, what is the nature of the universe?
> **Enterprise computer:** The universe is a spheroid region, 705 meters in diameter.

Character Arcs: Beverly Crusher

Tao is the essence of everything in the universe known and unknown. Yet when Dr. Crusher asks for the nature of it, the computer tells her – something that both astonishes and stuns the physician. No one knows the complete answer, and certainly the answer given is wrong, but a telling one that proves to Starfleet officer her world, her universe, is not what it appears. In this moment, Beverly realizes that her *Enterprise* is not the one in her real life. But what is it? Ah ha! The warp bubble Wesley created in Engineering!

Everyday Reflections

How do you define your world? What words would you use to name the unnamable? Do you understand it by your friends? Your clothes? Family? State or national laws? Church implicit ways of behavior with your fellow men and women?

Everyday Actions

Spend a few minutes of your day, or whenever you can find the time this week, and re-connect with a good friend from college or work you haven't spoken to in five years or longer. Take the time to listen to how their lives have evolved, for the better or worse, and share your experience with this friend as well. If possible, make a Zoom call or call a friend on WhatsApp or Facebook – anything with real time video and audio. If the warmth and love between you two is still there, make your talk a monthly or more than once a year promise to stay in touch.

Lesson 63

When many people are killed

They should be mourned and lamented.

Those who are victorious in war

Should follow the rites of funerals

Lao Tzu Chapter 31

Season 4 Episode 12: The Wounded

Story Summary

Unprovoked, Captain Picard's starship is fired upon by a Cardassian vessel – allegedly in retaliation for another Federation ship's attack on a science outpost a few days earlier. Gul Macet is unconvinced it was not *Enterprise*, but agrees to meet with Picard to discuss in detail what happened earlier that week.

Picard confirms with Starfleet that the USS *Phoenix* had indeed fired upon the station. Jean-Luc agrees to handle the problem directly to keep the fragile Cardassian-Federation peace accord in place. Gul Macet sees the value in the help, stands down, and tells his government that the *Phoenix* captain will be held responsible for the deaths of their science team.

Picard locates the *Phoenix*, but is unable to stop it before it fires on a Cardassian freighter and destroys it and kills over 650 crew members. Jean-Luc orders Captain Maxwell to stand down and transport to *Enterprise* immediately. After greeting O'Brien, an old friends from a way long ago, Maxwell meets with Picard and tells him that the Cardassians are reasserting themselves in the sector. He admits to destroying the science station because it was not that – but a military base. The freighter, too, was carrying weapons to the base for possible warlike battles in the future. Jean-Luc, though sympathetic with Maxwell, tells him to go back to this ship and join him on the way back to a nearby Starfleet base in Federation space where he will give up his command and stand trial for the crimes he committed against the Cardassians.

Although Maxwell accepts Picard's decision and beams back to his ship, the *Phoenix* steers away to destroy yet another freighter. Before Picard fires on the *Phoenix* to prevent it from killing more Cardassians, O'Brien asks his commander to beam him aboard Maxwell's ship so he can convince him to back of the freighter. Though a dangerous move, Jean-Luc grants the request.

Once onboard the *Phoenix*, Miles talks to his former captain. They reminisce about old times and sin a war song. Soon, O'Brien convinces his Maxwell to surrender to Picard and turn the ship over to his first officer.

After Gul Mecet thanks Picard for his help, Jean-Luc takes a moment to be honest and warns him that he believes Maxwell. It was only to preserve the peace that he did not look into the freighter's cargo bay that the *Phoenix* captain was sure held weapons. The captain then warns the Cardassian that the Federation will be watching closely in the days ahead.

Notable Dialogue:

> **O'Brien:** It's not you I hate, Cardassian. I hate what I became because of you.

Character Arcs: Chief Miles O'Brien

Chief Miles O'Brien still harbors the trauma by his experiences fighting against Cardassia. By observing his former commanding officer's unprovoked assault on a Cardassian ship, Miles recognizes that holding onto his anger feelings against the onetime enemies of the Federation are self-destructive. The Cardassians may be hiding armaments in civilian-like ships – and thus, readying for another war, but the greatest danger to O'Brien and others who fought against them in a battle long ago is not understand their hate and resentment towards the race itself. Miles' discrimination towards them as a group, and the despise he had for them must be set aside. The Starfleet officer recognizes it for what it is today, and does not allow it to eat away at the best part of his humanity.

Everyday Reflections

Lao was not a proponent of wars like Sun Tzu, a Chinese tactician who understood that such events were inevitable. Lao understood that too many of his people enjoyed the bloodshed and glory that went along with battle victories. Lao Tzu also believed that rulers, generals and other leaders who bask in glorious wins too soon forget the horrors that accompany any territory or materials gained in such conquests.

Do you know anyone in your family who has ever had fond memories of battles won overseas? Perhaps they may still have contact with their troop members at Veteran of Foreign Wars town halls or talk with them on the phone from time to time, but the lingering reminders of death and destruction is unlikely to remain a pleasant memory for any of them.

Everyday Actions

If possible, visit a military cemetery in your local town. Walk among the graves and tombstones. Read the names, and the ranks, who the dead have left behind.

Imagine yourself at that time or place in a war and how you would have reacted to losing a buddy to an enemy bullet or hand grenade.

Think about this story, and go back the notable dialogue Miles O'Brien made to the Cardassian solder. Do the words hit home a bit more now?

Lesson 64

In haste, the ruler is lost

Lao Tzu Chapter 26

Season 4 Episode 15: First Contact

Story Summary

The humanoid civilization of Malcor III is about to finish their warp technology research and soon investigate the galaxy.

Before the launch of any spacecraft, Captain Picard and Counselor Troi ask the planet's high minister, Durken for a private meeting. His best scientist, Mirasta Yale joins the discussion and is much more excited about life among the stars then Malcor III leader, who is suspicious of Picard and the Federation's intentions.

During the first contact discussion, Jean-Luc welcomes them into the exploration of space and hopes that their people and the Federation can come to a friendly agreement and alliance.

The *Enterprise* captain also asks for a personal favor – for Durken's help in retrieving Commander Will Riker. Riker had been observing the society for several weeks, a common thing for Starfleet to do before initiating first contact protocols. Several days earlier, the commander stopped communication with *Enterprise*. He is suspected injured, dead or in custody of Malcor III officials. Marasta volunteers to assist Picard and Troi locate their second in command.

While hospitalized, Chief of Planetary Security, Krola, who fears invasion from an alien race, revives a severely injured Riker. Krola places Will's phaser in his hand and tells him that his death will prevent his planet from accepting any negotiated peace dealings with a potential enemy race. Though nearly passed out, Riker changes the phaser setting to stun, thus saving Krola's life.

Finally located, both Krola and Riker are beamed to *Enterprise* where Dr. Crusher saves both men. Durken visits his friend and assures him that he will delay the warp drive technology project until their people are ready for first contact with other races. As a favor by Durken, Marasta is allowed to remain on *Enterprise* and joins Starfleet as a science consultant.

Notable Dialogue:

Chancellor Durken: I go home each night to a loving wife, two beautiful daughters. We eat the evening meal together as a family. I think that's important. And they always ask me if I've had a good day.

Captain Picard: And how will you answer them tonight, Chancellor?

Chancellor Durken: I will have to say: This morning, I was the leader of the universe as I know it. This afternoon, I'm only a voice in a chorus. But I think it was a good day.

Character Arcs: Chancellor Durken, Science Minister Marasta Yale and Security Minister Krola

Although Krola takes a drastic measure towards Riker's appearance to defend his home world from the outsiders, Marasta takes a different approach towards first contact. She is welcoming and embraces the Federation offer of an alliance. Both are proactive, but both are representative of the scientific, political and social culture of the planet.

The sage of the Malcorians is Chancellor Durken. He determines that although the planet may have technological advancements, the people are not ready for learning the truth about the galaxy quite yet. Warp drive technology is not the key to unveiling the truth to his people. First contact is postponed and the universe remains a mystery to Malcorians – except for Marasta, who joins Starfleet and a journey to the stars.

Everyday Reflections

How many times in your life have you been impatient and acted quickly only to find that if you had been quiet, reflected, and observed, you might have accomplished more?

According to Taoist expert Stephen Stuuden, Lao Tzu believed that a ruler must take his time and not rush into situations that may bring down his kingdom. Eagerness creates more problems than it ever can solve. In this story, Chancellor Durken uses a measured response to Picard's offer to join the UFP – and it is a justified one. When his chief of planet security nearly commits suicide to prevent an alleged alien takeover, Durken sees that his planet, his culture, is not ready for what lays ahead in the galaxy. By putting the warp drive research on hold, and allowing Marasta to leave, he forces his people to catch up with what awaits them among the stars in the heavens.

Everyday Actions

The very next time you 'feel' that you must make a decision quickly, and move forward with a decisive action, take a few minutes, an hour or a day to reflect. Will this guarantee exactly the best path for me to walk? What would a Taoist sage do in this exact moment? By observe stillness, perhaps, you will find what you truly need to satisfy you without pain, suffering and regret in the end.

Lessons 65

There is one appointed supreme executioner. Truly, trying to take the place of the supreme executioner is like trying to carve wood like a master carpenter. Of those who try to carve wood like a master carpenter, there are few who do not injure their hands.

Lao Tzu Chapter 74

Season 4 Episode 20: Half a Life

Story Summary

Dr. Timicin of Kaelon II boards *Enterprise* to be taken to a nearby sun to test an experimental approach to reignite a sun in his solar system. If his method works, his civilization will survive on their world; if not, everyone will need to move, but that seems an unlikely scenario.

Modification of several photon torpedo work, temporarily, but the sun explodes, demonstrating that Timcin's work needs further study before trying this action again.

Soon after Lwaxana, Counselor Troi's mother, boards the starship and falls for the soft spoken scientist. The two have dinner together, and both seem taken with the other.

In the morning, Timicin admits to Lwaxana that his latest effort has made him terribly disappointed, but hopes that others will carry on his work after he dies. The Betazoid laughs off the comment. Timicin goes on to say that his people perform he Resolution when a person turns sixty years old – a death ritual. With his day coming soon, he will not have time to finish his research.

Lwaxana argues with him over the concept of giving up a life so young. Timicin rejects her logic, but admits that now that his feelings for her have erupted, he wishes he could remain alive to be by her side.

The distraught Betazoid goes to Captain Picard for advice. Although Jean-Luc sympathizes with her, he reminds Lwaxana that he cannot violate the Prime Directive. He does add that if Timicin were to ask for asylum, he would honor the request.

When Timicin's analysis of the failed tests show other promising leads, his research is denied by the Science Minister on Kaelon II. Unless Timicin shows for the Resolution, no more of his finding or work will reach his planet, says the minister. Soon, two warships appear and tell Enterprise that it may not leave orbit unless it surrenders their citizen.

After Timicin's daughter arrives and pleads with her father, he accepts his role and decides to return to his world. By doing so, he says, he may save his planet and certainly follow the culture of his people that has made his life worth living. Lwaxana joins him for the ritual suicide and remains with her lover until the end.

Notable Dialogue:

Lwaxana Troi: We raise them, we care for them, we suffer for them, we keep them from harm their whole lives. Now eventually, it's their turn to take care of us.

Timicin: No parent should expect to be paid back for the love they have given their children.

Lwaxana Troi: Well, why the hell not?

Character Arcs: Timicin and Lwaxana

Lao Tzu would view this arbitrary submission to death as wrong – period. Nature is not at play here. A civilization's attempt to prevent disrespect and age-related illness and suffering by the murder of citizens at a certain date in their lives is arbitrary at best.

Lwaxana's protests and pleading with Timicin, a man she has fallen in love with, is justified. Her arguments were sound. She fought for the very survival of not only Timicin but the entire civilization on his home world. A valiant fight indeed, and one that almost swayed her lover, but in the end, family and culture prevailed. At least by submitted to the death ritual, the scientist ended was able to give his data to the ministry. By doing this, Timicin may have saved his doomed planet. Death, by a real executioner, one undeserved by a vital man, may have been the one sacrifice that was needed to save millions.

Everyday Reflections

Why did Timicin's home world sentence their citizens to death when they reached a certain age? Did Timincin's explanation to Lwaxana make sense to you? Can we simply judge a person's value by the age they reach or should we support all people, regardless of their physical timeclock? Do you think less of the aged due to their mental or physical infirmities or limitations? Would you feel like Timicin and give up your life when you were on the cusp of making a breakthrough to save a society, a world, due to tradition? Did his daughter do the right thing by begging him to return and go through the death ritual?

Everyday Actions

If you have a relative or friend in a retirement home, visit them. Look carefully at the conditions they must endure. Is he/she happy being away from the home they were raised in, or the one they had lived in for much of their happiest adult lives? Are such places where you would hope to live in in your golden retirement years? Even though Timincin's home world had a strict cultural norm of death when reaching a certain age, is it not true that the reality of America or other countries is harsh when serving the most humane of conditions for the poor and middle class elderly.

Lesson 66

The most fundamental seems fickle

Lao Tzu Chapter 41

Season 4 Episode 20: Q-Pid

Story Summary

In an odd scenario, Q visits *Enterprise* to repay Jean-Luc for recently saving his life from the Continuum. Typically the most narcissistic being in the universe, Q genuinely wishes to thank the human, but Picard declines his offer repeatedly.

While sneakily observing Captain Picard before a prominent gathering of archelogy experts, Q discovers Vash and Jean-Luc's torrid but secret love affair. To push the two lovebirds closer together, Q designs a scenario placing Picard and Robin Hood and Vash as Maid Marian in Sherwood Forrest. With real lives endangered, Q puts in motion the final wedding of Marian to the Sheriff of Nottingham. Picard must both rescue Vash from an arranged marriage to the vile sheriff while also assuring the safety of Worf, Troi, Riker, Data, Geordi, and Beverly as the story plays itself out.

Will Jean-Luc save his lover?

Will Data ever lose his Friar Tuck weight?

Will Troi learn how to shot an arrow straight without killing her friends?

Even Q is unsure who will win and survive and who will die.

Thus, Picard plays the role of a life time, as does the bridge crew, and rescue Vash from Sir Guy of Gisborn.

Q returns Jean-Luc and crew to their ship – but Vash does not join them. Eventually, Jean-Luc's lover returns, in archeological gear, as is Q, and explains to her boyfriend that she will explore the universe with the omnipotent being. Q assures her safety and both he and Vash leave *Enterprise* on their next exciting adventure.

Notable Dialogue:

> **Jean-Luc Picard**: I've just been paid a visit by Q.
> **William Riker**: Q? Any idea what he's up to?
> **Jean-Luc Picard**: He wants to do something nice for me.
> **William Riker**: I'll alert the crew.

Character Arcs: Vash and Jean-Luc

Even though the Taoist proverb could be interpreted as a sexist phrase when used for a woman as the fundamental element, it was Q himself who called her duplicitous when she aligned herself with the Sheriff of Nottingham midway through the story. In Taoism, this saying of opposites seem true to Vash's romantic leanings come and go, depending on how far she believes it will serve her purpose in life. Although Q finds this behavior surprising at first, when the scenario plays out, he enlists her company throughout the galaxy exploring archeological sites over the centuries. Fickle may be a fundamental flaw with Vash, but for Q, and attractive one indeed.

For Jean-Luc, he risked his life, and those of his crewmates, to save Vash from harm or possible death in the real-life play Q created for them. Picard acted out of love to save his part-time girlfriend. Acting as a Taoist, Jean-Luc's virtuous deeds should have shown Vash the best part of him, but to her, in the end, chose to be with Q, an all-powerful being over the mere mortal, Picard.

Everyday Reflections

Do you consider yourself a person of fundamentally sound behavior? Do you, at times, act upon your best interest over those of other people? Who do you know, publically or privately, who acts like Vash?

Everyday Actions

Here's your homework: View the 1938 classic original movie, *The Adventures of Robin Hood*, with Errol Flynn, Basil Rathbone, Olivia De Havilland, and other fine actors. The story has been around since the 13th century, and was told in ballads in England through the 15th century. Although Q has Jean-Luc and Vash playing on again off again lovers, the story goes far beyond their tortured love affair.

Lesson 67

Good leaders reach solutions, and then stop. They do not dare to rely on force.

Lao Tzu Chapter 30

Season 4 Episode 21: Drumhead

Story Summary

After an explosion on *Enterprise*, Admiral Norah Satie boards the starship with the sole purpose of proving a Klingon crew member planted a bomb to destroy the starship. Satie, well known in Starfleet for her ability to discovery conspiracies when no other can find them.

With more digging, Lieutenant Worf does find out that the Klingon exchange officer, J'Dan, was working with Romulans to encode secret information in syringes for transport off *Enterprise*. J'Dan does not admit to causing the explosion near the warp core to cover his tracks. Geordie and Data do their own investigation and find that a door near the core experienced fatigue, which allowed the explosion to occur. Picard is satisfied with their work and tells Admiral Satie she is no longer needed aboard his ship.

Nonetheless, Satie is not satisfied with the explanation. She decides to hold court on the starship to prove a conspiracy of wrongdoers aboard *Enterprise*. Satie conducts another interview of Tarses in a full courtroom. Picard assigns Riker to act as council to the crewman. After accusing Tarses with using a chemical compound on the hatch, and that he also falsified his academy entrance application, Satis accuses the man that he is ¼ Romulan, not ¼ Vulcan blood. Will invokes his client's right not to answer the questions as it may incriminate him.

Soon, Satie calls for Admiral Henry of Starfleet Security to attend the proceedings. Picard calls her action a tribunal, or a drumhead, that became infamous on Earth for its injustices for many soldiers in the 18th and 19th century.

> **Picard:** Five hundred years ago, military officers would upend a drum in a battlefield, sit at it and dispense summary justice. Decisions were quick, punishments severe, appeals denied. Those who came to a drumhead were doomed.

As a result of his defiance, Satie calls on Jean-Luc to testify.

Satie calls into question Picard's loyalty to the Prime Directive and other Starfleet actions. The sitting judge calls Lieutenant Worf's standing as Chief of Security considering his discommendation by the Klingon High Council. She also accuses Picard of his encounter with the Borg and how, under his leadership as Locutus, caused over 11,000 deaths and the destruction of thirty-nine Federation starships.

> **Jean-Luc Picard**: You know, there are some words I've known since I was a schoolboy. "With the first link, the chain is forged. The first speech censored, the first thought forbidden, the first freedom denied, chains us all irrevocably." Those words were uttered by Judge *Aaron Satie* as wisdom and warning. The first time any man's freedom is trodden on, we're all damaged.
>
> **Adm. Norah Satie**: How dare you! You who consort with Romulans! Invoke my father's name in support of your traitorous arguments! It is an affront to everything I hold dear. And to hear his name used to subvert the United Federation of Planets. My father was a great man. His name stands for *principle*, and *integrity*! You dirty his name when you speak it! He loved the Federation! But *you*, Captain, corrupt it! You undermine our very way of life! I will expose you for what you are! I've brought down bigger men than you, Picard!

After hearing this outburst, Admiral Henry leaves the proceedings and later calls a halt to any more investigations into J'Dan, Tarses or Picard.

As the courtroom empties, Worf apologies to his captain. Jean-Luc reminds him that vigilance is what humanity must pay in exchange for freedom from people like Satie.

Notable Dialogue:

> **Jean-Luc Picard**: We think we've come so far. Torture of heretics, burning of witches, is all ancient history. Then, before you can blink an eye, suddenly, it threatens to start all over again.
>
> **Worf**: I believed her. I... helped her. I did not see her for what she was.
>
> **Jean-Luc Picard**: Mr. Worf, villains who twirl their moustaches are easy to spot. Those who clothe themselves in good deeds are well-camouflaged.
>
> **Worf**: I think... after yesterday people will not be so ready to trust her.
>
> **Jean-Luc Picard**: Maybe. But she, or someone like her, will always be with us. Waiting for the right climate in which to flourish, spreading fear in the name of righteousness. [...] Vigilance, Mr. Worf. That is the price we must continually pay.

Character Arcs: Admiral Norah Satie, Captain Picard and Lieutenant Commander Worf

Admiral Satie reveals that she is not a good leader soon after the initial trial when she accuses an innocent Enterprise crewmember of espionage. When those charges do not stick, she attacks Jean-Luc's loyalty to Starfleet. Satie's force of will does not work – not when accusations are made against innocent and loyal members of the Federation.

Everyday Reflections

Admiral Satie's behavior illustrates how the use of McCarthyism can spread fear and distrust among the people. Like Joe McCarthy's deplorable accusations of politicians and Hollywood star ruined the lives of so many people, Satie was about to do the same thing to Jean-Luc. She thought she was protected by her high-ranking position in Starfleet, but when others saw her for what she really was, a fanatic pushing the agenda of fear-mongering, Satie was ruined, and Picard, absolved.

Everyday Actions:

Is the threat of communism lurking in the foreground today in the world? Are Joe McCarty's 1950's alive and well in America or other countries? What type of people and politicians use this form of fear to rally the troops to his/her side?

Do a little research on the internet or libraries to discover if such actions truly are all around us, no matter the era. If possible, find footage of a committee hearing led by Joe McCarthy.

Lastly, watch the 2015 movie, *Trumbo*, staring Bryan Cranston. The movie is based on a real life story of how McCarthy's Red Scare affected Hollywood – especially writers and actors. This story is frightening, but amazingly has a fairly happy ending for the real life Dalton Trumbo, who found a way to keep his career alive and ultimately a success again, in part, thanks to Kirk Douglas, a famous actor at the time.

Lesson 68

Hence it is only the enlightened ruler and the wise general who will use the highest intelligence of the army for purposes of spying and thereby they achieve great results

Sun Tzu Chapter 12

Season 5 Episodes 5 & 6: Unification (Parts 1 & 2)

Story Summary

Part 1

Starfleet has contacted Captain Picard to report Ambassador Spock has gone missing. What is most troubling is that the unofficial Federation spy agency, Section 31, has reported the ambassador has been spotted on Romulus, which could mean the Vulcan has defected to the enemy.

Soon, Captain Picard orders his ship to Vulcan, to speak with Spock's father, the aged Sarek, to see if he can shed light on his son's disappearance. Once there, Jean-Luc finds perhaps the most honored member of the diplomatic ranks near death. Though it is painful for the captain to interrogate his friend, he does so, and meets a defiant Vulcan who maintains his son's honor despite the reports of his defection. Regardless of his pride, Sarek does give Picard a name of a Romulan senator, Pardek, who his son has maintained a close relationship with over the decades. The two part company, Sarek turns on his side in bed, with Jean-Luc giving thanks to the honorable Vulcan before leaving his side.

Back on *Enterprise*, Data confirms a recent photo from Starfleet intelligence of Spock and Pardek in a recent conference. Picard knows what his next move must be: to locate Sarek's son and determine his intentions on Romulus.

Calling in a favor to Chancellor Gowron, Picard and Data board a Klingon Bird of Prey to travel to Romulus. Neither one are comfortable on the old warship, but spend time preparing for their mission. On the trip, the captain informs Jean-Luc that his friend, Sarek, has died.

Once on Romulus, the disguised Picard and Data meet with Senator Pardek. Romulan security capture the two spies, but are intercepted by Pardek. The Romulan informs the two that the Tal Shiar knew of their presence on the home world, so it was best to go underground quickly to avoid detection by the Romulan intelligence.

The three move to an underground facility, discussing the whereabouts of the Vulcan ambassador. To Jean-Luc's surprise, out from the shadow of a tunnel Mr. Spock appears. Resolute, but quizzical over the Starfleet officer's appearance, he politely but firmly tells both Picard an Data to leave Romulus immediately

Part 2

Captain Picard moves closer to the ambassador and demands to know why he is on Romulus. Jean-Luc also denounces *cowboy diplomacy* that has made Spock famous over the years. Spock tells Pardek to excuse the two, and Picard and Spock walk way in deep conversation. The Vulcan reveals that the last time he was involved with Romulans he endangered the lives of Kirk, McCoy and other trusted friends of the *Enterprise*. This time, in the midst of peace talks, he chose to be alone, putting only himself at risk in case the move turned ugly.

Captain Picard begins to see the logic of his argument, but questions the real possibility of the two embittered culture creating a workable peace accord. Spock reveals the nature of an underground movement towards peace and unification between the distant cousins. Although it is unlikely, it is possible, and or that slim chance he will risk his life for peace – as his father did many years ago. Picard's tone softens as he informs Spock of Sarek's death. The news does not shock the Vulcan as he had sensed it for days. Spock admits he and his father were never close, but news of Sarek's death still has stirred emotions in him.

Jean Luc warns Spock that both Pardek and the Romulan Procouncil's sympathy with him for reunification may be a ploy for darker motives. The Vulcan agrees, but says that if true, he would rather let the actor play out their roles to uncover their true intentions.

Soon, Spock, Picard and Data are captured by Commander Sela. She admits to planning of a Romlan conquest of Vulcan. Sela asks Spock to send an announcement to his people of a peaceful beginning of positive Romulan-Vulcan relationship. The stolen Vulcan ship and two others will carry an invasion force – not one of diplomacy. Spock declines to say anything, even though she threatens to kill him. Sela leaves the three in her office, but by the time she returns,

Data has hacked the computer system and created a holographic simulation of Riker rescuing his friends. The distraction works and the three captives overwhelm their captors.

When Enterprise arrives at Galorndon Core, they discover the three Vulcan ships, but move to block them from reaching the home planet. Spock's message is transmitted to Vulcan and discloses the true nature of the invasion force. A cloaked Romulan warbird destroys the three ships and leaves the system, not allowing any of its troops or secrets to be captured by Starfleet.

Spock informs Picard that he will remain behind and hope to work with the dissident movement towards reunification one day. Before leaving Romulus, Picard offers to mindmeld with Spock so he can share his father's final thoughts. The Vulcan is touched, and allows it as Data watches on with a wonder.

Notable Dialogue:

> **Spock**: Fascinating. You have an efficient intellect, superior physical skills, no emotional impediments. There are Vulcans who aspire all their lives to achieve what you've been given by design.
> **Data**: You are half human?
> **Spock**: Yes.
> **Data**: Yet you have chosen a Vulcan way of life?
> **Spock**: I have.
> **Data**: In effect, you have abandoned what I have sought all my life.
>
> ———————————————————
>
> **Data**: Ambassador Spock, may I ask a personal question?
> **Spock**: Please.
> **Data**: As you examine your life, do you find you have missed your humanity?
> **Spock**: I have no regrets.
> **Data**: "No regrets". That is a human expression.
> **Spock**: Yes. Fascinating.

Character Arcs: Spock, Picard, Commander Sela and Data

Spock, now in his later stage of his life, transforms his belief system by letting go of who he was to become who he might be if he embraces the notion of the Romulans changing their approach to warfare regarding the Vulcans and the Federation.

The first time we saw the Romulans in a fierce battle with Kirk, Spock recommended, like his father Sarek had advised Michael Burnham in the Battle of the Binary Stars, to fire first, then ask questions. In this tale, Spock is kinder, and hopeful that not only does the Romulan underground movement for peace and unification of his race but that the leadership at the highest levels sense it may be time for that as well.

Picard and Data, on the other hand, are unaware of this possibility. They use the Klingons to search for the Federation ambassador. Jean-Luc does not believe that Spock is a traitor, but he needs to clarify the Vulcan's intentions.

Commander Sela, Tasha Yar's daughter in a different timeline, designs a plan to capture not only Vulcan itself, but to gain a foothold in Federation space.

Everyday Reflections

How does Spock react to hearing about the death of his father? How does his conversation with Data bring out his humanity? Is his hope for unification between the Vulcans and the Romulans based more emotion or logic?

If you found it possible to change the essence of who you are regarding your behavior or belief system towards others, could you – would you today? What factors would change you this fundamentally?

Everyday Actions

Ambassador Spock is not alone in his quest to bring peace between people – distant cousins, in his case, of bringing his people, Vulcans, together with Romulans.

Any peace accord between nations – or worlds in this case of *Star Trek* – is a fluid process that takes years due to the constant change of people involved in the process and the potential for political gains and losses among the players.

In some cases, nations simply can be split apart for decades and reach sovereign status – like North and South Korea and North and South Vietnam; separated through wars and political leanings.

Take a few minutes to read through one online resource from the United States Institute of Peace. Here's the link: https://www.usip.org/grants-fellowships/grants/what-makes-effective-peace-processes-comparative-approach.

Lesson 69

Knowing the manly, but clinging to the womanly, you become the valley of the world

Lao Tzu Chapter 28

Season 5 Episode 17: The Outcast

Story Summary

The *Enterprise* is contacted by the J'Naii, a humanoid race, to help them locate a shuttle pod lost that is likely lost in a pocket of null space. Soren, a J'Naii scientist, comes aboard and proposes a way to use another shuttle to find the missing colleagues.

Working closely with Commander Will Riker, Soren finds the human attractive, though her species do not have relationships based on a genderless culture. Soren talks with Dr. Crusher about Will and explains that romantic coupling do happen, but they are rare and frowned upon by the government.

Soon, Riker and Soren fly an *Enterprise* shuttle in to null space – and although the energy drain on their vessel hits them immediately, they see the other ship. Riker beams the dying scientists aboard. Although their shuttle transport fails at first, Will finds a way to transfer all of life support into the transporter signal. In a desperate, final effort to transport, Riker, Soren and the other J'Naii make it back to *Enterprise* in time before life support ends and the shuttle explodes.

In Sickbay, Soren admits to Dr. Crusher that she is attracted to Will, but since her species is androgynous, she is unable to express either female or male gender. Any sexual liaisons are seen as perverse and viewed as primitive. If caught, the J'naii will use a forced psychotectic therapy that renders any sort of gender-specific preference and allow the person back into society.

Regardless of her fear, Soren admits her feelings to Will and both begin a sexual and romantic affair. The J'naii diplomats find out about the affair and Soren is put on trial, where she defends herself well, but has no effect on the final judgement of the court. Riker appeals at the trial, but is warned to stay out of J'naii affairs.

As her prepares to liberate Soren from her world, Worf volunteers to help him. Both beam down and find Soren, but she tells her lover that she was *sick*, and no longer has the same feelings for him. Although he professes his love for her, Soren apologizes for leading him to false conclusions. Riker leaves with only Worf, realizing that the therapy worked, and now suppresses yet another citizen of their personal freedom in love.

Notable Dialogue:

> **Soren**: I am female. I was born that way. I have had those feelings… those longings… all my life. It is not unnatural. I am not sick because I feel this way. I do not need to be helped, and I do not need to be cured. What I do need — what all of those like me need — is your understanding and your compassion. We do not injure you in any way. And yet we are scorned, and attacked. And all because we are different. What we do is no different from what you do. We talk and laugh… we complain about work and we wonder about growing old… we talk about our families, and we worry about the future…We cry with each other when things seem hopeless. All the loving things that you do with each other… that's what we do. And for that, we are called misfits, and deviants… and criminals. What right do you have to punish us? What right do you have to change us? What makes you think you can dictate how people love each other?

Character Arcs: Will Riker and Soren

Will Riker is the ever-charming lady's man throughout the series. Riker typically pursues the more feminine and standardly beautiful females – like Captain Kirk. Somehow, he changes and becomes smitten with Soren, an androgynous J'naii. We see a more mature first officer in his approach to females after he and Soren nearly die in the shuttle pod. What was it about Soren that brought out a more profound love for her?

As for Soren, Will provided her yet another chance to explore her femininity. Forbidden relationships aside, Soren could not resist the Starfleet officer's intellect, character and handsomeness. A gender attraction grew, and even with severe consequences likely, she took a leap of faith and kissed Will. From there, her life was forever changed.

Everyday Reflections

Is the LGBT community in America and across the world still prosecuted for their feelings? What political platforms or legal mandates have encouraged suppression or free expression of the LGBT community in the 21st century? Are you shocked to see a science fiction story illustrate punishment for gender restrictions? Is this story believable?

Everyday Actions

From the Internet, watch a video from any LGBT organization to understand the issues better in your country. Also, watch several news reports on how LGBT rights are different in nations across the world today. Do you see that human rights regarding this group are expanding or becoming more restrictive?

Lesson 70

First and last follow each other

Lao Tzu Chapter 2

Season 5 Episode 18: Cause and Effect

Story Summary

The USS *Enterprise* 1701-D is caught in a temporal causality loop, explodes, before returning to a few days in time before its destruction. At the key moment before each explosion – when another starship, the USS *Boseman*, shoots out of a time rift, heads towards and hits *Enterprise* – Commander Will Riker suggests Captain Picard decompress the shuttle bay to move the starship out of path of the careering vessel. Instead of taking Riker's advice, Jean-Luc goes with Data's suggestion – to push the ship out of the way with the *Enterprise's* tractor beam. *Enterprise* explodes, time and time again, because of Picard's constant error in choice.

The night before the explosion, Worf, Will, Data, Geordi and Beverly play poker – but on one occasion, Dr. Crusher is able to guess the exact hands each of her friends receive from the dealer. Data suggests that this cannot be a coincidence. Days pass, and Worf, Riker and Geordi, too, are able to predict the exact dealt cards.

The night before the incident, Dr. Beverly Crusher hears voices as she is about to fall asleep. Eventually, she asks others if they too heard voices, but none of her closest of friends share this experience. As the causality loop continues, Beverly reacts slightly differently to the voices. On one night in the loop, she records the voices and brings her evidence to Geordi in Engineering. Mr. Data is able to decipher them as voices of the crew, over 1,000, with one, Captain Picard shouting, "All hands abandon ship!" Data proposes that he send himself a message to his positronic brain, a short one that he can interpret in the next loop. When the disaster comes up yet again, the android sends the message to himself right after the collusion with the other ship.

In the poker game, Crusher and the others still express a feeling of déjà vu, but Data deals cards in threes, unlike the previous loops.

As the collusion is about to occur again, Riker calls for decompression of the main shuttle bay, Data realizes that Will's suggestion is best, and tells Picard that may be the best solution. Jean Luc complies, and this time, Enterprise finally avoids the other starship.

The loop ends. The time is now 17 days later for *Enterprise*, but the time loop has lasted 90 years for the USS *Bozeman*. Picard invites the *Bozeman's* captain to his ship for a talk.

Notable Dialogue:

> **William Riker**: Sometimes I wonder if he's stacking the deck.
> **Data**: I assure you, commander, the cards have been sufficiently randomized.
> **Worf**: *[surly]* I hope so.

> *[at a poker game]*
> **Worf**: I am experiencing nIb'poH, the feeling I have done this before.
> **Riker**: Yes, last Tuesday night.
> **Worf**: That's not what I mean.

Character Arcs: Beverly Crusher

Beverly Crusher's intuition, and scientific approach to a problem, leads her and others in questioning their existence in this never-ending time loop where the *Enterprise* hits a temporal rift in space, is hit by another starship, explodes, killing everyone aboard, and goes back and does it all over again.

Everyday Reflections

How does your intuition powers play a part in determining the actions you take? Are you more of a practical person, one who uses the scientific method to understand what goes on around you? In other words, is it pure emotion that drives you or scientific curiosity?

Everyday Actions

The notion of time loops are fictional plot devices to allow its characters to relive moments of their lives again and again with the hope of breaking themselves out of a dismal life or catastrophic events. In our story, *Cause and Effect*, Dr. Crusher alerts others and eventually Data brings this problem to an ending, in a positive way, for the Enterprise crew.

If you have not seen the 1993 movie, *Groundhog Day*, featuring Bill Murray, as a sarcastic, selfish weather man stuck in the same day until he learns how to live a more selfless, altruistic and meaningful life, you have missed one of the great stories of all time. Watch it soon. Imagine yourself in such a time loop – what lessons would you need to learn before a higher power allowed you to continue your life in the present day?

Lesson 71

Being a model to the world,

Eternal virtue will never falter in you,

And you return to the boundless

Lao Tzu Chapter 28

Season 5 Episode 19: The First Duty

Story Summary

Before Cadet Wesley Crusher is about to graduate, a deadly accident happens to his classmate, Joshua Albert, during a flying exhibition to impress the faculty and friends of Starfleet Academy.

Of importance to Captain Picard is Wesley Crusher, is injured, but not severely. Jean-Luc directs USS *Enterprise* to San Francisco to check in on their beloved, former crewmember. Once on Earth, Picard becomes suspicious of the incident, and attends a trail the next day to determine who was at fault for Joshua Albert's death.

In accordance with school policy, the court proceeding try identify any cadet responsible for the accidental death of a student. After deposing all members of Nova Squadron, it is suspected that the truth has been stretched, due to the video tape from Jupiter that shows a highly unusual maneuver from all the entire squad. Flight leader Mr. Locarno puts the blame on Joshua Albert, the dead cadet, for pulling out too soon from a normally a precise flying act called a Yaegar Loop. Locarno goes on to say that Joshua put him and all other team members at risk. Alberts father who is in attendance breaks down from brutal testimony.

Regardless of Locarno's word, Captain Picard does not believe him. The *Enterprise* commander goes back to his starship and begins his own investigation into the loss of Joshua Albert. When he determines the real cause the attempt of a Kolvoord Starburst – a reckless stunt that he knows all cadets wish they could accomplish – he calls Wesley into the ready room.

Wesley disavows any knowledge of such as order from his flight leader that day.

Picard knows better – and reprimands the cadet. Jean-Luc reminds him that the *first duty* of any cadet – any person – is the truth.

Cadet Crusher asks to be excused – without admitting the truth.

After returning to San Francisco, he tells Locarno that Picard knows what really happened that day. The flight leader sooths Wesley and reminds his partner that the captain has no evidence of his claim. Wesley argues that Picard will speak up tomorrow, and that they should tell the truth before they are caught in a lie.

The next day, before the judges render their final decision, Cadet Crusher admits the truth, incriminating all others from his squadron. Wesley apologizes to Mr. Albert for the loss of his brave son.

As Picard walks with Wesley on an outdoor garden path, Jean-Luc tells him of his punishment – his senior year credits are erased from the records and he must repeat his final year to graduate. Still, Picard commends him for performing the first duty and standing up for truth, honor and integrity of himself and the profession he hopes make a career of one day.

Notable Dialogue:

> **Jean-Luc Picard**: The first duty of every Starfleet officer is to the truth, whether it's scientific truth or historical truth or personal truth! It is the guiding principle on which Starfleet is based! If you can't find it within yourself to stand up and tell the truth about what happened, you don't deserve to wear that uniform!

Character Arcs: Wesley Crusher and Jean-Luc Picard

In Taoism, the truth is a perspective that may elude us, no matter how hard we seek it. Chasing answers will cause problems for the truth seeker. Endless searching for personal or universal truths can madden anyone. In Lao's belief system, there are two: inner and outer truth. Inner truth has a baseline for human judgement to prevail. Thus, truth is a personal story of facts. Taoists do not a search for ever-knowing, ultimate answers. There are none.

Jean-Luc finally realized that Wesley's version of the accident that killed a Starfleet cadet was untruthful. Wesley knew the difference between not telling a lie was untruthful. Still, he held onto the belief to protect the team. Picard made him face the factual truth. And in the end, it was Cadet Crusher's version of the facts that set him free from a guilty conscience and expulsion from Starfleet Academy.

Everyday Reflection

How many times in your life, as a child or teenager, do you remember coming to that crossroad of truth or deception, to protect yourself or others from admitting a crime or an indiscretion that would lead to punishment? What Taoist path did you take? Was it the proper one?

As an adult, do you find the line between truth and lies are grayer or are they clearer?

What actions have you taken as an adult are you most proud?

Everyday Action

As a parent, a teacher at school, or as a friend, take a moment to remind someone you care about as to the importance of virtue – that of developing character based on telling one's truth to power, to others of similar rank, and how it will lead to a peaceful ending.

Lesson 72

The sage desires no desire, does not value rare treasures,

learns without learning, recovers what people have left behind

Lao Tzu Chapter 64

Season 5 Episode 21: The Perfect Mate

Story Summary

A Kriosian Ambassador comes aboard *Enterprise* with valuable cargo for a peace agreement with the Valtians. As the starship heads toward the meeting point, a Ferengi ship sends out a distress signal that Captain Picard responds to, rescuing two crew members. Once aboard, the two Ferengi cause mischief and topple over the cargo, releasing a beautiful, female metamorph.

Prepared for the arranged marriage from birth, Kamala was in stasis, preventing her from releasing pheromones that drive all males around her crazy. The two Ferengi, though confined to quarters, plot to buy or steal her from the ambassador. In that attempt, the ambassador falls in a heated dispute, nearly dying from his injuries.

Picard takes over in the role as mentor to the metamorph and prepares her for the wedding. Kamala finds herself genuinely attracted to Jean-Luc, and the feeling is more than mutual. Regardless, both maintain a professional relationship, and Kamala marries the Valtian ambassador, cementing the political alliance between her people and his.

Notable Dialogue: None

Character Arcs: Kamala and Jean-Luc Picard

Although Jean-Luc Picard has urges like every other man, he does not allow himself to act on them with Kamala. Picard is sage-like here, and throughout the difficult trials, but here he once again shows that he sticks to an ethical stance that is important for any leader in Starfleet.

Kamala is a young metamorph, but although she is groomed to please men especially, she learns from Jean-Luc that her prime duty is to prevent a war and marry Chancellor Alrik. Essentially, Kamala learned sage-like wisdom from Picard, and serves her people well.

Everyday Reflections

In Taoism, there is no concept of 'love' in the ancient text. Contentment and happiness is possible, but the notion of love is never mentioned. For Taoist, the concept of femaleness and maleness (Ying and yang connection between men and women) is important, but the idea of infatuation as an emotion is disregarded. Why?

As demonstrated by the Ferengi, their infatuation with Kamala is a form of love that never could last because it focuses on the wrong form of the emotion.

Did Jean-Luc make the right choice by turning down the sexual advances of the metamorph?

Have you ever had an infatuation that has forced you to make poor decisions? Are you more mature, or can you tell the difference between what you want and what you should do, ethically speaking, when confronted with a romantic dilemma?

Everyday Actions

A different take on infatuation, romance and love than the Spock's story, *Amok Time*, Jean-Luc must resist Kamala and use diplomacy to help two waring planets unite.

Take a few minutes to look over the very popular book by Ray E. Short, *Sex, Love or Infatuation: How Do I Really Know?* A best seller, and one that teens and young adults refer to better understand their emotions in their early experiences.

Too bad the Ferengi didn't have a chance to read this one before boarding *Enterprise*!

Lesson 73

Who can wait in stillness while the mud settles?

Lao Tzu Chapter 15

Season 5 Episode 23: I, Borg

Story Summary

Enterprise discovers a small Borg cube with one survivor, a young drone, on a desolate planet. Dr. Crusher asks to treat the Borg, but is denied by Captain Picard. Beverly pleads with Jean-Luc, who then sees a chance to use it as a weapon against the entire Collective.

In a holding cell, La Forge helps Beverly Crusher set up a feeding station for the young male Borg. Later in sickbay, Geordi befriends *third of five*. Both share ideas on what it means to be a part of a collective and how individualism is the preferred state of being in the Federation. Geordi says that he would prefer to remain an individual because it gives him freedom to choose and autonomy. The Borg reflect on this for a few moments, disagrees, but accepts the wishes of his new 'friend.'

Since there are not five drones onboard *Enterprise*, Geordi asks the drone to take a name more fitting to his position on the ship. The young Borg picks the name, Hugh. Deceptively simple, the Borg now begins to understand the very foundational value of individualism vs. Collective welfare in the universe.

Regardless of his relationship now close relationship with Hugh, La Forge, with Data's help, design a mathematical equation that will destroy the entire Borg Collective when Hugh is sent back home to the Collective. Guinan vehemently disagrees with Picard's choice of destroying an entire civilization as akin to what the Borg has done to countless worlds in their conquests. Jean Luc disagrees just as strongly, but he does agree to meet with Hugh.

In the captain's office, Hugh immediately recognizes Picard as Locutus of Borg. Jean-Luc plays off this and tells Hugh he must assimilate everyone on *Enterprise*. Hugh, confused, says that the crew do not wish this – nor would his friend, Geordi. Picard commands he assimilate La Forge, but again, Hugh declines the order. The Borg tells him that Geordi wishes to be an individual and not part of the Borg. When the young drone refers to himself in the pronoun of 'I', Jean-Luc is stunned. Picard gives up his verbal assault on the young Borg. Hugh is escorted back to the holding cell, with Captain Picard wondering if destroying the Collective is the right choice.

Soon, Captain Picard decides to offer Hugh asylum on *Enterprise*, but the Borg declines. Even though he wishes to stay with his friend, Geordi, he knows that the Collective will look for him, and will stop at nothing – even if it means destroy *Enterprise*, to bring him home. The drone is returned to the crash site, picked up another Borg Cube, but before he beams up, looks to La Forge with gentle recognition.

Back on *Enterprise*, Captain Jean-Luc Picard wonders if the most pernicious program Hugh may have brought back with him to the Collective is a sense of individualism.

Notable Dialogue:

> **Beverly Crusher**: But even in war there are rules. You don't kill civilians indiscriminately.
> **William T. Riker**: There are no civilians among the Borg.

Character Arcs: Geordi, Guinan, Picard and Hugh the Borg

As a Borg, Hugh's first and prime interest should be on assimilating the entire *Enterprise* crew. In a very unusual move, the young Borg develops a sense of 'self' and individualism under the care of Dr. Crusher and his new friend, Geordi. His dedication to his friend is selfless, and through it, Hugh becomes the very first Borg that we see act like a sincere Taoist.

For Hugh, the Borg Collective is his 'Way' towards enlightenment and unity with a higher power. The joy in being part of something bigger than himself is part of the attraction to the drone. Of course, he is taken apart and put back together as something quite different than a human being. Still, he cannot name the Way – as any Taoist cannot put a label to perfect behavior or the calling itself.

Geordi La Forge is the first *Enterprise* crewmen to recognize the humanity in the drone. La Forge sees that the young man was transformed against his will, but still holds humanity in his heart. Their friendship is not that of a human and a pet, as Captain Picard claimed in his anger. Geordi saw the good in the enemy, and the potential of Hugh to be more than its programming.

LaForge saw the same in Commander Data, too. Data was not just positronic network, but had the potential to be more than what Dr. Soong created. Thus, it was not such a leap of faith to see Hugh grow beyond Borg programing, too.

For Guinan, she understands that one of the key concepts of Taoist is compassion. Even towards our mortal enemies, compassion must be given. How else can we ever learn to accept their current or past acts if we do not see them as human? To destroy the entire Borg Collective would make Captain Picard just like the enemy. Guinan knows this, and Jean-Luc learns this when he finally meets Hugh. The young drone is not a killer, or an assimilator like the Queen. Hugh represents the side of the Collective that may change the entire philosophy of those following the Borg Way.

Finally, Jean-Luc Picard thought he had the perfect opportunity to strike at the enemy who momentarily took away his humanity when they assimilated him and force him to lead the Borg into Federation space, killing over 11,000 and destroying thirty-seven starships. This seemed his final to chance to wipe out the enemy from the inside out. Yet, when the captain spent a few minutes with Hugh, even he realized that the death of all meant the death of one. Hugh was not the enemy, but only a follower of the Way of the Collective. Though the Borg Way is not the Taoist way, one cannot kill over difference of philosophy – even though the Borg assimilate and kill others that resist. As Jean-Luc realizes, individualism may be the most pernicious way to disable the selfishness of the Borg and start a revolution within the entire Collective. In essence, Picard must be patience as the germ of individualism spreads throughout the Borg.

Everyday Reflections

What made Hugh so much different that his Borg counterparts? Was his relationship with Geordi the key variable to his transformation of an individual rather than a collective mindset? When faced with Jean-Luc/Locutus (the Borg's former facilitator), and told to assimilate the *Enterprise* crew, why does Hugh decline the edit? Is it emotion (love and affection for a friend) that changes Hugh or is it more his realization that all individuals have the choice to say no – even to the Borg Collective?

Everyday Actions

Perform research on the Reformation Movement in Europe in the 16th century. The Catholic Church changed due to corruption and abuse within the higher ranks. Can you see any connection between the Borg Collective and the Catholic Church – or any churches for that matter – that demand obedience and unquestioning loyalty from its congregation? Is the Borg Collective simply a religious cult that brainwashes its followers by mechanical means? Do religions today employ certain techniques to create a following that will never question those in the highest of power?

Lesson 74

The sage knows without traveling,

Perceives without looking,

Completes without acting.

Lao Tzu Chapter 47

Season 5 Episode 25: The Inner Light

Story Summary

The USS *Enterprise* 1701-D comes across an alien probe after performing a routine magnetic wave survey of a nearby system. The unknown probe scans the starship, then shots a focused energy beam towards Captain Picard. Jean-Luc collapses.

Dr. Crusher rushed to the Bridge, but recommends not cutting off the beam for is may cause more injury to the captain, likening it to pulling out a knife and allowing a patient to bleed to death.

While the bridge officers can offer no more than comfort and monitoring to their ship's beloved leader, Jean-Luc experiences a lifetime in just over 25 minutes.

Under the influence of the alien energy beam, Picard wakes up as Kamin, a husband, friend, and community leader on Kataan, a planet with a sun that will soon go supernova.

For over 40 years, Kamin learns to love his wife, Eline, raise children, and make a life as a scientific researcher and local community activist. Over a lifetime Kamin, outlives his wife, his best friend, Batai, but also finds life sweet as a father, grandfather and respected elder.

When Kataan sends a rocket into the sky, Meribor walks her aged, complaining father out to view it. Kamin is greeted by his old friend, Batai, his wife, Eline, and finally told that his life on Kataan has been only a memory of a civilization that had hoped to find just one person who could tell their story to others after their planet's death.

Once Picard finally awakens, he is relieved to be what he believed he was all along – a Starfleet captain.

Contemplating his profound experience in his quarters, Jean-Luc invites Commander Riker inside his room. Will tells the captain nothing was found in the probe but a small box – which he hands to his close friend. As Jean-Luc opens the tiny box, Riker leaves quietly.

Ever so gently, Picard takes out a small flute and begins to play a song that he learned as a member of Kataan . . . and remembers.

Notable Dialogue:

> **Batai**: We hoped our probe would encounter someone in the future. Someone who could be a teacher. Someone who could tell the others about us.
>
> **Picard/Kamin**: Oh, it's me, isn't it? I'm the someone? I'm the one it finds. That's what this launching is. A probe that finds me in the future.
>
> **Eline**: Yes, my love.
>
> **Picard/Kamin**: Eline.
>
> **Eline**: The rest of us have been gone for a thousand years. If you remember what we were, and how we lived, then we'll have found life again.
>
> **Picard/Kamin**: Eline…
>
> **Eline**: *[the rocket rises into the sky]* Now we live in you. Tell them of us, my darling.

Character Arcs: Jean-Luc Picard

Ever the Starfleet officer, Jean-Luc's life is solely focused on his job. Protecting Federations worlds and their people, toting the line for Starfleet protocols, and setting an example for fellow officers consumes Picard's daily actions on the *Enterprise*.

Yet even for a Taoist of courage and virtue like Jean-Luc Picard, ignoring life around you is not ideal.

Everyday Reflections

Lao Tzu understood that for humans to truly gain wisdom and learn the Way, finding knowledge would never take them far from home. Even in the 21st century, Lao would see that traveling to distant places in the world is simply unnecessary – likely to believe that a person can lose his way on the search for new cultural experiences and exciting ways of thought in foreign countries.

Over the course of your life, what have you learned about the importance of a career and family? What did Jean-Luc learn from his experience? Could he use the lesson of becoming a husband, father, grandfather and valued community member in his *Enterprise* duties? Do you put too much emphasis in your job?

"According to Morgan Gendel, she named the episode, *The Inner Light*, after a song written by George Harrison in 1968 and while he was still a member of The Beatles. Lyrics of Harrison's song are based words found in Lao Tzu's 47th chapter. The particular words referred to are:

Without going outside his door, one understands (all that takes place) under the sky; without looking out from his window, one sees the Tao of Heaven. The farther that one goes out (from himself), the less he knows. Therefore the sages got their knowledge without travelling; gave their (right) names to things without seeing them; and accomplished their ends without any purpose of doing so.

According to freelance writer, the song "captured the theme of the show: that Picard experienced a lifetime of memories all in his head." (Wikipedia, August, 2020).

Everyday Actions

To live a day in the shoes of another is not an overused saying, but one that begs the question of putting oneself in the path of fellow human being, a road that is not the easiest one. In, *The Inner Light,* Jean-Luc Picard is placed in those shoes to experience the life of a simple man in a civilization that has been dead for thousands of years. His experience changed him at a profound level, and allowed him to better appreciate family, children, and a community in a way he never did onboard *Enterprise* or on Earth.

In the 1989-93 television series, *Quantum Leap*, staring Scott Bakula, aka, Captain Johnathan Archer of *Star Trek: Enterprise*, the main character moves through time and lives the lives of others to correct a wrong – an accident death, a murder, even an attempt to prevent the 63' assassination of President John F. Kennedy The series was nominated, like *Star Trek: The Next Generation*, for Best Drama in its five year run.

If you have not seen this show, please take an hour to watch at least one episode. When you do, compare a Sam Beckett story to Jean-Luc Picard's adventure in the shoes of another, less fortunate soul. Look for similarities and differences in character development and ultimate outcome. Picard cannot change what happened to the people of Kataan, but Sam can. As a viewer, you may even wish that somehow, Jean-Luc could have prevented the death of the simple, yet meaningful inhabitants of a planet long ago.

Lesson 75

If the sage wants to stand above people,

He must speak to them from below.

If he wants to lead people,

He must follow them from behind.

Lao Tzu Chapter 66

Season 6 Episode 4: Relics

Story Summary

Responding to a nearby Dyson Sphere, the *Enterprise* finds the USS *Jenolan*, a transport freighter crashed on the surface of the unusual object's surface. Riker, La Forge and Worf investigate the *Jenolan*, lost 75 years earlier, and find that the transporter has been locked into a reintegration cycle. La Forge believes that the crew must have done this to survive the long wait for a rescue. Examining the transporter more closely, Geordi tells Riker that two of the patterns may be salvageable, and reintegrates one – that happens to be Captain Kirk's Chief Engineer, Mr. Scott from the old USS *Enterprise* 1701-A. Scotty appears, arm in swing, but otherwise mentally and physically well. Kirk's former's friend tries to bring back his partner, but finds his pattern has disintegrated beyond recognition.

Back on Picard's *Enterprise*, Jean-Luc visits Scotty in sickbay as Dr. Crusher tends to his arm. The captain praises his ingenuity on the Jenolan, but Scotty replies that his friend died on the ship, so his work was not quite genius after all. Jean-Luc nods, but gives Mr. Scott the run of the ship. Off to the side, he asks his Chief of Engineering, Commander Geordi La Forge, to bring Mr. Scott up to speed on Starfleet technology. Geordi obliges, but soon wishes he had not because of Scotty's constant questions and meddling into the Warp Drive Engines and the rest of engineering.

Meanwhile, Captain Picard hopes to investigate the inside of the Dyson Sphere. Jean-Luc makes plans to examine the sphere more closely, but not until he has more specific information on it.

A bit bored without much to do aboard this *Enterprise*, Mr. Scott goes to Ten Forward to drink and meets Mr. Data, who has taken over for Guinan. Scotty asks for any old Earth beverage, as long as it is strong. The android bartender pulls out one of Guinan's oldest bottle, one that is green, and pours Scotty a glass. The old engineer approves, thanks Data, and takes the bottle out of Ten Forward, and wanders the hallways.

Scotty goes to the holodeck and boards his USS *Enterprise* NX 1701-A. Captain Picard joins him and listens to the famous engineering expert. Sadly, Mr. Montgomery Scott feels his age, longs for the good old days with his friends, but acknowledges that time has passed for him and he does not wish to live in the past like all other old men beyond their usefulness.

Sensing that Mr. Scott needs to feel valued and wanted today, Captain Picard assigns him to work with Commander La Forge for an assignment on his old ship. The next morning, Scotty, hung over from Data's green beverage, he and Geordi beam to the *Jenolan* to gather its data logs on the Dyson Sphere.

After a failed hail to *Enterprise*, La Forge and Scotty guess that the *Enterprise* must have been pulled into the Dyson Sphere. Both devise a plan to call the port, let it open, then wedge the *Jenolan* inside the door to allow the starship to escape. Picard sees the chance for escape and follows the plan, blowing up the *Jenolan*, but retrieving both La Forge and Scott before the photon torpedoes destroy the smaller ship.

In appreciation, Captain Picard gives Scotty a shuttlecraft for his retirement. The former *Enterprise* engineer admits that he may postpone his plans and look for more adventures as he bids his farewell to his friends.

Notable Dialogue:

> **Scotty**: *[inspecting his drink]* What is it?
> Data: It is… *[sniffs the bottle]* it is… *[sniffs the bottle again, looking puzzled]* …it is green. (An echo of Scotty's comment to the Andromedan/Kelvan alien Tomar in TOS' *By Any Other Name*)

Character Arcs: **Captain Montgomery Scott and Chief Engineer Geordi La Forge**

Lao Tzu would see this story as one that illustrates humbleness is most important for not only rulers in a kingdom, but in any sectors of life – even on a futuristic starship.

Captain Montgomery Scott tastes the humbling experience of learning his knowledge of warp drive and ship engineering is ancient, with none of it useful in the 24th century. Although he merely wants to help on the newer version of his former *Enterprise*, he soon realizes that old men with even older ideas are unwelcome and unnecessary in the present day.

Commander Geordi La Forge, arrogant and impatient with Mr. Scott, learns to be humble, by listening to Scotty, and respecting his sage wisdom, especially when Geordi's friends stuck in the Dyson Sphere with no way out.

Working together, they save Captain Picard's starship and over 1,000 crew members.

Scotty found his way, by showing his unique creativity in a tough scenario. Likewise, Geordi finally sees the value in his new friend, and through his humbleness, rescues his crewmates in a style only Scotty could have imagined.

Everyday Reflections

Why was Geordi disrespectful to Commander Scott at first? What triggered his new-found respect for him later on in the story?

Have you ever been disrespectful to an older co-worker, teacher, or relative simply because of their age?

Everyday Actions

Over the years, I had never met anyone as lively as my neighbor, Alma, then 74 years old, had the energy of someone half her age. We would play bocce in her backyard, talk, have meals together, and just laugh at nothing important. My parents were one of her closest friends, so I had easy access to her. Alma was caring, loving, and sensitive . . . and the older she aged, the more graceful she was to me and others. A month after her 99th birthday we played the old-time favorite Italian game in her backyard, had lunch – she loved to make bean soup, and laughed about nothing important. When I hugged her goodbye that afternoon she seem especially frail. She passed away just before Christmas.

This week, if possible, see in person or contact an older, senior friend. Remember their value to not only the community but the world around them. Talk to them about their personal history and how life is so much different today than what it was in their youth. You'll be amazed how vibrant the memories may be – and how valuable this friend is to your perspective on life itself.

Lesson 76

Do not repeat the tactics which have gained you one victory,

but let your methods be regulated by the infinite variety of circumstances.

Sun Tzu Chapter 7

Season 6 Episodes 10 & 11: Chain of Command (Parts 1 & 2)

Story Summary

Part 1

Starfleet Command assigns Captain Picard, Lieutenant Worf and Dr. Crusher to investigate and destroy a possible Cardassian biogenic weapon project on Celtris III. While in training before leaving for the planet, Admiral Jelico is reassigned to take over *Enterprise*. Jelico's style is brash, arrogant and demanding – much different the Jean-Luc's manner. Commander Riker continually challenges Jelico's decisions, which irks the admiral.

Eventually, *Enterprise* reaches Celtris III and the three officers beam to the underground site of the alleged weapon. A cave-in deters the team momentarily, but the three receive a sensor reading pointing toward the installation. Once inside the area, it is obvious there is no weapon and that team has been set-up for capture. Cardassians run towards the room, but Picard holds them off while Worf and Crusher escape and beam up to *Enterprise*.

Picard surrenders and is taken to an interrogator, Gul Madred, who warns the Starfleet commander that his stay will be challenging and highly uncomfortable. Jean-Luc is resolute, but knows his tormentor will push him to a breaking point – one that he hopes will not lead to his death.

After stripping off Picard's clothes and hanging him by his hands on a metal pole, Madred leaves his human captive alone for the night to contemplate his fate.

Part 2

Admiral Jelico receives word of Picard's capture from the Cardassians. Regardless of the news, the *Enterprise* acting captain refuses to acknowledge Jean-Luc's presence on Celtris III, and by doing this, the prisoner of war code will not be implemented for Picard's safety. Seeking a way to force the enemy's hand, Jelico demands a strategy to force Cardassia to return Picard. Riker protests Jelico's action of non-acknowledgement of Picard's mission, thus protecting him from torture. Visibly upset, Jelico relieves Riker of duty.

After receiving information from Starfleet, Jelico believes that the Cardassians are planning an attack on Minos Korvo, and are likely hiding in a nebula before the upcoming raid. After asking Gordi to help him place mines in the nebula to flush out the enemy, the chief engineer declines the offer, and recommends Riker to pilot a shuttlepod. Very reluctantly, Jelico approaches Riker, who makes the situation eve more uncomfortable for his superior, but still accepts the mission for Starfleet and to save his captain.

After Jelico succeeds in his plan, he demands that the Cardassians return Picard immediately or see their entire fleet blown-up by the minefield. The enemy accepts the terms.

Madred learns of the failure and prods his prisoner to tell him he sees five lights above him – an obvious attempt to finding break his mind and spirit. The captain shouts out defiantly, "there are four lights!"

After Picard returns home to his ship, he admits to Counselor Troi that he did see five lights, but never admitted it to his torturer.

Notable Dialogue:

> **Gul Madred**: I remember the first time I ate a live taspar. I was six years old and living on the streets of Lakat. There was a band of children, four, five...six years old—some even smaller, desperately trying to survive. We were thin, scrawny little animals, constantly hungry, always cold. We slept together in doorways, like packs of wild gettles, for warmth. Once I found a nest. Taspars had mated and built a nest in the eave of a burned-out building. And I found three eggs in it. It was like finding treasure. I cracked one open on the spot and ate it, very much as you just did. I planned to save the other two. They would keep me alive for another week. But of course, an older boy saw them and wanted them. And he got them. But he had to break my arm to do it.
>
> **Jean-Luc Picard**: Must be rewarding to you to...to repay others for all those years of misery.
>
> **Gul Madred**: What do you mean?
>
> **Jean-Luc Picard**: Torture has never been a reliable means of extracting information. It is ultimately self-defeating as a means of control. One wonders it is still practiced.
>
> **Gul Madred**: I fail to see where this analysis is leading.
>
> **Jean-Luc Picard**: Whenever I look at you now, I will not see a powerful Cardassian warrior; I will see a six-year-old boy who is powerless to protect himself.
>
> **Gul Madred**: Be quiet!
>
> **Jean-Luc Picard**: In spite of all you have done to me, I find you a pitiable man.
>
> **Gul Madred**: Picard, stop it. Or I will turn this on and leave you in agony all night!
>
> **Jean-Luc Picard**: Aha! You called me "Picard!"
>
> **Gul Madred**: What are the Federation's defense plans for Minos Korva?
>
> **Jean-Luc Picard**: There are four lights!

Character Arcs: Picard, Riker, Madred and Jelico

Riker vs. Jelico and Picard vs. Madred – both sets of opponents use different tactics to defeat the other.

At first, Riker is passive, and accepts Jelico's command style. When Picard is found to be a prisoner of war, Riker changes his stance and challenges his superior officer. Although Will is relieved of command, Riker does find a way to aid in Picard's release by helping a more compliant Jelico

For Picard, his tactics are to never let his torturer, Madred, see his mental anguish. When Madred gives his prisoner a bowl of food and gives him a glimpse into his past, Jean-Luc uses it to his advantage. The captain puts his spin on his torturer's pain as a youth. Picard how him that whatever methods he may use to cause him pain is only an extension of the anguish Madrid felt as a lost, afraid child on Cardassia.

Everyday Reflections

How does Jean-Luc eventually get the upper hand on Madred? Is torture a useful tool to extract information from enemies during war? Can you think of anything in recent history that shows such tactics in war/military incursions in foreign conflicts abroad?

Everyday Actions

Romulan torture techniques used on Jean-Luc Picard were prohibited as cruel and inhumane in the 24th century as they in the 21st century by American law. Regardless of this universally agreement, Gul Madred delighted in using any and every form of psychological and physical method to break Captain Picard for Starfleet and Federation military strategies.

Any form of torture is prohibited under U.S. federal law. Other forms of detainee abuse, such as cruel, inhuman, or degrading treatment is also prohibited by American law. On his second day in office in 2009, President Obama issued an executive order strengthening the ban on torture.

Regardless of worldwide agreement that social, political or military dissidents have rights protected by the Geneva Convention, torture exists in many countries around the world. Sudan, Democratic Republic of Congo, Afghanistan, Iran, Iraq, Ethiopia, Turkey, Syria, Cameron and Egypt. Ethnic and religious minorities are often targeted, as well as LGBTQ groups that threaten cultural belief systems. Torture on these detainees will include physical and psychological techniques such as sleep deprivation, electrocution, and even rape.

Lesson 77

Do not swallow bait offered by the enemy

Sun Tzu Chapter 7

Season 6 Episode 12: Ship in a Bottle

Story Summary

Doctor Moriarty is inadvertently revived from his computer generated sleep in the holodeck. Equipped with cunning and with nothing to lose, he devises a plot to fool Captain Picard to find a way to make him a 'real' man, not a photonic, sentient character in a holodeck program. Picard, Data and Barkley are left to figure out this ruse before Moriarty uses his control of the ship computer to threaten *Enterprise's* destruction yet again, endangering all crewmen. In a double switch, Picard our maneuvers his adversary, but also give him and his lover, the Countess, their dream – a trip among the stars in a never ending program.

Notable Dialogue: None

Character arcs: Barclay, Picard, Data and Moriarty

Moriarty has always been focused on criminal activities as written in the Sherlock Holmes novels. Even on the *Enterprise*, as a holodeck character designed to defeat Data, he has acted selfishly and without conscience. In this instance, the professor only wishes to become 'human', with substance, so he can travel the galaxy with his love, the Countess Regina Bartholomew. For Moriarty, he merely wishes to feel contentment and bliss, and leave the criminal life behind him.

Everyday Reflections

Have you ever wondered, as a child or now, that you are part of a dream that someone is having? In the Deep Space Nine story, *Far Beyond the Stars*, Captain Sisko asks that same question to his father in the final scene. Therefore, is Barkley's action in the final scene of this tale a reasonable one to make, considering Professor Moriarty's new holographic life adventure?

Everyday Actions

Pick up a Sherlock Holmes book at a library, or read a chapter of one online, and do a character study of Professor Moriarty. How is the villain on the pages different than the one you see in this story? Which Moriarty is more devious?

Lesson 78

Having inward spies and making use of officials of the enemy

Sun Tzu Chapter 13

Season 6 Episode 14: Face of the Enemy

Story Summary

Similar to the second season episode in DS9, *Second Skin*, *Face of the Enemy* forces another *Star Trek* hero must participate in an uncomfortable scenario for the sake of completing a mission. In this story, surgically-altered Deanna Troi must portray a Romulan Tal Shiar officer to transfer two high level political dissidents to the USS *Enterprise*.

Like Kira of DS9, Troi wakes up to find her face changed to serve the purpose of transporting Vice Proconsul M'Ret and two of his aides to the Federation. The Romulan dissidents are kept in stasis, and held as cargo, and is planned to be exchanged with a Corvallen cargo ship. When the ship does shows, Troi tells her capture that the ship's captain cannot be trusted" – so N'Vek blows it up. Troi later tells him that she recognized the captain as a known Federation spy. N'Vek changes the plan and tells Troi that she must use her Starfleet secret codes to contact *Enterprise* for the pick-up. Deanna refuses to give N'Vek her codes, and devises another way to transfer the cargo.

When *Enterprise* arrives to meet the cargo ship, they only find the wreckage. Toreth commands the Romulan ship to a safer distance so as not to be detected by Picard. Troi, worried that *Enterprise* will lose them asks N'Vek to leave a trail so it can follow the cloaked ship. As expected Picard picks up the clues and follow the Romulan ship. Toreth orders a collision course towards Enterprise to determine whether they know their position. When Enterprise moves away,

Toreth orders to fire, but N'Vek fires, but only low-powered setting. Finally realizing that N'Vek has deceived her, she executes him. Just before Toreth can take Troi as a prisoner, she and the dissidents are transported aboard *Enterprise*.

In Sickbay, after cosmetic surgery, Troi laments the loss of N'Vek's life with Beverly.

Notable Dialogue: None

Character Arcs: Counselor Deanna Troi

Sun Tzu understood an *inward* spy was a brilliant tactic to defeat an enemy. In this story, Deanna Troi is the reluctant, secretly transformed spy used to bring the *real* inward spies to the Federation. As this plot is thrown into her lap without any warning, Troi warms up to the job and even finds commanding the Romulan captain a dangerous but exciting moment. Deanna has always wished to be more than a counselor, and this undercover assignment, even though a life and death one, is thrilling to the Betazoid who has been playing it safe aboard the *Enterprise*. Now, with everything won or lost by her strategy teamed with N'Vek, Deanna finally shows that she is more than a telepath.

Everyday Reflections

Why are inward spies, as Sun Tzu points out, work to a distinct advantage against the enemy? Why was the kidnapping of Counselor Deanna Troi the most effective way of delivering the real spies to Federation? Could Sub Commander N'Vek have kidnapped Dr. Crusher, or Geordi La Forge, who may have been better prepare for such a mission?

Why are spies so valuable in the 21st century?

Everyday Actions

Pick one, or both assignments for this TNG story . . .

First, write in your journal the times you played spy in your youth.

As a child, did you ever play James Bond against Dr. No? If you are a bit older, perhaps you made believe you were Austin Powers fighting Dr. Evil? In my youth, I often played Napoleon Solo from *The Man From Uncle* (1964-68) with my neighbor – I even had the secret agent case with camera and gun!

Second, watch the DS9 episode, *Second Skin*, and compare the how Major Kira and Counselor Troi change during the story. Which episode do you like better? Which character is most believable as an enemy spy?

Lesson 79

When wisdom and knowledge appear, great pretense arises

Lao Tzu Chapter 18

Season 6 Episode 15: Tapestry

Story Summary

Captain Jean-Luc Picard is rushed to Sickbay after being shot at a diplomatic meeting. Apparently dead from his severe wounds, Jean-Luc awakens in an all-white waiting area – and is greeted by a white robbed, God-like being with open arms. As Picard walks towards the image he finds Q, who welcomes him to the after-life.

The captain's arch rival, Q, tells Jean-Luc that he died under Dr. Crusher's haphazard care onboard *Enterprise*. Q holds Picard's artificial heart in his hand and tells him that if he had a real heart, the injuries would not have killed him. Picard replies that he needed the mechanical one after a very tall and angry Nausicaan plunged a dagger in his back at a bar fight. Jean-Luc regrets the brawl, and tells Q that he was a very different person in his younger years; arrogant, prideful and immature, but read for his first deep space assignment after graduating from Starfleet Academy.

Coming up with a unique challenge, Q says that he will give Picard his life back if he can avoid the being stabbed in the back and losing his heart to an artificial replacement. Jean-Luc accepts the challenge – and finds himself back on a starbase with his close friends, Corey and Marta, a day before the fight.

As before, Corey is cheated by a Nausiciaan at *Dom Jat*, a pool game, and plans revenge by rigging the table for the next match. When the same player loses to Corey the next night, a fight begins, but this time Jean-Luc holds Zweller back, and avoids the tragedy, but infuriates his friend who leaves the bar. Marta, now seeing Picard in a different light, falls for him and spends the night with him, further complicating their friendship.

As promised, Q returns Jean-Luc to his starship, but no longer as captain, merely a junior science officer under La Forge. When Picard asks both Riker and Troi if he has any chance of a promotion to the commander rank, they both agree that he has not shown that type of leadership in the past, and as such, is unlikely to rise to such a prominent level in the future.

In a turbolift, Jean-Luc angrily chastises Q, saying that he hopes he is enjoying his predicament. The elevator opens to the heavenly scene once again and Q reminds him that he never took chances as the man he hoped to be by avoiding the bar fight. As Q turns his back on his friend, Jean-Luc asks to have a redo, and take the knife through the heart as before he changed his history. Q warns him that he will surely die in sickbay if he chooses this path. Picard accepts the challenge, telling Q that he would rather die the man he was than live out an existence in a pathetic remake. Q grants Picard's request, and the Jean-Luc is stabbed, and laughs in a macabre, gleeful way.

Jean-Luc awakens in Sickbay, still laughing, and the bridge crew around them are eased by his good cheer. In the Ready Room, Riker wonders if his friend had a livid dream or it was Q who intervened to help him. Picard wonders, too, but says he owes Q a great debt. Picard admits to Will in private that his young life was undisciplined, but made up the fabric of what he would become in later life. Soon, Jean-Luc begins to regale Riker with stories about other Nausicaan encounters.

Notable Dialogue:

> **Q**: You're dead, this is the afterlife...and I'm God
>
> **Jean-Luc Picard**: You are not God!
>
> **Q**: Blasphemy! You're lucky I don't cast you out or smite you or something. The bottom line is, your life ended about five minutes ago... under the inept ministrations of Dr. Beverly Crusher.
>
> **Jean-Luc Picard**: No. I am not dead. Because I refuse to believe that the afterlife is run by *you*. The universe is not so badly designed!
>
> --------
>
> **Jean-Luc Picard**: There are many parts of my youth that I'm not proud of. There were loose threads - untidy parts of me that I would like to remove. But when I pulled on one of those threads, it unraveled the tapestry of my life.

Character Arcs: Jean-Luc Picard

For Captain Picard, his youth is a forgettable voyage. His arrogance, far too many romantic interludes, and a pre-occupation with rank and status were qualities less becoming of the man he is today. Jean-Luc defines himself today, but not who he has become but of what he was years earlier.

As Lao Tzu realized, great wisdom and knowledge does not necessarily mean a person is better than others. Arrogance often comes with the acquisition of status and power – often gained through life experience. Jean-Luc may have thought of himself an arrogant young man, and perhaps he was in his youth, but by re-visiting his past, Picard learns that everyone needs a little bit of cockiness – a character trait that pushed oneself into personal challenges. Fortunately for Jean-Luc, he never became a man of pretense when leading his crew on dangerous missions. His tempered way of facing life as an adult served him well on a starship and as a good friend.

Everyday Reflections

Mistakes are a part of life for everyone. We only learn from the mistakes we make in life, not the victories.

When did Jean-Luc finally realize that his life was not so bad after all? Did he make the right choice, to put his life back the way it was, even though it had supposedly led to his death? Would you have been so brave?

Everyday Actions

Take a few minutes and write down a personal story or two as a journal entry of several events that have shaped your life today. Your choices can be positive or negative – it's your story. If you could cross out, delete or erase parts of your life, like Jean-Luc tried to do in Q's reality (or Picard's dream?), would you? What would you change about you today that was created in the past?

Lesson 80

My words have an origin.

My deeds have a sovereign.

Truly, because people do not understand this,

They do not understand me

Lao Tzu Chapter 70

Season 6 Episode 20: The Chase

Story Summary

Picard's mentor, Professor Galen, "a father who understood me," boards the *Enterprise* to ask Jean-Luc to come along with him on a mission of not merely archeological importance of profound universal significance. The captain politely declines, and is accused of doing nothing but dull servitude to the Federation. When Dr. Galen's ship is attacked a few hours later, *Enterprise* rescues him, but the professor still dies in sickbay. Picard decides to follow the Galen's quest and goes on the adventure, hoping to find the murderer and the mystery to the universe his mentor promised him.

Soon, Jean-Luc understands what the puzzle represents, but must put together other DNA samples to solve the mystery. As the *Enterprise* travels to a uninhabited planet that Galen had talked about earlier, a Romulan, Klingon and Cardassian ship appear as well, seemingly to believe that Galen's search was for a weapon of immerse power.

Picard asks the two ship captains for a meeting and they agree to combine DNA sample that all the parties have not pieced together yet for a complete picture of the mysterious puzzle. Eventually, the evidence reveals that the samples also indicate yet another planet with the final DNA sample.

All three groups assemble on a distant planet and once Beverly inputs the DNA strand into her medical tricorder a holographic image of a humanoid alien in front of the group. The hologram explains that they seeded the galaxy with their DNA eons ago to leave themselves a legacy. The alien pleads with the group to work together as one species.

The Cardassians and Klingons leave after a few angry words, but later on, the Romulan talks with Picard. The commander speaks highly in the value of the alien's words and remarks that perhaps in a not so distant time, humans and Romulans may indeed become friends.

Notable Dialogue:

> **Ancient Humanoid**: You're wondering who we are. Why we have done this. I stand before you, the image of a being from so long ago. Life evolved on my planet, before all others in this part of the galaxy. We left our world, explored the stars, and found none like ourselves. Our civilization thrived for ages. But what is the life of one race, compared to the vast stretches of cosmic time? We knew that one day we would be gone, and that nothing of us would survive. So we left you. Our scientists seeded the primordial oceans of many worlds, where life was in its infancy. The seed codes directed your evolution towards a physical form resembling ours. This body you see before you, which is of course shaped as yours is shaped, for you are the end result. The seed codes also contained this message, which was scattered in fragments on many different worlds. It was our hope that you would have to come together in fellowship and companionship to hear this message. And if you can see and hear me, our hope has been fulfilled. You are a monument, not to our greatness, but to our existence. That was our wish. That you too, would know life, and would keep alive our memory. There is something of us in each of you. And so, something of you in each other. Remember us.

Character Arcs: Professor Richard Galen, Jean-Luc Picard and the Ancient Humanoid

Ever wonder why so many species on *Star Trek* look humanoid? Is it a coincidence, a common denominator for the Alpha Quadrant, or is it DNA that was spread across the galaxy in the primordial soup of the cosmos?

Professor Galen surmised a connection to the words of the Ancient Humanoid – but his secret nearly died with him. The archeologist in him sought out his favorite student, Jean-Luc, who took the torch and lit the way for himself and others. By working together, they solved the most profound of questions: Where did life begin and why did it bring us into existence.

The words, sadly, were lost on the Klingons and the Cardassians. Neither military leader dare admit the commonality between mortal enemies. Surprisingly, the Romulan commander sent a message to Captain Picard stating that one day peace may be a reality between them and the Federation.

For the ancient one, putting a context of their origins in words were of vital importance. Their hope was for mutual understanding, acceptance and compassion towards among all races in their galaxy.

Lao Tzu would be pleased if the warring factions in the *Star Trek* universe were to take the words to heart.

Everyday Reflections

Does the Klingon's reaction to the notion that all beings were created from a supreme-being sound familiar to you? Does the ancient humanoid character seem like a real possibility or is it just science fiction to you? What does the phrase, 'being made in my image' mean to you?

Everyday Actions

Perform a quick study on world religions. Comparative religious studies can be all consuming, but for this task, look at the major religions to see similarities and differences. Where are the intersections – are the crossovers so different from one another?

As we all know, religious battles have accounted for nearly 75% of all the deaths in world history. If we begin to see others as we would like others to see us, humanity's combative, hateful and vengeful nature could be eliminated.

Ironically, it is the Romulan who secretly communicates with Picard about groundbreaking news of the Ancient one's words. Two mortal enemies, conceiving by the same species? Even in *Star Trek*, there are always signs that peace may be right around the corner.

Lao Tzu would be happy to see the promise of hope between alien cultures, humanity and Romulan, in the 24th century.

Lesson 81

Having converted *spies, getting hold of the enemy's spies*
and using them for our own purposes
Sun Tzu Chapter 11

Season 6 Episode 21: Frame of Mind

Story Summary

Before embarking on a top secret mission for Starfleet, Commander Riker practices for a play onboard *Enterprise*. Riker's role is to play an inmate of a mental institution. Towards the end of the drama, Will gives a short monologue on the importance of sanity in the world.

In between rehearsal and the actual performance, Riker trains for his secret mission, but is injured by Lieutenant Worf. Dr. Crusher heals the wound, but Will feels the pain on the side of his head during his first performance. The small audience gives the actor rousing applause, but one officer in the crowd. Will is a bit bewildered, but lets it go. Turning around to the set behind him, Riker realizes that it has turned into an actual cell. The humanoid alien, the one in the audience who hated his performance, says, "I see we still have much work to do," before locking the cell door in front of the inmate.

Will continues to question his own sanity as the physicians claim that he is delusional and at the institute for his own good. Dr. Crusher, Worf, and Data appear to him while eating, but this, too is only an illusion. Time and time again, different scenarios play out in his mind until Will realizes that the painful wound to his temple must be from something alien.

Riker recovers consciousness and finds himself on an operating table with a device inserted in head. Will frees himself from the table, grabs his communicator and phaser that rests on a nearby medical tray, and calls Enterprise.

Once home, Dr. Crusher tends to his injury and learns that he was captured while on an undercover mission. The aliens had tried to scan his brain for the strategic information, but his subconscious fought the probe. After Will is well enough to leave Sickbay, he goes to the theater and tears apart the play set piece by piece.

Notable Dialogue: None

Character Arcs: Will Riker

In this story, Will's state of mind is fraught with questions of what *is* and *isn't* reality. Was he ever a Starfleet officer or was it all a lie, a dream that his mind created to protect him from the murder of innocent man.

What William Riker fails to realize is his nightmare was created by those he was sent to spy on in a Starfleet espionage assignment. Turning him into a test experiment to retrieve Federation secrets is something Sun Tzu might be interested in evaluating – for its success would have been a remarkable achievement in Chinese military circles over 1,000 years earlier.

Everyday Reflections

Do you believe that enemies of the state can and regularly do try to brainwash their captured spies in this way? Can the CIA and other US intelligence agencies turn a spy with the right type of technological equipment?

Everyday Actions

In our story, Will Riker was unsure he was going mad, had reached insanity or was slowly being driven insane by an alien group. Fortunately for Will, he overcame the delusions and fought back against his attackers and returned to *Enterprise* before he finally gave up important military secrets and lost his sanity.

As we know, hundreds of thousands of us, young and old, experience mental challenges throughout our lives. Do you have a friend or family member going through this sort of illness? Go to the internet or the library and perform a search on the subject of schizophrenia.

There are several older and contemporary books on the subject such as, *I Never Promised You a Rose Garden*, by Joanne Greenberg (1964), *Mad in America* by Robert Whitaker (2001), *The Looney Bin Trip* by Kate Millet (1978), *The Voices Within* by Charles Ferneyhough (2016) and *Outside Mental Health: Voices and Visions of Madness* by Will Hall (2016). Each one of these texts provide either first-hand accounts of schizophrenia or professional analysis of how this illness can devastate, but not totally destroy those suffering from this affliction.

Lesson 82

Not knowing is true knowledge

Lao Tzu Chapter 71

Season 7 Episode 11: Parallels

Story Summary

After a very proud Lieutenant Worf wins a bat'leth tournament on Forcas III, he is still hesitant to enter his quarters on the *Enterprise*, anticipating a much loathed birthday. Commander Riker greets him in the hallways and promises nothing awaits him in his quarters – but as the Klingon opens the door, and turns a corner in his room, the bridge crew scream, "Surprise!" Counselor Troi places a pointy hat on her friend, and Will tells his good friend that he lied – that he *loves* surprise parties.

Soon afterwards, Worf experiences dizziness on the bridge when *Enterprise* investigates a communication array that may have been sabotaged by the Cardassians. The Klingon goes to sickbay, but Dr. Crusher finds nothing out of the ordinary with her patient – but again, Worf feels disoriented, and the universe he exists in changes once more.

Further investigation reveals that Worf's RNA signature does not match the one in the current universe. It is assumed that he must have passed through a time-space fissure on his return from the Bat'let tournament, causing Worf to experience quantum flux between multiple universes. Enterprise retraces Worf's steps, attempting to find the fissure, but are attacked by a Bajoran ship, and creates a worst case scenario, allowing over 285,000 *Enterprises* to appear in that area of space.

Worf boards the same shuttle craft and heads directly for the time-space fissure. Although he is fired upon by a badly damaged *Enterprise* that does not wish to return to their reality where the Borg are dominant, the Klingon makes it back to his universe and closes the fissure. Finding his championship standing trophy besides him, Worf knows that he has made it home.

After docking with *Enterprise*, the Klingon walks sheepishly to his quarters, expecting a surprise birthday party. When only Troi greets him inside, Worf asks her to stay and have dinner with him, bring a smile to the counselor's face.

Notable Dialogue: None

Character Arcs: Worf, Troi and Geordi

The more a person knows, the less knowledge he/she possesses because it becomes very apparent that more questions exist on a variety profound issues of science (physics, biology, chemistry, et. al.) than were thought of before.

Worf is not only confused by the events in different the various multiverses, but has a difficult time arguing his case to Geordi and Picard. Only when Dr. Crusher finds the answer through Geordi's visor does she and the bridge officers realize that Worf has indeed been travelling through parallel universes.

Counselor Troi's perspective changes too, in a sad way, to know that the Worf she loved and had children with in one universe was not the love of the Klingon's life in his universe. She reluctantly accepts the fact, and hopes that the husband she married in her timeline returns.

Everyday Reflections

Do you believe that there could be alternate timelines, or multiple universes? Have you done any reading on this theory, one accepted by prominent scientists, like the late Stephen Hawkins? Have you ever felt that if your life could have been changed in just the smallest of fashions that you would be living a completely different lifestyle today?

Everyday Action

Is this possible? Could we visit out counterparts in another mirror universe? Maybe Captain Kirk did *not* do the impossible?

Exactly like Worf's mind-blowing predicament, the late physicist, Stephen Hawkins, believed the Big Bang Theory could have produced an uncountable number of universes with its explosion. Find Stephen Hawkins final paper on theoretical possibility of multi-verses across the galaxy.

For a summary of the article go to the BBC online discussion of Hawkins's theory:
https://www.bbc.com/news/science-environment-43976977

Lesson 83

Prohibit the taking of omens, and do away with superstitious doubts.

Then, until death itself comes, no calamity need be feared.

Sun Tzu Chapter 11

Season 7 Episode 6: Phantasms

Story Summary

In the recent past, Commander Data's dream programming has taken him on personal and illuminating adventures, but recently his nighttime experiences have given him pause as to the deeper messages in the highly symbolic stories. In his latest dream, after he meets with Dr. Sigmund Freud, Data walks upon old fashioned workmen, banging heavy equipment on a warp plasma conduit panel. As he speaks to the men, Data can only shriek a high pitched sounds, which prompts the angered men to rip off his arm, and then, his head.

Meanwhile on the starship, Geordi La Forge is having a tough time starting *Enterprise's* engines after installing a new warp drive.

After consulting with Counselor Diana Troi on this odd nightmare, Data feels a bit better, and is pleased that he may be developing a neurosis, too.

Yet, in an almost deadly attack, Data stabs at the counselor and nearly kills her in the turbolift before Riker and Worf stops him.

Dr. Crusher, after attending to Diana's serious injury inflicted on her by a sleep walking Mr. Data, the physician stunning discovers a peptide-sucking, interphasic creature attached to not only Troi's neck, but on others in Sickbay as well. Beverly calls Captain Picard, and First Officer Riker to show them the odd being on Troi's neck, but also finds them on Jean-Luc's neck and Will's temple. Dr. Crusher informs them that if they cannot rid themselves these parasitic beings, everyone on the ship will be nothing more than a handful of chemicals.

Picard and La Forge, working with Mr. Data, hook-up the android to the holodeck in hopes of seeing a way to combat the parasites. Data goes to sleep, dreams about the invaders as workman, and wakes up, understanding the symbolic nature of the people and a way to kill the creatures. The commander asks Geordi to hoop him up to allow an interphasic pulse to go through the ship – an act that should destroy the creatures. The act works immediately and the intruders return to their own universe. Later, Troi visits Data later and accepts her friend's apology for the earlier attack. They share a cake, in Data's image, as Deanna jokingly says, "Turnabout is fair play."

Notable Dialogue:

> **Picard**: What type of cake is that?
> **Data**: It is a cellular peptide cake.
> **Worf**: [*With mouth full*] With mint frosting.

Character Arcs: Commander Data and Counselor Diana Troi

As Sun Tzu rightly claimed, omens of death and superstitions have no place in wars nor in the minds of soldiers on the battlefields. Mr. Data's highly symbolic nightmare counter Sun Tzu's claims. Data's dreams mask a subconscious sensitivity to the danger aboard *Enterprise* – something a Chinese war philosopher could not have possibly imagined thousands of years ago. Soldiers may have predictive, or intuitive hunches upon entering a particular dangerous maneuver in an upcoming battle, but with Mr. Data, the battle was waged not in plain sight, but on level even he did not understand until Captain Picard and Chief Engineer Geordi La Forge helped him interpret through lucid dreaming in the holodeck.

Counselor Troi, who had little training in interpreting android dreams, went about helping her client in the wrong way. Even though she was correct in a general sense that dreams allow us to playout routine problems in everyday life, Mr. Data's nightmares were so much more intense and showed his need to alert himself to the real threat on *Enterprise*.

Everyday Reflections

Have you ever had a lucid dream? What happened to you in it? Do you believe such dreams allow us to live out a fantasy or a real life problem? If so, can you recall such a dream that you had recently or one that has stuck with you for many years? What was the importance of that dream to you – or others?

Everyday Actions

For one week, keep a pad a paper nearby and write down your dreams immediately after you wake up. Likely, you will only remember the endings, but write as much down as you can. Interpret the stories, the characters and the symbolism. Whatever you believe your nightmares or sweet tales to be, that's fine. If you find a recurring pattern, write that down as well.

Lesson 84

When the government is quite unobtrusive,

People are indeed pure.

When the government is quite prying,

People are indeed conniving

Lao Tau Chapter 58

Season 7 Episode 12: Pegasus

Story Summary

Admiral Pressman, Riker's former commander on the USS *Pegasus*, comes aboard *Enterprise* to find their lost ship before it falls in the hands of the Romulans. Picard asks his first officer about the alleged destruction of the ship long ago. Will reveals that he was young, stood up for Pressman and against the mutineers as he and the captain made it to the shuttlepods to escape, surviving the ship's explosion, but adds nothing substantial to the captain's inquiry as Jean-Luc presses him on the highly classified mission. Picard warns Will that even though he respects the first officers right to keep his secrets, he will reevaluate the ship command structure if certain facts come to light about Riker's actions on the *Pegasus*.

Unmoved by the danger of the attempt, Pressman leads Picard to an asteroid and demands that the captain enter a fissure deep inside. Once inside, it is revealed that the Pegasus is partially fused in the rock. Riker and Pressman beam to Engineering and find the experiment still intact. At the same time, Commander Sirol of a Romulan Warbird fires at the opening of the fissure, trapping Enterprise inside the asteroid. Sirol offers safe passage of the crew back to Romulus if they surrender.

After this impending disaster for the ship and crew, Riker tells Picard of the Federation cloaking device that can also phase-shift through solid objects. Picard turns livid, and challenges Pressman's authority, and tells him that he is in violation of the Treaty of Algeron. Regardless of the treaty policy, Picard is forced to engage the cloaking device and pray that it works so *Enterprise* can leave the asteroid safely.

Commander La Forge makes minor adjustments to the device, and it works, freeing the ship. Picard admits to Sirol of the treaty violation before sending both Pressman and Riker to the brig. Soon afterwards, Jean-Luc has a heart to heart with his imprisoned first officer, telling him that his career goals will not be smooth from then on, but allows him to resume his duties aboard Enterprise.

Notable Dialogue: None

Character Arcs: Commander Will Riker and Admiral Pressmen

Blaming others for one's action – or lack of it – in this case the truth about cloaking technology banned by Starfleet, is a secret that Will Riker must come to terms with when his former commanding officer comes aboard the *Enterprise*.

After discussing the real facts with Counselor Diana Troi, Will learns from his mistake of covering up the cloaking device and protecting the current Starfleet Intelligence officer. Will admits his mistake to Picard, saves his career, and starts a journey to accepting his role in a lie many years ago.

Everyday Reflections

Have you ever taken orders from your superior at work knowing that the person was in violation of company ethics? If so, did you report that person?

Everyday Actions

If there is anything you feel ashamed of, and can own up to it, do so. Write it down in your journal, reconcile the reason(s) why you acted a certain way, and admit the truth to the offended person. The only way to move past shame and guilt is to face it – and as we saw in this *Trek* tale, it took a burden off of Commander Riker's shoulder, too.

Lesson 85

The sage has no concern for himself, but makes the concerns of others his own

Lao Tzu Chapter 49

Season 7 Episode 13: Homeward

Story Summary

Lieutenant Commander Worf's brother meets with Picard and other senior officers in a last ditch plea to save the Boraalan civilization that he has been observing for the past few years. Due to an atmospheric disaster on the cusp, Nikolai Rozenko's words carry meaning, but are still rejected by Jean-Luc who professes the Prime Directive must be carried out regardless of the circumstance.

Not accepting that answer, Rozenko transports the small community directly to the *Enterprise* holodeck, complete with a rendering of their planet. When Worf figures out the power drain to the ship is caused by his brother's direct disobedience to his Starfleet oath, both battle over regulations and ethical behavior towards the Boraalans. Picard tells Rozenko he will be stripped of his Starfleet rank, but agrees that what is done is done, and works with him to find another world for the civilization to move to without much more cultural interference.

Sadly, the community historical chronicler, Vorin, discovers the ruse, and steps out of the holodeck. Although he is counseled and given a choice to return to his people or remain aboard Enterprise, the Boraalan commits ritualistic suicide. His loss to the village

Eventually, Mr. Data searches and finds a suitable and favorable planet to transport the unsuspecting civilization before the holodeck completely loses its power.

Nickolai remains with the villagers, taking on a wife and their unborn child, accepts Vorin's job as historian. With this act, Worf finally accepts the outcome and the principles Nikolai stood on to save the courageous, pre-warp society.

Notable Dialogue: None

Character Arcs: Starfleet Anthropologist Nikolai Rozhenko

Lao Tzu understood that a sage was caring, loving and self-sacrificing in all actions towards others in the world. Like Lao's definition of a sage, Nikolai has no worries about his rank or responsibilities to follow unsympathetic rules regarding Federation interference in alien civilizations.

Everyday Reflections

Would you have gone against rules and regulations to save people in trouble? Have you done this, to a less significant, but yet important way in your past?

Everyday Actions

Culture shock, what Vorin, the Boraalan village chronicler experienced and ultimately led to his death, is a real problem for immigrant and refugee groups. People from foreign lands will immigrate typically under oppressive government laws regarding religion, social or political freedom. More often, too, refugees flee their home countries to escape war, torture and poverty.

Spend time in the library or online and examine how different waves of immigrants react to their new homes. For example, at the end of the Vietnam War, the first several groups of Vietnamese who landed in America were the healthiest – and were professionals, such as physicians, business owners, and well-educated. Following these groups are the poorer classes without savings, nor a profession or highly educated. Which of these groups have a better chance of adjusting to their new surroundings?

Everyday Actions

For one week, keep a pad a paper nearby and write down your dreams immediately after you wake up. Likely, you will only remember the endings, but write as much down as you can. Interpret the stories, the characters and the symbolism. Whatever you believe your nightmares or sweet tales to be, that's fine. If you find a recurring pattern, write that down as well.

Lesson 86

The sage never strives for greatness,

And can therefore accomplish greatness

Lao Tzu Chapter 64

Season 7 Episode 15: Lower Decks

Story Summary

Four young and lower ranking crew officers, vying for promotions aboard *Enterprise*, find their relationship strained during the evaluation process headed by their supervising officers of Riker, Crusher and La Forge. In particular, Ensign's Sito and Lavelle, competing for the same position at Ops, find themselves more stressed because only one of them can earn the bridge promotion.

More importantly of the starship's concern is a secret operation the must be handled with the utmost secrecy.

Lieutenant Commander Worf spots an escape pod inside Cardassian space. Worf, Crusher and La Forge must work in secrecy to bring the passenger aboard and complete a dangerous mission with grave repercussions if handled even slightly wrong. What makes the task difficult is the young officer's curiosity about the nature of the covert mission and their roles in making it successful without their colleagues catching on to the nature of it.

For example, Nurse Ogawa must assist Dr. Crusher with the immediate surgery with a Cardassian operative. In Engineering, the young Vulcan officer must work with Geordi to create the appearance of a distress shuttle pod. Even though their friends question the mystery onboard, neither can tell the others the truth.

Eventually, Ensign Sito is called into Captain Picard's office, questioned, and scolded by Jean-Luc. Sito, one of the cadets with Wesley Crusher who had tried to cover-up the death of a fellow classmate, is reprimanded by the *Enterprise* commander. Though she wonders why he was question her dedication to Starfleet, she still stands up for herself when questioned about her standing on the ship.

Not so long afterwards, the young Bajoran accepts a dangerous role of helping a Cardassian dissident. Sito must pose as a captured Maqui terrorist so Joret, a Starfleet operative, can return to his people without suspicion.

Right before she leaves with Joret, Jean-Luc admits that he was testing her resolve earlier in his ready room. He also admits that it was he who requested she be placed on *Enterprise*, because like Wesley, Jean-Luc believed she deserved a second chance. Sito thanks him, and walks towards the shuttle bay, proud that her captain believed she had what it takes to be a success in Starfleet.

Hours later to rendezvous with *Enterprise*, Data locates the remains of a shuttle, destroyed by the Romulans.

Notable Dialogue:

> **Picard**: [over ship's intercom] "To all Starfleet personnel, this is the Captain. It is my sad duty to inform you that a member of the crew, Ensign Sito Jaxa has been lost in the line of duty. She was the finest example of a Starfleet officer and a young woman of remarkable courage and strength of character. Her loss will be deeply felt by all who knew her. Picard out."

Character Arcs: Ensign Sito Jaxa, Nurse Ogawa, Engineering Officer Taurik and Ensign Lavell

Of all the lower decks members hoping for career advancement, Ensign Sito Jaxa's journey has been the toughest. Along with Wesley Crusher, Sito faced scorn from Starfleet for her complicity in the cover-up at the academy.

For the other officers, Ogawa, Taurik and Lavell dealt with their careers in a less stressful way that Sito, but still had to negotiate their superiors for recognition and advancement.

Everyday Reflections

Lao Tzu believed that any wise person did not crave recognition – and because of humbleness, achieved greatest regardless.

The work of the subordinates in any occupation, even on a starship, goes under-appreciated. Rising through the ranks to bridge officers or heads of departments is not an easy feat as well. For those who train and put in the time to be better at their jobs, their heads and hearts are seldom on the present, but more on the future. The worry, anxiety and fears often creep into their lives and overwhelms them, thus, sometimes destroying their confidence and potential to achieve success.

With the *Enterprise* crew, especially, Ensign Jaxa had a lot to prove, due to the incident at Starfleet Academy with Wesley Crusher. Picard gave her a chance, and she earned the respect from him and Worf, but gave her life. Sito pushed ahead and did not play it safe – and in her final moments, one would hope she was at peace with this brave decision.

Everyday Actions

Re-watch, *Star Trek: Next Generation* episode, *The First Duty*, and focus on the Starfleet Academy student Jaxa Sito. Does the character seem like she is convinced lying is the only way to go to save her career? Do you see any hope that she or Wesley could come through this tragedy without losing self-respect and the admiration of their peers?

If you had lived through this type of problem in college – being caught breaking a severe social or academic rule, could you have come through it like Jaxa Sito?

Lesson 87

A climb of eight hundred feet starts where the foot stands

Lao Tzu Chapter 64

Season 7 Episode 22: Journey's End

Story Summary

Captain Picard must make a delicate diplomatic maneuver to a Native American tribe over a disputed Cardassian world on a newly negotiated treaty with the Federation. Admiral Nechayev tells Jean Luc to find a home for the Dorvan V colonists even though they may resist the move. On the way to the planet, *Enterprise* picks up Wesley Crusher who is on a break from the academy.

During a short vacation, Cadet Wesley Crusher visits his mother and friends onboard the USS *Enterprise*. Dr. Crusher, Chief Engineer Geordi La Forge and even Commander Data notice that Wesley is not the young man they have grown fond of during his stay on the starship. Wesley lacks enthusiasm, respect for his superiors and even becomes combative and angry when confronted by his mother and friends.

As Picard prepares for the transport of the colonists to the *Enterprise*, Wesley hears the news and transports down to the colony to warn them. A riot occurs. Transported back to the ship, Captain

Picard warns the cadet that any more interference from him will not be tolerated. Crusher quits Starfleet and leaves for the planet after a heartfelt conversation with his mother. Beverly tells him that the Traveler told her that he was destined for great adventures – and that no matter what he did with his life, she would be proud of him.

As the Cardassians survey the planet, a fight breaks out with the colonists. Wesley tries to stop the battle, but freezes time. Lakanta, the colonist who brought him on a vision quest earlier, reveals to be the Traveler. Both leave the groups to fight.

On *Enterprise*, Captain Picard and Gul Evek agree to stop hostilities under a settlement can be reached with the colonists. Soon, Anthwara tells the captain that they will forgo their Federation citizenship and stay on Drovan V – and Evek agrees that his people will not bother the colonists if they remain peaceful as well.

Wesley gives his goodbyes to his friends, Jean-Luc, and his mother before transporting off the ship to join the Traveler on his new adventures.

Notable Dialogue: None

Character Arcs: Wesley Crusher, Captain Picard and Gul Evek

Wesley Crusher takes his final steps in a Starfleet uniform – a journey he imagined would never end until he retired from his scientific/military career in the Federation. Even though he had a tough time at the academy, he rebounded from the incident, and almost had his commission. Yet something was not right. His passion changed from investigating stars systems to the inner exploration of his soul.

Jean-Luc Picard's journey stems back generations. His curse, his blood-stained ancestry must be rectified by choosing the best course for the Native American colony on the soon to be Cardassian planet. Captain Picard finally finds his way and convinces Gul Evek to calm down his troops before an incident brings both Federation and Cardassians to war.

Everyday Reflections

Was Captain Picard's pushback on Starfleet's demand that he remove the American Native Indian colony correct? Was it guilt or a sense of honor that drove him to stand by the Earth colonists? Did he, in fact, remove a blood stain from former Picard generations against the Native American colonists?

Was Wesley's decision to leave Starfleet Academy the right one? Have you ever made an important decision that went against the wishes of your parents, friends or co-workers? What factors went into such a decision?

Everyday Actions

Wesley Crusher made the hard, but necessary decision to take his own path, his Way in another direction – partly due to his dream vision in the Native American village, but mostly due to his sense of what he knew all along – that Starfleet success was more related to his father and mother's wishes for him.

How many times in your life have you taken the Way both or one of your parents have given you as road markers for personal growth? Certainly, one would hope, that nudge in the right direction was the best for you, too.

My father was a professional musician for part of his career, a pianist, singer and composer all of his life. I learned piano for five years, off and on, starting in grammar school and ending in junior high school. I still sing in the office, but not professionally.

Yet my love for the written word has propelled me in successful directions in school as well as in other directions. My father's love for reading and telling stories stuck with me, unlike learning the keyboard.

In your journal, write down at between five to ten memorable events in your early life that has brought you to the place you are in today. Instead of negative, traumatic events which all of us face in life, choose more life-affirming ones.

What conscious decisions did you make early on in your young life steered you to academic and occupational success? What type of personal choices did you make concerning hobbies, or friendships, or volunteer activities brought you a sense of pride and pushed you along to be a stronger, more creative version of yourself today?

After finishing your list, make another one for your present and future path to find your own Way through life. Lao Tzu would be proud of you taking control over your actions, behavior and peaceful approach to making yourself one with nature, others, and society.

Lesson 88

Heaven's Way

Is to benefit and not to harm.

The sage's Way

Is to act and not to contend.

Lao Tzu Chapter 81

Season 7 Episode 16: Thine Own Self

Story Summary

Data is sent to the planet Barkon IV, a pre-industrial world, to retrieve a deep space probe that has crash landed on the surface. The android is injured while recovering pieces of the probe, and wanders from the mountains many miles to the Renaissance-like society. Once there, the *Enterprise* crew member meets a father and young daughter. Data acts strangely when they meet, simply repeating Garvan's questions. When asked his name, he does not remember, so Gia, the nine year old gives him one: Jaden. Both take him home to help him recover from whatever it is that has interfered with his memory. Along with him, the android carries a small container filled with highly toxic pieces from the destroyed radioactive probe.

When evaluating Data for physical trauma and illness, Talur, the local healer, determines that the Ice Man must be suffering from a loss of memory due to some accident the pale-skinned man suffered on his long journey to their village. She is somewhat correct, but her recommendation he eat and drink to recover more quickly is obviously wrong.

Slowly, Data becomes more of himself when he attends Talur's school the next morning, correcting her scientific claims about minerals and elements on the planet's surface. Perturbed, but not truly angry, Talur dismisses Data's scientific approach to merely observational opinions.

When the village begin to show signs of radiation poisoning, Data uses scientific methods to determine the cause and finds out that the metal fragments he brought with him are the factor. Risking his life, he concocts a curative solution and pours into the town's well, but succumbs to an attack. Data is buried, but retrieved by *Enterprise* and with no recollection of his experiences on the planet.

In another story arc, Counselor Deana Troi decides that she needs another challenge in her life. Due to her friends who have also made late-life career changes, the ship counselor takes a Command Test that would allow her to take over the captain's chair in a ship emergency. Troi figures out the no-win solution in a holographic scenario, which means sacrificing a crewmate – and passes the test.

Notable Dialogue: None

Character Arcs: Commander Data and Counselor Deanna Troi

Lao Tzu believed the wisest sage is a person who does not fight nor act aggressively. It is also the way of a sage to help and never harm others in any way. And as we know, Mr. Data is a sage of immeasurable wisdom, empathy and compassion for others.

Commander Data, even in his limited and impaired way, makes sure helps the family who took him in – Garvan, Jia, and the others in the small village who become ill from the radioactive pieces he sells to help support himself. When he is confronted by the blacksmith and a small band of angry and suspicious villagers, he neither defends himself nor lashes out in anger when he is attacked. Data is eventually 'killed' by the blacksmith for his find act of bravery when he slips a chemical solution to cure the townspeople in the local well.

As it was with Doctor Beverley Crusher in the story, *Cause and Effect*, Commander Data needed to use the scientific method to determine the serious health problem that he created in the village. In this way, he was true to his internal programming and the 'person' he became while aboard *Enterprise*.

With Counselor Deanna Troi, she had to go against her training and learn that putting the welfare of the ship's compliment was most important over the value of an individual member of the crew. Thus, Deanna moved beyond her limited notion of sacrifice.

As for Data, he simply turned to his scientific training to re-learn who he was before he lost his memory.

Everyday Reflections

What defines you? Is it your sense of fair play? Are you a leader in your specialized field of study or profession? If you asked your friends or family, what would they say is your most endearing or best personal qualities?

Everyday Actions

Lieutenant Commander Data was true to himself, once he realized he understood how to help villagers of the planet, even sacrificing his life for them. He was true to his nature, regardless of his lack of memory of where he stood in the universe.

In your journal, keep track of important decisions or action you have made in the past month. Have these choices reflected the real you, or have you made compromises to accommodate your lifestyle, boss, or friends? Are you the person you need or wish to be today?

Granted, the world pandemic of 2020 may have been a major factor in changed many of us professionally speaking – over 100,000 small businesses alone have closed in America as of October 15th. Therefore, you may have lost your family store and occupation – and your line of work temporary.

If you are a teacher, you likely have learned to teach at home. Has this expanded your approach to education and interacting with your students? How has this new challenge made you a better educator?

Try to take a positive approach in your life regardless of tough, life altering choices thrust upon you.

Lesson 89

At the critical moment, the leader of an army acts like one who has climbed up a height and then kicks away the ladder behind him. He carries his men deep into hostile territory before he shows his hand.

Sun Tzu Chapter 11

Season 7 Episode 24: Preemptive Strike

Story Summary

With Captain Picard's blessing, Ro Laren, a Bajoran, but also a specially-trained operative, must choose to go against a small terrorist cell to prove herself to Starfleet and her commanding officer. Laren goes on an undercover mission to infiltrate a Maquis cell but slowly she realizes her dedication to Bajor is more important that her oath to the Federation. Once she realizes what needs to be done, she leads the Maquis to safety, out of the grip of both Federation and Cardassian forces. Her only regret is not turning her back on Starfleet, but of letting her down commanding officer.

Notable Dialogue: None

Character Arcs: Starfleet Officer Ro Laren and Captain Jean-Luc Picard

As Macias, the informal leader of the Marque cell Laren infiltrates is mortally wounded by Cardassians, he tells Ro that his death does not matter as long as others like her take up the cause for the Bajorans. This touching moment solidifies Ro's decision on just whose side she must pledge true allegiance.

As Sun Tzu says, if you take your forces deep into the battle before you show your plan you gain a distinct advantage. Ro Laren had to do so, with Riker by her side, to prevent him from alerting Picard or the Federation ships capturing her compatriots. At the proper moment, she saves the Maqui cell by exposing the Starfleet trap.

Captain Picard also understands the Sun Tzu code of war well, too. That is part of the reason he is so angry at her. Jean-Luc is angrier at himself for assigning Laren to a mission, that on retrospect, he should not have entrusted to a Bajoran.

Ro Laren did as her heart told her – to save the true heroes of her story. Although at first enraged by Ro's actions, Jean-Luc undoubtedly accepted Ro's ultimate betrayal to Starfleet for her people. How long it took him to come to peace with it is anyone's guess.

Everyday Reflections

When did you last change course dramatically in your life? Was in in a job that you hated but held onto until a pivotal point that forced your hand to resign? Were you in a long term relationship that you ended because it no longer satisfied you?

Everyday Actions

In your journal, discuss personal or professional choices you have made that may have been tough to make, but now, years later, you realize that if you had a chance, you would still make them. Be as honest as you can in this recollection. No anger, no bitterness allowed. Remind yourself of the importance of these choices and how you have moved on in life regardless of the short term pain you went through to find your way to happiness and success today.

Lesson 90

Knowing the future is the flower of the Way,

And the beginning of folly

Lao Tzu Chapter 38

Season 7 Episodes 25 & 26: All Good Things

Story Summary

The finale begins with Diana and Worf about to have their first kiss. Before the two take the emotionally bold act, they see a befuddled Jean-Luc walking towards them from the turbolift. Captain Picard asks for day at the very late hour aboard the ship. Neither of the soon to be lovers understand Jean-Luc's confusion and attribute it to a nightmare.

For Jean-Luc, who has been travelling back and forth through time, he knows that he cannot reveal his adventures for now until he figures out the reason for his odd time skips, as not to alter the timeline for himself nor his crew.

And so the USS *Enterprise* 1701-D crew's adventures end –in this series, as it began – with Q's meddling into their lives. With Captain Picard time jumping from the past, when he first was assigned to command *Enterprise*, to the present, seven years later, to twenty five years into the future tending his vineyard in France, Jean-Luc is befuddled as to why he life is a mixture of confusion. Is it the progressive brain disease manifesting itself, or is there something beyond his control, pushing him into temporal shifts? Only he finds himself in Q's Mid-evil courtroom does he figure out that he is not going mad, but is being played with by his nemesis, but for what reason, he has no idea except that whatever he faces must be met with the patience he has developed as a follower of Taoism principles for much of his adult life in Starfleet.

Eventually, with Q's help, Jean-Luc understands the chicken-and-the-egg riddle about the temporal disruption causing the space-time that threatens to destroy the history of humanity. With the help of the *Enterprise* crews in all three timeframes, the ships go the center of the anomaly, creating a static warp bubble, and it implodes, helping to maintain the barrier between anti-time and time.

At the end of the story, Jean-Luc Picard tells the current *Enterprise* bridge crew about his experiences. With this knowledge, the captain hopes that each one of his friends will not make the same mistakes they made in the alternate timeline. After the captain walks into the poker game and is invited to play, Jean-Luc says, "The sky's the limit," as we end the adventures of this *Star Trek* series.

Notable Dialogue:

Q: You just don't get it, do you, Jean-Luc? The trial never ends. We wanted to see if you had the ability to expand your mind and your horizons. And for one brief moment, you did.

Jean-Luc Picard: When I realized the paradox.

Q: Exactly. For that one fraction of a second, you were open to options you had never considered. That is the exploration that awaits you. Not mapping stars and studying nebulae, but charting the unknowable possibilities of existence.

Jean-Luc Picard: Q, what is it you're trying to tell me?

[Q considers, then opens his mouth as if to answer...but changes his mind, steps back and smiles]

Q: You'll find out. In any case, I'll be watching. And if you're *very* lucky I'll drop by to say hello from time to time. See you...out there.

[Picard is playing poker with the senior staff for the first time.]

Jean-Luc Picard: I should have done this a long time ago.

Deanna Troi: You were always welcome.

Jean-Luc Picard: So, five-card stud, nothing wild... and the sky's the limit.

[Final line of the series]

Character Arcs: Q, Picard, Data, Riker, Geordi, Worf, Deanna and Beverly

As Lao Tzu implies, if one were to know the future, the enjoyment of the present moment may pass by too quickly. Also, we may somehow miss living in the moment – which is what many of us do today. As Stefan Stenudd (2020) says, "Tao is not about the future, although it rules that, too. It's about how everything works and should work at every moment of time. To follow its fruit instead of its dazzling flower is to adapt to Tao now, not at some other time."

Although Jean-Luc Picard reveals to his bridge officers and friends their future, it is only one possible outcome, according to Mr. Data. Knowing the future allows them to change personal relationships for the better now and avoid conflicts later on. For example, Worf and Will Riker coming to an agreement with Troi's affection for the both of them may only strengthen their friendship. Since Jean Luc sees his future with Beverly, perhaps the two can better appreciate their lives together in the present so divorce never occurs.

For Jean-Luc, perhaps the most important lesson Q taught him is to live in the moment. As Picard walks in on the weekly poker game, he admits that he should have been more open and friendly as a commanding officer. Deanna admits that he was always welcome, and the officers embrace him as a friend.

Everyday Reflections

Disregarding the fact that he solved Q's biggest conundrum, and thus "saved the galaxy, once again", what does Jean-Luc finally learn in this grand story? Is the morality tale more about relationships and how to manage them properly than being heroic? What Taoist path will Picard likely take now that he values his friendships more dearly?

Remember that Tao is not about knowing the future, or predicting it – it's about living life, the voyage that we embark on each and every day. Understanding the main principals of the Way is most important so we can implement them in our daily lives. The future will come as we step along the path each day. Enjoy the fruit of not merely the bloom of the blossom. It is the deepest of personal revelations that must prevail over the superficial knowledge of what we think out future must become, based on status, power, or money.

Everyday Actions

In your journal, write down actions you believe your future self could make to save your family, friends, and the world. Of course, Captain Jean-Luc Picard's choice nearly destroyed the known universe for him, the Federation, and countless other worlds in the galaxy. Thanks to the Continuum, Q tricked him into causing a problem for everyone and thing around him. Yet, once Jean Luc realized the conundrum and the solution to it, Picard chose his true path, even if it meant his death in three different timelines.

One day soon, you may need to become the hero of your own story today – and tomorrow, for those around. Your strength and courage may bring others exactly what they need to survive. Do not doubt yourself, no matter the challenge.

Lesson 91

The good fighters of old first put themselves beyond the possibility of defeat, and then waited for an opportunity of defeating the enemy

Sun Tzu Chapter 4

Feature-Length Movie: Star Trek: First Contact (1996)

Story Summary

Even though the Borg is threatening to attack Earth, Admiral Hayes brushes off Captain Picard's request join in the defense of his home world. Hayes, like others in Starfleet, are worried that Picard would be emotionally compromised to engage with the enemy based on his past assimilation not long ago.

Therefore, *Enterprise* is sent to patrol the Neutral Zone for Romulan aggressive movements during a potential Borg attack. When word comes in to Picard that the Borg have attacked and are winning their fight against Starfleet, the captain breaks-off his patrol and heads toward Earth. Once in the battle, *Enterprise* rescues Commander Worf from the USS *Defiant*.

As the Borg create a temporal vortex, Picard and crew sees earth's history change before their eyes. The planet is now completely overwhelmed with the enemy – with no signs of human life. Aware that the Borg have changed the timeline, Captain Picard follows the Borg cube through the vortex and end up on earth in the year of 2063, the day before Zefram Cochrane historic first warp flight.

Shortly after arriving on the monumental day in Earth's history, Picard and others realize that the Borg has gone back in time to prevent Cochrane from his historic warp drive accomplishment. An away team transports to the site in Montana and renders emergency aid to Lily Sloan, Cochrane's assistant, then sends her back to the *Enterprise* for further medical procedures.

At this time, a Borg invasion party board *Enterprise*, murder dozens of crew members, but not before being repelled by Picard's forces. In the melee, the enemy captures Commander Data. The Borg are held to a few decks of the ship, and Worf suggests that the captain order a self-destruct of *Enterprise* – which infuriates Picard. Regardless of the idea of losing the ship to his sworn enemy, Jean Luc finally agrees with the chief of security and evacuates the *Enterprise* crew down to Earth.

In Montana, Riker and La Forge help Cochrane prepare for his flight on the *Phoenix*.

After finding Mr. Data, Picard offers himself to the Queen for the compromised android who has reluctantly given the computer codes to her to prevent the self-destruction order of *Enterprise*.

As ordered by the Borg Queen, Data sends two torpedoes towards the *Phoenix* with Cochrane, Riker and Geordi aboard. Picard watches helplessly as the missiles miss the target – and Data ruptures a coolant tank that corrupts her human components, killing her.

As Picard retrieves his crew from earth, all watch the Vulcan ship meet Cochrane, Sloane and the small camp back in Bozeman, Montana. With the timeline restored, *Enterprise* returns to the 24th century.

Notable Dialogue:

> **Zefram Cochrane**: Let me just make sure that I understand you correctly, *Commander*. A group of cybernetic creatures from the future have traveled back through time to enslave the human race... and you're here to stop them?
> **William Riker**: That's right.
> **Cochrane**: Hot damn! You're heroic.

William Riker: Someone once said, "Don't try to be a great man. Just be a man and let history make its own judgements."

Zefram Cochrane: That's rhetorical nonsense. Who said that?

Riker: *[smiling]* You did. Ten years from now.

Character Arcs: Captain Picard, Data, Geordi, Riker and Zefram Cochrane

Zefram Cochrane and Captain Jean-Luc Picard give themselves a chance at achieving a miracle; one man who believes he can reach the warp threshold and another man trusting his instincts on how to stop the Borg from destroying humanity. Both men are fighters Sun Tzu would be proud of, and both work towards impossible victories.

Of the three characters of this story, Data best represents Sun Tzu's saying about the ancients who waited for the moment to best strike and defeat the enemy. It was not until he pretended to target Cochrane's ship that he put his plans to best use. By allowing Zehram to achieve his dream as was first played out in history, and flooding the compartment with coolant that quickly killed the Queen, Data won a battle that seemed impossible only moments before.

Everyday Reflections

Have you ever positioned yourself to win in a seemingly impossible situation? What was it? How did you strategize your victory?

Everyday Actions

Re-watch the key Borg episodes of the TNG entire series before watching the movie to better understand the relationship between Picard and the Queen as well as the enemy's culture and method of attack. Such stories as *The Best of Both Worlds* (Parts 1 & 2), *Q-Who*, *I, Borg*, are just a few of the best ones.

Also, you may wish to watch Borg episodes featuring Seven of Nine and Captain Janeway in *Star Trek: Voyager*. *Scorpion (Parts 1 & 2)*, *Dark Frontier (Parts 1 & 2)*, and *Endgame* are the best ones of that series.

Chapter Five

Walking the Taoist Path

Which *Star Trek* Characters Earn the Highest Marks?

From the Alpha to the Delta Quadrant: Searching for the Best and the Worst from Human and Alien Civilizations

Over the ninety stories we've reviewed from *Star Trek: The Original Series, Star Trek: The Animated Series* and *Star Trek: The Next Generation* and movies, too we have followed very brave men and women of the Federation. We have also seen the very worst of behavior exhibited by humans and aliens in each and every story.

In terms of awful behavior and unethical treatment of others, both humans and alien species are relentless in their pursuits to dominate or destroy innocent, peaceful civilizations and people. As we move from the worst, we find certain villains actually turned their cheeks, recognizing their evil ways and became budding Taoists. Some, as we see, truly turned to good acts, working with the Federations officers to bring justice to the quadrant, galaxy and universe.

Let's review which Federation and non-Federation members who have demonstrated the best and worst of Taoist principles illustrated in the *Star Trek* saga over the eight television series and other cannon stories we have covered in this book and come to enjoy over the past fifty five years.

Lesson 92

The precept against killing is: All living beings, including all kinds of animals, and those as small as insects, worms, and so forth, are containers of the uncreated energy, thus one should not kill any of them

Lao Tzu – First of the Five Precepts

Worst of the Worse *Star Trek* Characters

Lao Tzu believed that all living creatures had an energy force that must be protected and respected by humanity. In *Star Trek*, individual villains and alien races exhibiting warlike tendencies represented the very worse of humanity. As fans of the series, viewers were asked to evaluate the enemies by their unremorseful nature. The following groups and vile antagonists were seen in the various plotlines of each of the Trek series – and should be examined for the deadly and destructive actions they took on innocent people and Starfleet heroes. Without remorse or self-reflection on their hideous deeds, none of these alien races nor their awful creations would ever seem likely to change their ways and live a more peaceful, harmonious life with nature or humanity.

Star Trek: Original Series

Creators of the Doomsday Machine – whichever civilization created such a weapon, whether it was meant as a symbolic deterrent or a true weapon of mass destruction of planets and their people, the scientists and military leaders should be shocked as the destructive power of it before it was deactivated by Kirk and Spock – and Matt Decker's sacrifice of life and his starship.

Khan Noonien Singh – the ultimate villain of the origin *Enterprise* adventures.

Nomad – a nomadic computer that evaluates the worthiness of civilizations and individuals before it decides to execute – sterilize – the people or person under examination.

Gorn – a lizard-like race that attacked a Federation outpost over a territory dispute. Although this race is only featured twice in all of the *Star Trek* series, it is possible they learned to better co-exist within the United Federation of Planets.

Romulans – an offshoot of the Vulcan race, this civilization is more focused on conquest, like the Klingons, than reconciliation. The Romulans eventually side with the Federation in the Dominion War in *Star Trek: Deep Space Nine*, but their alliance is only a temporary one.

Trelane – a childlike Q, he tormented Kirk and crew – and nearly murdered the *Enterprise* captain if not for the interference of his parents.

Tholians – an impatient alien race, who when confronted over territorial boundaries, trap their enemies and destroy them in an energy beam web. Like the Gorn, we only see this race twice in the Trek series.

Star Trek: Next Generation

The Borg – the most menacing, dangerous, and nearly undefeatable villains in all four quadrants of the galaxy.

The Borg Queen – leader of the Borg Collective, the Queen and her Collective nearly changed Earth's history by going back in time before Warp Drive. Fortunately, Captain Picard leads Enterprise to the same time, and with key help by Mr. Data, who was temporarily seduced by the Queen, assists Jean-Luc to doom the Queen's evil plan.

Lore – Commander Data's evil twin brother. In the two-part story, *Descent*, Lore becomes a threat to humanity when he becomes a cult-like leader to small bang of Borg who have found individuality intoxicating, and the prospect of leading the Alpha Quadrant equally as alluring. Data, again seduced, this time by an emotion chip, is temporarily transformed into believing his brother's ideals. When it comes down to murdering Picard, Troi, and nearly killing his best friend, Geordi, Data realizes the crimes and refuses to follow his brother. Led by Hugh and Commander Riker and a rogue Borg group, Data and the rest overcome Lore and his small terrorist group. Data defeats his brother, and disassembles him, hopefully preventing him from ever rising to power ever again.

Professor James Moriarty – a self-aware holo-character programmed to defeat Commander Data. His criminal background bleeds through his actions, and twice threatened to destroy the ship. Once, Picard reasoned with him to return the ship to his control, the second time, he fooled the professor to believe he was a mortal being, and allow him to leave the Enterprise with his female companion, the Countess Regina Bartholomew.

Dr. Soran (TNG movie: Generations) – scientist who destroyed planets and civilizations just to return to the energy ribbon and live his life with his deceased family.

Duras – Unethical and treacherous Klingon of the House of Toral. This Klingon eventually loses his life to Worf in a hand to hand battle of honor over the death of Ambassador K'ehleyr.

Duras Sisters – Lursa and B'Etor are sworn enemies of Commander Worf after the Starfleet officer killed their brother, but only after he had murdered Ambassador K'ehleyr, Worf's beloved and mother of their child, Alexander. They also side with the Romulans, Commander Sela in particular, and try to cause a civil war on their home planet and try to install their brother's son into the chancellor role. Eventually they lose their lives after siding with Dr. Soran and his struggle to reach the Energy Ribbon in the movie, *Star Trek: Generations*.

Lesson 93

Although there are weapons

For tens and hundreds of soldiers,

They will not be used

Lao Tzu Chapter 80

Transitional Characters – Despicable Turned Respectable

As Lao Tzu noted, weapons of war need not be used if rulers realize that the threat alone may be good enough to keep enemies away. Too often in China during the time Lao Tzu wrote, battles were fought with spears, bows and arrows, knives and sheer manpower to overcome the opponent. In the Star Trek universe, photon torpedoes, hand phasers, and other military arms are not the only way to fend off the enemy. Civilizations keen on keeping their natural resources or independence from hostile takeovers not only use weapons, but other ways to prevent other races from taking advantage of their people or home world for strategic military uses.

Let's look at how originally powerful races used their weapons of choice against others – only to realize their cruelty need not be applied to innocent and selfless civilizations.

Star Trek: Original Series

The Talosians – an advanced race originally seen in the episode, *The Cage*, then in *The Menagerie*, who helped Vina live a life of normalcy after her space craft crashed landed on their planet. They deceive Captain Pike and his crew of the USS *Enterprise*, and intended to keep the star officer prisoner as company for Vina. They learn that kidnapping and holding anyone a hostage is wrong. When Pike is seriously injured many years later, they offer him a home with Vina where both can live out their natural lives in a pleasant, imaginary world.

The Klingons – originally only shown as a warrior species with little sympathy for any other race, the species evolved and became an important ally during the Dominion-Federation War.

Vians – Although they murdered Federation scientists and tortured Kirk, Spock and McCoy to test their research subject, they learned the intrinsic value of Gem and her people and rescue her race from a supernova.

Star Trek: Next Generation

Q – A supreme being with extraordinary powers over time, space and material objects, Q change, ever so slightly, to become more of a mentor to Jean-Picard than the inquisitor and judge he was in his first encounter with the *Enterprise*. Even though he put Captain Picard and the Federation in dire peril by throwing the *Enterprise* light years ahead to encounter the Borg, this action actually helped prepare Earth and their allies for the biggest battle against them a short year later. Even when the Q Continuum put Picard and humanity on trial again in yet another test – one that determined whether Jean-Luc and crew could figure out the deadly riddle of the tachyon pulse in three different time frames which almost destroyed Earth – Q allowed Picard to retain his memories from one time period to another, thus helping him solve the mystery. As Data remarked in the final television adventure, even though Q thought of Jean-Luc as a beloved pet, he gradually came to believe that the human race showed promise, and in that brief moment when Picard figured out the puzzle, he realized that the humanity was worthy of existence along with his Continuum counterparts.

Hugh the Borg – never truly menacing when recuperating on the *Enterprise*. His congenial personality and dedication to his friend, Geordi, after Picard orders him to assimilate the engineer, shows that even a Borg, whose primary purpose in life is to absorb individuals into the Collective, demonstrated people, even half-machine, can change.

Garak – the one time spy for the Obsidian Order, he gradually became more of an ally to the Federation, based on his friendship to Bashir and realization that his loyalty to his father and the secret police was not as important in his life on DS9.

Romulans – After Captain Sisko's unethical and illegal maneuvering with a Romulan commander, the military decided to join the Federation in their fight against the Dominion. Though enemies of the Klingons and Vulcans, they put aside their centuries of hatred and distrust to combat an even greater foe to them during the conflict against the Founders.

.

Lesson 94

Not knowing of the eternal leads to unfortunate errors.

Knowledge of the eternal is all-embracing.

To be all-embracing leads to righteousness,

Which is majestic.

To be majestic leads to the Heavenly.

To be Heavenly leads to the Way.

Lao Tzu Chapter 16

Best of the Best: Federation Heroes

As you may have guessed, the Starfleet crews represent the very best of what Lao Tzu proposes humanity strive for in their lives. Not all of the character are 100% pure of heart and purpose, but their actions, in the end, are guided by principles that both Starfleet and Lao Tzu has promoted for centuries.

Who are the Tao Masters on the Path to Enlightenment for each series?

In the *Star Trek* series, there are three distinct types of characters who best represent the best of both Lao Tzu and Sun Tzu. First, there are men, women, holograms, and even a Denobulon who assist everyone with physical or emotional problems on starships or space stations.

Healers: Counselors and Physicians

In *Star Trek: The Original Series*, Doctor McCoy is the closest thing to a counselor on the ship for the crew and the bridge officers – especially Captain James T. Kirk, who turns to 'Bones' during tough choice scenarios. Although Nurse Chapel helped McCoy, Bones was more of a counselor to the captain as well as others on *Enterprise*.

Star Trek: The Next Generation is the only series with a ship's counselor, the Betazoid, Diana Troi, can not only read minds, but offer a soothing voice, compassion, empathy and advice to all crew members – children and parents, bridge officers, aliens and humanoids alike. Of course, there is also Dr. Beverly Crusher who tends to the injured and also has a full medical staff behind her as well.

Leaders: The Taoist and Militaristic Duality

TOS

In the original series, Captain James T. Kirk is the prototype leader of how to manage both peaceful negotiations and tactical ingenuity when dealing with alien civilizations. The famous Starfleet leader is first a Taoist in dialogue with others, without the use of intimidation or threat of violence. In the episode, *The Corbomite Maneuver*, the James uses guile when an aggressive alien threatens annihilation. The strategy works, and soon Kirk, Spock, McCoy board the enemy vessel to negotiate a peace pack and a crewman exchange. This is just one example of dozens of times when James T. Kirk uses his mind, and not the arsenal of weapons of the *Enterprise*, to create the opportunity for peace with an unknown alien race.

Of course, Captain Kirk was not always the most peaceful Starfleet officer. In the story, *Balance of Terror*, Kirk believes he must engage the Romulans to prevent future war. Pushed by Mr. Spock, *Enterprise chases* down the warbird after they have destroyed a Federation outpost. Although Kirk finally defeats the Romulans, he does offer to rescue the crew and captain before their ship explodes. Kirk repeatedly offers mercy to all opponents – something that both Sun Tzu would see as the right thing to do in battle situations. Even Lao Tzu, who never saw wars as a necessary way of life, but accepted them for what they were, would applaud James for his humanity.

Captain Kirk's first officer, Mr. Spock was the most logical of the crew, and always balanced military strategies with the humane aspect of battles. It was never a win-at-all-costs contest for the Vulcan, and as such, in every conflict, the least amount of causalities occurred under his watch. *The Doomsday Machine* story illustrates Spock's brilliance, as does *The Tholian Web* conundrum, which pits his intellect with compassion, and ends with him saving James T. Kirk's life.

Chief Engineer Montgomery Scott, too, is the third most important leader of the *Enterprise*. Scotty uses tactically insightful maneuvers to rescue his Kirk, Spock and McCoy, among others in too many adventures to count. Mr. Scott always found a way to save the ship, too, from descending into strong gravity wells, and came up with a cold engineer restart that eventually made the tech manuals for its originality. Working with Mr. Spock, Scotty develops a slingshot maneuver that also makes time travel possible, too. After saving himself in the story, *Relics*, Scotty places his bio-pattern in a feedback loop that keeps him alive for seventy five years. Geordi La Forge learns that ingenuity and fearlessness is essential for his *Enterprise* just as it was for Mr. Scott's nearly a century earlier.

TNG

Unlike Captain Kirk, Jean-Luc Picard seeks advice first before making a monumental decisions involving potential conflicts. Essentially, Picard seeks negotiated, peaceful settlements instead of intimidating others – a difference in leadership style, say, to Commander Jellico, who intimidated the Cardassians to return Jean-Luc to *Enterprise* after his imprisonment and torture. Picard studies his opponents before making any provocative moves, and often has back-up plans coordinated with allies to prevent a capture or loss in the battle field.

Commander Will Riker proves his value to Jean-Luc, Starfleet and the Federation when he retrieved Picard from the Collective and helped defeat the Borg before it annihilated Earth's population. Offered his own command, Riker stays aboard *Enterprise* to learn more from Captain Picard and remain close to his Starfleet friends.

After Jean-Luc saved his friend, Commander Data, from becoming a lab rat under the misguided research hands of Commander Maddox, the sentient android shows his brilliance on numerous occasions throughout his years under Captain Picard.

Data's best friend, Chief Engineer Geordi La Forge, saved *Enterprise* and crew from countless impossible situations as well. Always willing to talk through problems with Data, Geordi uses theoretical application to practical problems in a way that prevented system overloads, and provided tactical weapon use against enemy attacks – even weaning a space baby off the energy field surrounding the starship, with help from Leah Brahms' hologram. Once, La Forge, acting as a peaceful follower of Lao Tzu, befriended a young Borg, who became one of the first to display individuality after his assimilation into the Collective. In essence, Geordi La Forge used both Sun Tzu and Lao Tzu philosophy to become the best chief engineer in the fleet.

Followers: Walking the Path with Unsung Heroes

From TOS all the way through *Star Trek: Picard*, supporting characters have shown us that the lower ranked officers, or merely civilians, have what it takes to be courageous and righteous as they battled their own demons and enemies to the Federation. Let's look at these characters we may have forgotten for their contributions to the *Star Trek* saga.

TOS

Although Helmsman Hikaru Sulu was not considering the highest ranking of officers, his dedication to duty, along with that of Helmsman Pavel Chekov, proved steady under enemy attacks. Both men navigated the ship as well as necessary under James T. Kirk, never wavering under the most deadly conditions. Communications Officer Nyota Uhura, too, translated the most impossible of languages from her post on the bridge. Even in away missions with Sulu and Chekov, Uhura provided perhaps the most important of information to the captain of anyone during first contact and primary negotiations with alien civilizations.

We should not forget the most memorable of characters in the *Star Trek* universe, Edith Keeler – a pacifist who was ahead of her time, who helped a drug-induced, hysterical and weary Leonard McCoy. Keeler's kindness saved the physician and reunited him with Spock and Kirk. Her death, destined, was fulfilled, and although her ideals and principles were correct it was just the wrong time. Edith was ahead of her time, but walked path to the Way Lao Tzu would likely have been proud of for her humanitarian vision.

TNG

Of all the members of the crew Picard relied on the most who was not a bridge officer, it was Guinan. Her guidance in advising her friend through the grim and alternate reality in *Yesterday's Enterprise* storyline proved her value not only to Jean-Luc but the Federation. Guinan's wisdom was also important in saving Mr. Data's life in the story, *Measure of a Man*, and in Picard's decision not to put a pernicious program in Hugh to destroy the Borg Collective. Acting out of profound love and respect for Jean-Luc, after he saved her in San Francisco in the late 1880's, paid back Picard and the *Enterprise* crew for years.

Chief Security Officer Tasha Yar, too, should not be forgotten. Tasha may have died in a Prime timeline, but her devotion to duty, and in respect for Guinan's advice, helped the USS *Enterprise* 1701-C return to the temporal juncture that ultimately restored the normal timeline, reestablishing a peaceful and honorable relationship between the Federation and the Klingons.

Star Trek Heroes: Do you see yourself as a Healer, Leader, or Follower?

As I started this book, I admitted my passion for Roddenberry's science fiction franchise of the mid-1960's was based on a desire to look towards role models in the characters Gene and the writing staff created in the original series. Whether it was Kirk, Spock, or McCoy, I felt comforted by their behavior and actions, knowing that their choices were made with forethought, compassion and wisdom. Soon after the series ended, I realized that their actions could be linked to both Lao Tzu's and Sun Tzu's principles of living at peace, or at war in the unknown regions of the galaxy.

More precisely, I understand Gene's outer space adventures are still symbolic of what we as human beings need to base our lives on to live more peacefully in contentious times. Whether it is James T. Kirk, Jean-Luc Picard, Benjamin Lafayette Sisko, Kathryn Janeway, or Johnathan Archer, their actions still reflect the basic principles Lao Tzu and Sun Tzu articulated thousands of years ago in China – and still are relevant in societies around the world, especially in 2020.

Final Reflections and Actions

As we conclude this book, I ask you to consider this one, basic question: Do you see you true nature as a one of taking three basic paths – that of a healer, a leader, or a follower in life? Is your nature one of helping others resolve their problems with common, everyday conversations, in essence, therapy, such as what ship's counselor Deanna Troi's does for her crewmates? You do not need to be an empath to see that your friends and family need a shoulder – especially since COVID-19 spread across the globe.

Teaching is also a profession a healer takes in life. Are you inherently a mentor, educating the young or adults, in their quest to better understand their world around them? Whether you instruct biology, chemistry, history, sociology, political science or language, you make a difference in the world around you – whether it be in a well-known college like Stanford University in Palo Alto, California or an inner city school in the Bronx of New York. Your contributions matter no matter the status location of the institution simply because you are molding minds to become critical thinkers in a society that does not always appreciate others questioning authority.

Perhaps you see your role in life more as a leader by making tough decisions for yourself and others? Is leading a business your biggest goal? Is working on Wall Street the perfect job for you? Do you dream of becoming a politician to change the system so it better serves the entire community, state or nation so that every citizen has a louder and more distinct voice in the laws, policies and practices no matter their gender, race or age?

If you see yourself as a supporting cast member in life such as Helmsman Hikaru Sulu or Communication Officer Nyota Uhura, you are a pathfinder in 2020. Your contribution to any community, whether it has only 30,000 men, women and children like Portales, New Mexico or over 3 million like Chicago, Illinois, will make a difference. You may only become a baker, a truck driver, or a custodial worker, but each person can, in their own unique way, contribute to the betterment of any society.

Just remember one important idea: You ARE the hero of your own story. Whatever it is, make it one that you are proud to tell others.

Afterward

The Future is the Past: My Favorite *Star Trek* Stories

With more *Star Trek* promised for the near future due to its popularity on the CBS streaming service, we will see more adventures of Captain Christopher Pike in *Star Trek: Strange New Worlds* and Mirror Philippa Georgiou in *Star Trek: Section 31* over the next few years. For example, *Star Trek: Picard* has been guaranteed for seasons 2 and 3; *Star Trek: Discovery*, just completed season 3 and will start season 4 after pandemic restrictions allow the actors to return to the set. And for the younger audience and animation fans, *Star Trek: Lower Decks* is here and *Star Trek: Prodigy* is nearly ready. Overall, in the next few years, there is much to look forward to in the Roddenberry franchise.

Yet, as we look towards the future, what best represents the past of the Trek saga? And with previous series, which ones include your favorite stories?

With currently have 750+ television episodes of cannon series stretching across nine separate programs, I have selected the best episodes based on my personal taste. For me, these tales best illustrate the complexity of human nature, and tell important stories about life not only in the 24th century, but about the world we live in today.

Here are my Top Fifty, plus a few honorable mentions:

1. City on the Edge of Forever (TOS)
2. Far Beyond the Stars (DS9)
3. In the Pale Moonlight (DS9)
4. Balance of Power (TOS)
5. Inner Light (TNG)
6. All Good Things (TNG)
7. The Visitor (DS9)
8. Timeless (VOY)
9. In a Mirror, Darkly (ENT)
10. Duet (DS9)
11. Yesterday's Enterprise (TNG)
12. Best of Both Worlds (TNG)
13. Star Trek II: The Wrath of Khan (TOS Movie)
14. The Trouble With Tribbles (TOS)
15. Trials and Tribble-ations (DS9)
16. Chain of Command (TNG)
17. The Doomsday Machine (TOS)
18. The Measure of a Man (TNG)
19. Similitude (ENT)
20. Star Trek: First Contact (TNG Movie)
21. Carbon Creek (ENT)

22. Endgame (VOY)
23. Magic to Make any Man Insane (DIS)
24. Arena (TOS)
25. The Menagerie (TOS)
26. Yesteryear (TOS – Animated)
27. Waltz (DS9)
28. Tacking into the Wind (DS9)
29. Past Tense (DS9)
30. Space Seed (TOS)
31. Drone (VOY)
32. Darmok (TNG)
33. Faith, Treachery and the Great River (DS9)
34. Sacrifice of the Angels (DS9)
35. Nepenthe (Picard)
36. Zero Hour (ENT)
37. The Corbomite Maneuver (TOS)
38. Shadows and Symbols (DS9)
39. Little Green Men (DS9)
40. Terra Firma (DIS)
41. Take me out to the Holosuite (DS9)
42. The Tholian Web (TOS)
43. Year of Hell (VOY)
44. His Way (DS9)
45. Siege of AR-558 (DS9)
46. It's Only a Paper Moon (DS9)
47. Once More Unto the Breach (DS9)
48. Rocks and Shoals (DS9)
49. The Magnificent Ferengi (DS9)
50. Bride of Chaotica (VOY)

Honorable Mentions: Carpenter Street (ENT), North Star (ENT), Blink of an Eye (VOY), Dr. Bashir, I Presume? (DS9), Shattered (VOY), Time's Arrow (TNG), The Forge (ENT), The Awakening (ENT), Kir'Shara (ENT), Unification I & II (TNG), Unification III (DIS) and Calypso, The Escape Artist, Q & A and Ephraim & the Dot (Short Treks).

Enjoy the past, current and future *Star Trek* adventures – and continue to learn life lessons, no matter if they focus on peace or war – and do your best apply them to your everyday life challenges.

As Mr. Spock would say, "Live long and prosper."

References

Abatemarco, F. (Writer). Landau, L. (Director). (1992, December 21st). Chain of Command: Part 2. (Season 6, Episode 17). [137]. In R. Berman (Executive Producer), *Star Trek: The Next Generation*, Paramount Studios.

Armen, M. (Writer). Taylor, J. (Director). (1969, February 28th). The Cloud Minders. (Season 3, Episode 21). [74]. In Gene Roddenberry (Executive Producer), *Star Trek: The Original Series*, Paramount Studios.

Armen, M. (Writer). Sutherland, H. (Director). (1973, September 29th). The Lorelei Song. (Season 1, Episode 4). [4]. In G. Roddenberry & D. C. Fontana (Executive Producers), *Star Trek: The Animated Series*, Paramount Studios.

Aroeste, J. L. (Writer). Chomsky, M. (Director). (1969, March 14th). All Our Yesterdays. (Season 3, Episode 23). [78]. In Gene Roddenberry (Executive Producer), *Star Trek: The Original Series*, Paramount Studios.

Austen, Jane. (1813). *Pride and Prejudice*. T. Egerton, Whitehall. London, England.

Bates, R. & Wise, D. (Writers). Reed, B. (Director). (1974, October 5th). How Sharper Than a Serpent's Tooth. (Season 2, Episode 5). [21]. In G. Roddenberry & D. C. Fontana (Executive Producers), *Star Trek: The Animated Series*, Paramount Studios.

Beagle, P. S. (Writer). Landau, L. (Director). (1990, May 14th). Sarek. (Season 3, Episode 23). [71]. In G. Roddenberry (Executive Producer), *Star Trek: The Next Generation*, Paramount Studios.

Behr, I. S. (Writer), Manning, R. (Writer), Beimier, H. (Writer) & Moore, R. D. (Writer). Carson, D. (Director). (1990, February 19th). Yesterday's Enterprise. (Season 3, Episode 15). [63]. In G. Roddenberry (Executive Producer), *Star Trek: The Next Generation*, Paramount Studios.

Bellisario, D. (Executive Producer). Quantum Leap. (May, 1989 - May, 1993). Los Angeles, CA, Bellisario Productions and Universal Television.

Berman, R. (Executive Producer). Piller, M. & Behr, I. S. (Showrunners). (1993-99). *Star Trek: Deep Space Nine*.

Berman, R. (Executive Producer). Piller, M., Taylor, J., Braga, B., & Biller, B. (Showrunners) (1995-2001). *Star Trek: Voyager*.

Berman, R. (Executive Producer). Braga, B. & Coto, M. (Showrunners). (2001-05). *Star Trek: Enterprise*.

Berman, R. (Writer). Bowman, R. (Director). (1990, October 8th). Brothers. (Season 4, Episode 3). [77]. In R. Berman (Executive Producer), *Star Trek: The Next Generation*, Paramount Studios.

Braga, B. (Writer). Frakes, J. (Director). (1992, March 23rd). Cause and Effects. (Season 5, Episode 18). [118]. In R. Berman (Executive Producer), *Star Trek: The Next Generation*, Paramount Studios.

Braga, B. (Writer). Weimer, R. (Director). (1993, October 29th). Parallels. (Season 7, Episode 7). [163]. In R. Berman (Executive Producer), *Star Trek: The Next Generation*. Paramount Studios.

Braga, B. (Writer). Conway, J. L. (Director) (1993, May 3rd). Frame of Mind. (Season 6, Episode 21) [147]. In R. Berman (Executive Producer), *Star Trek: The Next Generation*, Paramount Studios.

Braga, B. (Writer). Kolbe, W. (Director). (1993, February 2nd). Birthright: Part 1. (Season 6, Episode 16) [142]. In R. Berman (Executive Producer), *Star Trek: The Next Generation*, Paramount Studios.

Coon, G. (Writer). Pevney, J. (Director). (1967, January 19th). Arena. (Season 1, Episode 18). [19]. In Gene Roddenberry (Executive Producer), *Star Trek: The Original Series*, Paramount Studios.

Coon, G. (Writer) & Wiber, C. (Writer). Daniels, M. (Director). (1967, February 16th). Space Seed. (Season 1, Episode 22). [24]. In Gene Roddenberry (Executive Producer), *Star Trek: The Original Series*, Paramount Studios.

Coon, G. (Writer). Pevney, J. (Director). (1967, March 9th). Devil in the Dark. (Season 1, Episode 25). [26]. In Gene Roddenberry (Executive Producer), *Star Trek: The Original Series*, Paramount Studios.

Crawford, O. (Writer). Taylor, J. (Director). (1969, January 10th). Let That be Your Last Battlefield. (Season 3, Episode 15). [70]. In Gene Roddenberry (Executive Producer), *Star Trek: The Original Series*, Paramount Studios.

Culver, J. (Writer). Reed, B. (Director). (1974, October 12th). The Counterclockwise Incident. (Season 2, Episode 6). [16]. In G. Roddenberry & D. C. Fontana (Executive Producers), *Star Trek: The Animated Series*, Paramount Studios.

Daniels, M. (Writer). Sutherland, H. (Director). 1973, September 22nd). One of Our Planets is Missing. (Season 1, Episode 3). [3]. In G. Roddenberry & D. C. Fontana (Executive Producers), *Star Trek: The Animated Series*, Paramount Studios.

David, Peter. (1994). *Star Trek: The Next Generation: Q-Squared*. Pocket Books. NY, New York.

Danus, R. (Writer). Landau, L. (Director). (1990, February 5th). Deja Q. (Season 3, Episode 13). [61]. In G. Roddenberry (Executive Producer), *Star Trek: The Next Generation*, Paramount Studios.

De Palma, B. (1989). *Casualties of War*. Columbia Pictures.

Echevarria, R. (Writer). Frakes, J. (Director). (1990, February 12th). The Offspring. (Season 3, Episode 16). [64]. In G. Roddenberry (Executive Producer), *Star Trek: The Next Generation*, Paramount Studios.

Echevarria, R. (Writer). Singer, A. (Director). (1993, January 25th). Ship in a Bottle. (Season 6, Episode 12).   [138]. In R. Berman (Executive Producer), *Star Trek: The Next Generation*, Paramount Studios.

Echevarria, R. (Writer). Beaumont, G. (Director). (1994, February 7th). Lower Decks. (Season 7, Episode 15. [167]. In R. Berman (Executive Director), *Star Trek: The Next Generation*, Paramount Studios.

Echevarria, R. (Writer). Curry, D. (Director). (1993, March 3rd). Birthright: Part 2. (Season 6, Episode 17). [143]. In R. Berman (Executive Producer), *Star Trek: The Next Generation*, Paramount Studios.

Echevarria, R. (Writer). Stewart, P. (Director). (1994, May 16th). Preemptive Strike. (Season 7, Episode 24). In R. Berman (Executive Producer), *Star Trek: The Next Generation*, Paramount Studios.

Echevarria, R. (Writer). Lederman, R. (Director). (1992, June 11th). I, Borg. (Season 5, Episode 23). [123]. In R. Berman (Executive Director), *Star Trek: The Next Generation*, Paramount Studios.

Ellison, H. (Writer). Pevney, J. (Director). (1967, April 4th). City on the Edge of Forever. (Season 1, Episode 29) [29]. In Gene Roddenberry (Executive Producer), *Star Trek: The Original Series*, Paramount Studios.

Fields, P. A. (Writer). Lauritson, P. (Director). (1992, June 1st). The Inner Light. (Season 5, Episode 25). [125]. In R., Berman (Executive Producer), *Star Trek: The Next Generation*, Paramount Studios.

Fineli, D. (Writer). Reed, B. (Director). (1974, September 28th). Albatross. (Season 2, Episode 5). [20]. In G. Roddenberry & D. C. Fontana (Executive Producers), *Star Trek: The Animated Series*, Paramount Studios.

Fontana, D. C. (Writer). Lucas, J. M. (Director). (1968, September 27th). The Enterprise Incident. (Season 3, Episode 2). [59]. In Gene Roddenberry (Executive Producer), *Star Trek: The Original Series*, Paramount Studios.

Fontana, D. C. (Writer). Pevney, J. (Director). 1967, November 17th). Journey to Babel. (Season 2, Episode 10). [39]. In Gene Roddenberry (Executive Producer), *Star Trek: The Original Series*, Paramount Studios.

Fontana, D.C. (Writer). Sutherland, H. (Director). (1973, September 15th). Yesteryear. (Season 1, Episode 2) [2]. In G. Roddenberry & D. C. Fontana (Executive Producers), *Star Trek: The Animated Series*, Paramount Studios.

Fontana, D. C. (Writer) & Roddenberry, G. (Writer). Allen, C. (Director). (1987, September 28th). Encounter at Farpoint (Season 1, Episode 1). [1]. In G. Roddenberry (Executive Director), *Star Trek: The Next Generation*, Paramount Studios.

Frank, S. (Director). (2020). *The Queen's Gambit*. United States. Flitcraft, LTD.

Frakes, Jonathan. (Director). (1996). *Star Trek: First Contact*. Paramount Pictures.

Fromm, Eric. (1956). *The Art of Loving*. Harper and Brothers. NY, New York.

Fuller, B., Semel, D., Roddenberry, E., Roth, T., Goldsman, A., Kaden, H., Osunsanmi, O., Berg, G., Harbarts, A., Kurtzman, A., Siracusa, F., Weber, J., Lumet, J., & Paradise, M. (Executive Producers). (2017-present). *Star Trek: Discovery*.

Gerrold, D. (Writer). Sutherland, H. (Director). (1973, October 6th). More Tribbles, More Troubles. (Season 1, Episode 5). [5]. In G. Roddenberry & D. C. Fontana (Executive Producers), *Star Trek: The Animated Series*, Paramount Studios.

Goldstone, J. (Writer) & Peoples, S. (Writer). (1966, September 22nd). Where No Man Has Gone Before. (Season 1, Episode 3) [2b]. In Gene Roddenberry (Executive Producer), *Star Trek: The Original Series*, Paramount Studios.

Hatton, C. (Writer). Kolbe, W. (Director). (1994, February 14). Thine Own Self Be True. (Season 7, Episode 16). [168]. In R. Berman (Executive Producer), *Star Trek: The Next Generation*, Paramount Studios.

Hamner, R. (Writer) & Coon, G. (Writer). Pevney, J. (Director). (1967, February 23rd). A Taste of Armageddon. (Season 1, Episode 20) [23]. In Gene Roddenberry (Executive Producer), *Star Trek: The Original Series*, Paramount Studios.

Harmon, D.P. (Writer) & Coon, G. (Writer). Komack, J. (Director). (1968, January 12th). A Piece of the Action. (Season 2, Episode 17). [49]. In Gene Roddenberry (Executive Producer), *Star Trek: The Original Series*, Paramount Studios.

Hoff, Benjamin. (1982). *The Tao of Pooh*. Dutton Books

Kandel, S. (Writer). Sutherland, H. (Director). (1974, January 12th). The Jihad. (Season 2, Episode 16). [16]. In G. Roddenberry & D. C. Fontana (Executive Producers), *Star Trek: The Animated Series*, Paramount Studios.

King, Stephen. (1987). *Misery*. Viking Press, NY, New York.

Koenig, W. (Writer). Sutherland, H. (Director). (1973, October 20th). The Infinite Vulcan. (Season 1, Episode 7). [7]. In G. Roddenberry & D. C. Fontana (Executive Producers), *Star Trek: The Animated Series*, Paramount Studios.

Lucas, J. M. (Writer). Daniels, M. (Director). (1967, September 29th). The Changeling. (Season 2, Episode 3). [37]. In Gene Roddenberry (Executive Producer), *Star Trek: The Original Series*, Paramount Studios.

Mc Clough, Coleen. (1977). *The Thorn Birds*. Harper and Row. NY, New York.

Matheson, R. (Writer). Penn, L. (Director). (1966, October 6th). The Enemy Within. (Season 1, Episode 5). [5]. In Gene Roddenberry (Executive Producer), *Star Trek: The Original Series*, Paramount Studios.

Melville, Herman. (1851). *Moby Dick*. Richard Bentley. London, England.

Menosky, J. (Writer). Kolbe, W. (Director). (1991, September 3rd). Darmok. (Season 5, Episode 2). [102]. In R. Berman (Executive Producer), *Star Trek: The Next Generation*, Paramount Studios.

Meyer, Nicolas (Director). (1982). *Star Trek II: The Wrath of Khan*. Paramount Pictures.

Moore, R. D. (Writer) & Moran, R. (Writer). Landau, L. (Director). (1990, March 19th). Sins of the Father. (Season 3, Episode 17). [65]. In R. Berman (Executive Director), *Star Trek: The Next Generation*, Paramount Studios.

Moore, R.D. (Writer). Scheerer, R. (Director). (1990, January 1st). The Defector. (Season 3, Episode 10). [58]. In G. Roddenberry (Executive Producer), *Star Trek: The Next Generation*, Paramount Studios.

Moore, R. D. (Writer). Landau, L. (Director). (1990, October 1st). Family. (Season 4, Episode 2). [76]. In R. Berman (Executive Producer), *Star Trek: The Next Generation*, Paramount Studios.

Moore, R. D. (Writer). Bole, C. (Director). (1991, June 17th). Redemption: Part 1. (Season 4, Episode 26). [100]. In R. Berman (Executive Director), *Star Trek: The Next Generation*, Paramount Studios.

Moore, R. D. (Writer). Carson, D. (Director). (1991, September 23rd). Redemption: Part 2. Season 5, Episode 1. [101]. In R. Berman (Executive Producer), *Star Trek: The Next Generation*, Paramount Studios.

Moore, R. D. (Writer). Singer, A. (Director). (1992. October 10th). Relics. (Season 6, Episode 5). [130]. In R. Berman (Executive Producer), *Star Trek: The Next Generation*, Paramount Studios.

Moore, R. D. (Writer). Scheerer, R. (Director). (1992, December 14th). The Chain of Command: Part 1. (Season 6, Episode 12). In R. Berman (Executive Producer), *Star Trek: The Next Generation*, Paramount Studios.

Moore, R. D. (Writer). Landau, L. (Director). (1993, February 15th). Tapestry. (Season 6, Episode 15). [141]. In R. Berman (Executive Producer), *Star Trek: The Next Generation*, Paramount Studios.

Moore, R. D. (Writer). Allen, C (Director). (1994, March 28th). Journey's End. (Season 7, Episode 20). [172]. In R. Berman (Executive Producer), *Star Trek: The Next Generation*, Paramount Studios.

Moore, R.D. & Braga, B. (Writers) Kolbe, W. (Director). (1994, May 23rd). All Good Things: Parts 1 & 2. (Season 7, Episode 26). [176]. In R. Berman, (Executive Producer), *Star Trek: The Next Generation*. Paramount Studios.

Muskat, J. (Writer). Erman, J. (Director). (1968, December 6th). The Empath. (Season 3, Episode 12). [63]. In Gene Roddenberry (Executive Producer), *Star Trek: The Original Series*, Paramount Studios.

Nabokov, Vladimir. (1955). *Lolita*. Olympia Press, Paris, France.

Nimoy, Leonard. (Director). (1984). *Star Trek III: The Search for Spock*. Paramount Pictures.

Nimoy, Leonard. (Director). (1986). *Star Trek IV: The Voyage Home*. Paramount Pictures.

Niven, L. (Writer). Sutherland, H. (Director). (1973, December 8th). The Slaver Weapon. (Season 1, Episode 14). [14]. In G. Roddenberry & D. C. Fontana (Executive Producers), *Star Trek: The Animated Series*, Paramount Studios.

Okrad, Marc. (1996). *The Klingon Way: A Warrior's Guide*. Pocket Books. NY, New York.

Peoples, S. (Writer). Sutherland, H. (Director). (1973, September 8th). Beyond the Farthest Star. (Season 1, Episode 1). [1]. In G. Roddenberry & D. C. Fontana (Executive Producers), *Star Trek: The Animated Series*, Paramount Studios.

Perry, J. (Writer). Sutherland, H. (Director). (1973, November 17th). The Time Trap. (Season 1, Episode 11). [11]. In G. Roddenberry & D. C. Fontana (Executive Producers), *Star Trek: The Animated Series*, Paramount Studios.

Piller, M. (Writer). Bole, C. (Director). (1990, June 18th & 1990, September 24th). Best of Both Worlds: Parts 1 & 2. (Season 3, Episode 26 & Season 4, Episode 1). [74 & 75]. In R. Berman (Executive Producer), *Star Trek: The Next Generation*, Paramount Studios.

Piller, M. (Writer). Bole, C. (Director). (1991, November 11th). Unification: Part 2. (Season 5, Episode 8). [108]. In R. Berman (Executive Producer), *Star Trek: The Next Generation*, Paramount Studios.

Piller, M. (Writer). Bole, C. (Director). (1992, April 27th). The Perfect Mate. (Season 5, Episode 21). [121]. In R. Berman (Executive Producer), *Star Trek: The Next Generation*, Paramount Studios.

Ramis, Harold. (1993). *Groundhog Day*. Columbia Pictures.

Roddenberry, E., Roth, T., Duff, J., Kaden, H., Goldsman, A., Chabon, M., Kurtzman, A., Matalas, T., Aarniokski, A., Massin, O., & Stewart, P. (Executive Producers). (2020-present). *Star Trek: Picard*.

Roddenberry, G. (Executive Producer). (1966-69). *Star Trek: The Original Series*.

Roddenberry, G. & Fontana, D. C. (Executive Producers). (1973-43). *Star Trek: The Animated Series*.

Roddenberry, G. (Executive Producer: 1987-91) & Berman, R. (Executive Producer: 1991-94). (1987-94). *Star Trek: The Next Generation.*

Roddenberry, G. (Writer). Butler, R. (Director). (1988, October 4th). The Cage. (Original unaired Pilot). [1]. In G. Roddenberry (Director), *Star Trek: The Original Series*, Paramount Studios.

Roddenberry, G. (Writer). Daniels, M. (Director). (1966, November 10th). The Menagerie: Parts 1 & 2. (Season 1, Episodes 11 & 12). [16a & 16b]. In Gene Roddenberry (Executive Director), *Star Trek: The Original Series*, Paramount Studios.

Saberoff, R. (Writer). Pevney, J. (Director). (1968, January 19th). The Immunity Syndrome. (Season 2, Episode 18). [48]. In Gene Roddenberry (Executive Producer), *Star Trek: The Original Series*, Paramount Studios.

Schneider, P. (Writer). McEveety, V. (Director). (1966, December 15th). Balance of Terror. (Season 1, Episode 14). [9]. In Gene Roddenberry (Executive Producer), *Star Trek: The Original Series*, Paramount Studios.

Schneider, P. (Writer). McDougall, D. (Director). (1967, January 12th). The Squire of Gothos. (Season 1, Episode 17). [18]. In Gene Roddenberry (Executive Producer), *Star Trek: The Original Series*, Paramount Studios.

Segal, Eric. (1970). *Love Story*. Harper and Row. NY, New York.

Shakespeare, William. (1597). *Romeo and Juliet*. England.

Shanker, N. (Writer). Frakes, J. (Director). (1992, November 16th). The Quality of Life. (Season 6, Episode 11). [135]. In R. Berman (Executive Producer), *Star Trek: The Next Generation*, Paramount Studios.

Shanker, N. (Writer). Singer, A. (Director). (1994, January 17th). Homeward. (Season 7, Episode 13). [165]. In R. Berman (Executive Producer), *Star Trek: The Next Generation*, Paramount Studios.

Shanker, N. (Writer). Beaumont, G. (Director). (1993, February 8th). Face of the Enemy. (Season 6, Episode 14). [140]. In R. Berman (Executive Producer), *Star Trek: The Next Generation*, Paramount Studios.

Sheldon, L. (Writer). Bole, C. (Director). (1990, October 22nd). Remember Me. (Season 4, Episode 5). In R. Berman (Executive Producer), *Star Trek: The Next Generation*, Paramount Studios.

Snodgrass, M. (Writer). Scheerer, R. (Director). (1989, February 13th). Measure of a Man. (Season 2, Episode 9). [35]. In G. Roddenberry (Executive Director), *Star Trek: The Next Generation*, Paramount Studios.

Sohl, J. (Writer). Sargent, J. (Director). (1966, November 10th). The Corbomite Maneuver. (Season 1, Episode 10). [3]. In Gene Roddenberry (Executive Producer), *Star Trek: The Original Series*, Paramount Studios.

Spinrod, N. (Writer). Daniels, M. (Director). (1967, October 20th). The Doomsday Machine. (Season 2, Episode 6). [35]. In Gene Roddenberry (Executive Producer), *Star Trek: The Original Series*, Paramount Studios.

Stenudd, S. (2011). *The Taoism of Lao Tzu Explained*. Kindle Books, Amazon. United States.

Sturgeon, T. (Writer). Pevney, J. (Director). (1967, September 15th). Amok Time. (Season 2, Episode 1). [34]. In Gene Roddenberry (Executive Producer), *Star Trek: The Original Series*, Paramount Studios.

Taylor, J. (Writer). Chalmers, C. (Director). (1991, January, 28th). The Wounded. (Season 4, Episode 21). [86]. In R. Berman (Executive Producer), *Star Trek: The Next Generation*, Paramount Studios.

Taylor, J. (Writer). Landau, L. (Director). (1991, November 4th). Unification: Part 1. (Season 5, Episode 7). [107]. In R. Berman (Executive Producer), *Star Trek: The Next Generation*, Paramount Studios.

Taylor, J. (Writer). Frakes, J. (Director). (1991, April 29th). The Drumhead. (Season 4, Episode, 21). [95]. In R. Berman (Executive Producer), *Star Trek: The Next Generation*, Paramount Studios.

Taylor, J. (Writer). Sheerer, R. (Director). (1992, March 16th). The Outcast. (Season 5, Episode 17). [117]. In R. Berman (Executive Producer), *Star Trek: The Next Generation*, Paramount Studios.

Tivers, B. (Writer). Oswald, G. (Director). (1966, December 8th). The Conscience of the King. (Season 1, Episode 13). [13]. In Gene Roddenberry (Executive Producer), *Star Trek: The Original Series*, Paramount Studios.

Tolstoy, Leo. (1877). *Anna Karenina*. The Russian Messenger. Russia.

Tzu, Lao. (6th Century). *Tao Te Ching*. China.

Tzu, Sun. (5th Century). *The Art of War*. China.

Weinstein, H. (Writer). Reed, B. (Director). (1974, September 7th). The Pirates of Orion. (Season 2, Episode 1) [17]. In G. Rodenberry & D. C. Fontana (Executive Producers), *Star Trek: The Animated Series*, Paramount Studios.

Wikiquotes, (2020). Character dialogue for various *Star Trek* episodes and television series that includes: *Star Trek: The Original Series, Star Trek: The Animated Series, Star Trek: The Next Generation, Star Trek: Deep Space Nine, Star Trek: Voyager, Star Trek: Enterprise, Star Trek: Discovery* and *Star Trek: Picard*.

Wise, R. (Director). (1979). *Star Trek I. The Motion Picture*. Paramount Pictures. United States.

Made in the USA
Middletown, DE
15 December 2021

55685855R00119